Praise for *The Wealthy Fra*

As one of our most successful and dynamic fra:
what it takes to grow a franchise business. In *The Wealthy Franchisee*,
Scott gets to the heart of what it takes to succeed as a franchise
owner going beyond the obvious, like stable finances and prime
real estate, and focusing on the personal characteristics and
values needed to become a leader in today's highly competitive
marketplace. This is a must-read for anyone looking
to embody the ideal franchisee persona.

—Tariq Farid, Founder and CEO of Edible Arrangements

Scott is one of the best motivational speakers out there and has
had a real impact on me and my thinking. It is one thing to be able
to motivate in person from the stage, but Scott has managed to put
that motivation into one of the best books I've come across for small-
business owners. It's loaded with great advice, inspiring examples,
and timeless wisdom. It'll shave years off your learning curve.
This is the book the franchise industry has been waiting for.

—Doc Cohen, Multi-Unit Franchise Owner,
Great American Cookie Company & Pretzelmaker,
Former IFA Chair & Franchise Hall of Fame Inductee

There are a lot of business books out there, but none that are so spot
on for franchisees. If you're running a franchise business and
want to grow, this is the book you've got to read.

—Frank Garrido, Senior Vice President, Team USA at Domino's

Most franchisees take years to learn these ideas. One reading of this
book will save you time, reduce your stress, and make
you more money!

—Dan Harmon, President & Chief Operating Officer, Smoothie King

The Wealthy Franchisee is an excellent resource for anyone looking to build a franchise business. Scott Greenberg lays it all out there to help franchisees improve their mindset and operate more profitably.

—Tim Bisbocci, U.S. VP of Franchise Operations at Subway

Scott does an excellent job describing the connection between how leaders think and how much they earn. His book is an informative, inspiring read that's perfect for anyone wanting to succeed within a franchise system.

—Rob Price, CEO, School of Rock

I am so excited Scott finally put in writing the brilliant ideas he shares on stage. This insightful book is going to change the lives of a lot of franchisees.

—Jenn Johnston, President & Chief Brand Officer, Global Franchise Group

A captivating journey of self-awareness, this book unlocks the deep connection between attitude and achievement; the key elements to the wealthy success of any franchisee. Simply a must-read for any franchisee looking to take their business to the next level of prosperity.

—Tad Mollnhauer, Multiple Center Owner (MCO) Franchisee with The UPS Store, Executive Director of the National TUPSSO Franchise Owners Association

I've seen Scott speak and took away so many ideas for leading more effectively and running my company. This book captures everything he shared and so much more. I recommend it for anyone who runs a franchise business.

—Kati Buckland, 2009 Franchisee of the Year, Chem-Dry

Scott provides authentic and pragmatic advice for new, struggling, and successful franchisees alike. This book inspires the self-reflection and mindset shift essential to enjoying wealth beyond the balance sheet.

—Anna Larson, "Franchise of Distinction" Owner, Soccer Shots

Can a book really change your life? It can if it is *The Wealthy Franchisee*! Whether you are exploring the path of franchise ownership, a new franchisee, or an experienced franchise professional, this book has tips and tools that will drive your business to the next level! My advice: Don't operate your business without it!

—Alesia Visconti, CEO & President, FranServe

In *The Wealthy Franchisee*, Scott Greenberg hits all the marks on the key principles that enable franchisees to make a meaningful difference in their lives and the lives of their family and employees. Those franchisees who live and lead with passion, attitude, awareness, and confidence build high performance teams that deliver outstanding customer service. That is wealth that goes far beyond dollars and sense. Scott provides real-world best practices that give every franchisee the opportunity to design his or her own future as part of a franchise network.

—Brian Schnell, Partner and Chair of Franchise Practice, Faegre Drinker

Scott's roadmap to becoming a Wealthy Franchisee has been confirmed over and over by numerous franchise authorities. His unique insights on how to leverage the opportunity offered franchise business owners are practical, tactical, and grounded in the science of cognitive behavior and peak performance. Scott has given the franchise community an extraordinary gift in the pages of this book.

—Katrina Mitchell, Owner & Founder, SPEAK! Franchise Speaker Bureau

Scott Greenberg goes right to the heart of franchisee success. Lots of people run franchises, but only some get wealthy. This book clearly explains why and shows you exactly what to do to get the best return on your investment.

—Kim Haidacher, Franchise Owner, The Little Gym

THE
WEALTHY
FRANCHISEE

Game-changing steps to becoming
a thriving franchise superstar

SCOTT GREENBERG

Entrepreneur Press®

Entrepreneur Press, Publisher
Cover Design: Andrew Welyczko
Production and Composition: Eliot House Productions

This publication is designed to provide accurate and authoritative information
in regard to the subject matter covered. It is sold with the understanding that
the publisher is not engaged in rendering legal, accounting, or other professional
services. If legal advice or other expert assistance is required, the services of a
competent professional person should be sought.

Entrepreneur Press® is a registered trademark of Entrepreneur Media, Inc.

An application to register this book for cataloging has been submitted to the
Library of Congress.

ISBN 978-1-64201-124-1 (paperback) | ISBN 978-1-61308-445-8 (ebook)

Printed in the United States of America

25 24 23 22 21   10 9 8 7 6 5 4 3 2 1

For Rachel

Contents

PART III
Mastering the Wealthy Franchisee Skill Set

Foreword

by Chuck Runyon
Anytime Fitness Cofounder, Self Esteem Brands CEO

One benefit of being an entrepreneur and franchisor is that I've had a courtside seat to human success and failure. I've done my best to remain both a student and a teacher throughout my career, and I could fill volumes with what I've learned over my three decades in business. But one question has always nagged me:

In franchising—and in life—how can you accurately predict who will succeed and who will fail?

My particular frame of reference is the fitness industry, where you'd think it would be easy to forecast a person's success based on their dedication and work ethic. But it isn't.

Early in my career, I was a membership salesperson and gym owner. I sold literally thousands of gym memberships to every kind of person on the planet. I watched people of all ages, shapes, sizes, education levels, and life experiences join a gym with the best intentions—they wanted to lose weight, gain muscle, train for events, or look their best for a special event, like a wedding or reunion. They all had access to the same weights, cardio machines, group exercise classes, and personal trainers. Yet some achieved their fitness goals while others didn't. People whom I expected to fail would surprise me. Others whose success I would have staked my life on would quit and never come back.

I later parlayed my experience into cofounding Anytime Fitness with my partner, Dave Mortensen. We revolutionized the fitness industry by paring down gyms to their essentials, placing them in convenient locations, making them affordable, and offering 24/7 access to members. We opened our first club in May 2002 in Cambridge, Minnesota, and we've now grown into the largest coed fitness franchise in the world, with nearly 5,000 clubs in 40 countries on 7 continents. (Yes, we even have a gym in Antarctica. We're the only franchise brand in history to have operating units on every continent.)

In many ways, a franchisor acts like a personal trainer for its franchisees. We design a business like a workout. We provide coaching and support. But ultimately, the franchisee—like a gym member—has to show up and do the work. Anytime Fitness franchises have had a remarkably high success rate, but no franchise system is immune to failure.

Is there an algorithm for predicting a top-performing franchisee vs. an average or below-average one? No, but I've always had a hunch about some of the intangibles that play into it. And after reading this book, I'm happy to say that Scott Greenberg not only confirms that hunch, but also expands on it in smart, creative, unexpected, and practical ways.

I first met Scott in fall 2018 when we hired him to speak at our annual conference in Louisville, Kentucky. Prior to attending his seminar, I had only seen a summary of his content from our conference planning team. I thought I'd stop in for about 20 minutes, check out his delivery, assess the engagement from our franchisees, and move on to another session. Instead, I was instantly riveted. I ended up staying to the end.

Scott's message grabbed me because it was exactly what every franchise owner needed to hear. As a successful franchisee himself, he could talk credibly about issues like franchisor-franchisee accountability.

He brilliantly weaved in inspiring and funny stories from real life. And when I looked around the room to gauge the audience's reaction, I saw the ultimate measure of success in today's attention-deficit world: no phones.

At the end of Scott's talk, I waited at the end of a long line to meet him, eavesdropping on the questions and comments he was getting from our franchisees:

"Thank you, that's exactly what I needed to hear!"

"I see my business differently now. This was a game changer!"

"You changed my mindset in 60 minutes. This session alone was worth coming to the conference!"

When I finally met Scott, his attitude told me everything I needed to know about why he was so successful. For a guy from Los Angeles, he was totally un-Hollywood. He had a confident but down-to-earth demeanor that didn't change a bit when I told him I was the CEO of Anytime Fitness (nor should it have). Our conversation was no different from the ones he had had with our franchisees—we were just two guys looking to improve our businesses. Scott and I agreed to connect after the conference; we saw each other when he came to Minneapolis a few weeks later, and then many times after that.

When Scott eventually showed me the manuscript of this book, I was excited at the thought of my franchisees reading it. He shares the secrets of success like no one else in the industry. He draws on personal, real-world experience. He tells it like it is and speaks from the heart. He hands you the keys to unlock your full potential. And he explodes a lot of myths along the way—myths you often hear from franchisees who don't understand (or refuse to acknowledge) the real issues behind their lack of success.

Why should you read this book? Because it will teach you what it means to be a wealthy franchisee. You'll learn the specific traits that give wealthy franchisees their edge. You'll learn common franchisee "mind traps" that get in the way of success. And you'll learn ways you can operationalize the wealthy franchisee mindset within your organization.

Whether you're a franchisee or franchisor—or if you're just passionate about getting better at anything you do—you'll love reading the insights Scott shares from his own life, as well as those he's discovered by working with big and small franchises throughout the world.

This book will change you. You'll feel different. Your old excuses will melt away. Your brain will feel energized. And you'll see nothing but potential in front of you. That's how I felt when I saw Scott's presentation at our conference two years ago, and I guarantee that's how you'll feel when you've turned the last page of this book.

Now get reading!

—Chuck Runyon, Anytime Fitness Cofounder,
Self Esteem Brands CEO

Introduction

'd just come offstage from keynoting the opening session of a quick-service restaurant franchise convention in New Orleans. The presentation had gone well and now, on break, a small group had gathered around to chat. But John, one of the franchisees in the audience, patiently waited until I was alone.

"Hi, Scott," he said. "I really enjoyed your speech. Do you have a minute to talk?"

"Sure. Want to sit?"

The ballroom was now empty, so we grabbed a couple of chairs up front. "How can I help you?" I asked.

John shared his story of quitting his banking job to buy into this franchise. It wasn't going as well as he'd hoped. Things started OK, but sales had petered out over the past few years. Managing the restaurant himself had kept labor costs down, but it had also consumed all his time. He struggled to keep good employees; it didn't help that he'd been late with payroll a few times. He'd been in survival mode for a while and no longer trusted corporate to help him. (He figured they'd probably just tell him to market more, like he could afford it.) He still had six years on his franchise agreement and his lease. There was no way he could sell the business for enough to pay his debts. He had been limping along by using the equity in his house, which had taken a toll on his marriage.

John blew out his breath in a long exhale once he had finished his story. His despondence was palpable. It was obvious his problems were as personal as they were professional.

I listened with much compassion and little judgment. After 10 years as a franchisee myself, I could certainly relate. I've had those moments. I shared them with John. Then I explained how I moved through them and how he could, too.

That evening I was invited to a reception for the "President's Circle" franchisees, the brand's top performers. I'd noticed many of these folks earlier in the convention. These were the franchisees with ribbons hanging from their name tags, displaying phrases such as "Presenter," "Multi-Unit Owner," and "Million Dollar Club." They were a chummy bunch, perhaps a little tipsy. Their mood was festive.

Diane had just won "Franchisee of the Year" and was getting lots of attention. She fended off the praise with jokes: "The people they really wanted to award just couldn't make it to the convention!" I asked her if she had time for an interview, and she had to check her schedule. She didn't want to miss any of the breakout sessions. Meeting after the convention wasn't an option—she and her husband were leaving directly for the airport for a 10-day vacation in the Bahamas. We agreed to have breakfast together the next morning.

Over breakfast, I learned Diane had been in the system for seven years. She'd built two restaurants before picking up two existing locations in the past 18 months. The recent acquisitions hadn't yet matched the numbers of her original stores, but sales were definitely on the uptick. She was pleased.

"Seems like you know what you're doing, Diane," I said. "What's your secret?"

"Honestly, your guess is as good as mine!" she said. "I just really love this business, and it seems to be working."

John and Diane sell the same products in similar territories. They follow the same procedures under the same brand name. They pay the same royalties and buy from the same suppliers. They share the same opportunities and face the same threats. John and Diane are essentially running the same business. But their *experiences* of the business? Day and night.

Every franchise system I work with has franchisees like John, Diane, and the less extreme majority in between. Lots of people are running identical operations but getting different results. Through decades of professional business speaking and 10 years of running my own Edible Arrangements franchises, I've worked to understand this disparity. Why would so many people running the same business vary so much in their success? *The Wealthy Franchisee: Game-Changing Steps to Becoming a Thriving Franchise Superstar* will answer that question.

There's no denying that marketing, location, and operational skill are critical factors. But when you look at top franchisees across many companies and compare them with their lower-performing counterparts, you start to see some other patterns as well. It's not just where they're located. It's not just how they work. What really stands out is how they *think*.

Top performers have mental grit, enabling them to navigate through the complicated, stressful, and often lonely endeavor that is running a franchise. They see opportunities others don't. They respond well to adversity. They cultivate productive relationships with customers, employees, and their franchisor. Most of all, they control their thoughts.

This mental advantage translates to operational superiority. They engage in the same tasks and face the same problems as their peers. But they do it better because their mind is an asset to their business, not a liability. All franchisees think about their work. Top franchisees also work on how they think. That's their edge.

The Wealthy Franchisee will help you develop this edge. Incorporating concepts from interviews, surveys, anecdotes, cognitive behavioral therapy, brain science, and my firsthand experience as a franchisee, this book will help you adopt the habits of high-performance franchisees. You're going to explore your own mental responses and become more self-aware. You'll learn ways to optimize your thinking for better business leadership. Then you'll learn how to infuse your refined philosophy into daily operational procedures. This book will help you grow your business.

The use of the word "wealthy" in the title isn't just a hook. We'll define this word soon, but I assure you, there's a financial component to it. If all you care about is money, this book can help you make it and/or save it. But our approach to becoming wealthy may be different from what you expect.

Maybe you're hoping for practical tactics. Yes, you will get concrete ideas for running your business. But tactics are only as good as the execution. And their efficacy may be short-lived. Pick up a marketing book from five years ago and tell me how many of those tactics still work.

This book is about something bigger. It's about timeless, universal concepts that have always given top performers their edge. It's not just about building the business around you but the leader *inside* you. With a wealthy franchisee mindset, you'll get the most out of any tactics, no matter how quickly they come and go. You might even be the one who invents them.

Why Top Franchisees Can't Always Help Struggling Franchisees

It's common in franchising for someone like John to reach out to someone like Diane. She's getting wealthy in this business. Why not ask her how she's doing it?

The problem is that while high performers know what they're doing, they don't always know what they're doing differently. They're just running their business the only way they know how. They may not be able to articulate the real reasons for their success.

Outdoor Living Brands once brought me in to keynote a convention for their multiple franchise brands and asked me to emcee their awards banquet, where they recognized their top franchisees, based purely on sales. I suggested we keep the award winners onstage and interview them as a panel to see if we could squeeze out a few great ideas to share with the company. The award winners knew in advance they'd won and were asked to think of one thing they'd done in the past year that enabled them to succeed.

The first winner said, "We do a lot of marketing."

The second said, "We treat our employees really well."

The third said, "We go out into the community and get involved."

That's their big secret? That's their special sauce? Who *isn't* doing that stuff?! A few had some interesting ideas, but nothing mind-blowing. The discussion was pretty underwhelming.

But there were some things the top franchisees onstage had in common. All of them seemed positive, confident, and in control of their business. They were curious and committed to learning. They were focused on their customers. They were strong leaders. They took responsibility for their circumstances. They stuck to the system. They were the kind of people you like to do business with.

This distinction was never acknowledged (until my keynote the next morning). The entire conversation focused on operations. None of the award winners articulated their mindset, but all of them exuded it.

I always ask franchisees for the cause of their stress. What do they worry about? What keeps them up at night? I then try to speak to these issues during my programs.

Most people have plenty to say. They worry about sales and the competition. Their employees aggravate them. Their corporate office neglects them. These complaints are very common among franchisees.

But then I met Abdul Karim. Abdul is a multi-unit franchisee with Precision Tune Auto Care. His two units consistently rank number one and two in Washington state for revenue, operations, and customer service. His customers love him. His employees are loyal. His businesses are profitable. This guy is a high performer.

No matter how I asked the question, Abdul refused to complain about anything. He sleeps well at night. He solves any problems that arise. His employees consistently perform. I asked him what other franchisees complain about. In reply, he told me everything franchisees need to do to succeed in their system. His optimism was unbreakable and clearly the foundation for his success.

Across town from Abdul, Vinnie Sposari runs a Mr. Rooter Plumbing operation. Vinnie went from working as a single "man in a van" to overseeing a team of 65 employees who've helped him build the number-one Mr. Rooter franchise in America. Vinnie has earned countless performance and service awards, including multiple wins of "Franchise of the Year."

Like Abdul, Vinnie is upbeat. He's humble. He's grateful for his team. He runs a tight operation that gets great results. His business is completely different from Abdul's, but his attitude is identical. I asked him what he does to succeed.

"I believe there's something in me that allows me to be positive about things," he said.

OK, but what is that "something"?

Twenty-six hundred miles away, Danna Vach runs a Bruster's Real Ice Cream franchise in Georgia, which she acquired from a previous owner. After she took over the business, annual sales doubled. How'd she do it? "I don't know!" she confessed with a laugh. She couldn't identify any operational or marketing strategy that made a difference. Things just started working, and she had no idea why.

I do. Danna is just like Abdul from Precision Tune Auto Care and Vinnie from Mr. Rooter Plumbing. She's like those award-winning franchisees from Outdoor Living Brands. She's like the many other franchisees profiled throughout this book. She's positive. She's engaged. Danna has the qualities I consistently see among great business owners.

The best franchisees may not be able to tell you what makes them special, but this book can. I'm here to report my findings to you. We're going to explore in detail the thoughts and behaviors of the franchise industry's superstars. We're going to look at what they do and how they think. We're going to understand their methods and replicate them. Soon you'll be among them. And if you're already among them, you'll understand why. Even if you're great, you can always get better.

There are always some businesses that won't succeed. Their location, the competition, or other factors may render wealth-building impossible. The right person doing the right things in the wrong situation will not succeed. This book isn't about performing miracles.

But it is about maximizing potential. We control more than we realize. Most of our obstacles are excuses. They're real, but they don't tell the whole story. Wealthy franchisees turn around low-performing locations all the time. They scoop up these gold mines at rock-bottom prices from desperate franchisees who don't realize how much potential they're sitting on.

My money says you've got a better business than you think you do. You can lead better than you are. You can *serve* better than you are. Unless you're operating like a wealthy franchisee, you're in no place to judge what you have. Your business performance is as much a reflection of how you think as what you have.

So let's find out what you really have. Let's work together. Let's get you in shape and get you thinking and leading and serving like a wealthy franchisee. Only then can we put your business to the test and find its true value.

What to Expect in this Book

Our journey through these chapters will take us to three places. Each is a necessary stop to reach our final destination. We've got to build you before you can build your business. Don't look for shortcuts. Each section requires mastery of the previous one. To get what wealthy franchisees have, you must do everything they do. *Everything*. As so many franchisors say, stick to the system.

In Part I, we'll take a close look at the franchise experience. Who are wealthy franchisees and how are they different? What's the real reason they succeed? What's it really like to run a franchise, and why do wealthy franchisees thrive within the system? Part II will explore the specific internal dynamics of wealthy franchisees. We'll discuss some common mental traps hindering business execution, and then we'll address the strategies necessary to manage them.

These first two parts are the foundation for Part III, which is about external behavior. That's the actual work that launches businesses to the next level. What do wealthy franchisee customer service and leadership look like? How do wealthy franchisees cultivate productive partnerships with their franchisors? What do they do—what can we *all* do—to get wealthy?

Before we start, I want to be crystal clear about my intentions. This isn't a personal-growth book. I'm not here to motivate you. I am here to help you get wealthy. If this book warms your heart but doesn't build your business, I've failed.

But warmer hearts and clearer heads correlate with better execution. This is the common denominator among all wealthy franchisees. I'm not saying this because I want it to be true. It is true. It's the key to franchise success. So please trust me, lean in, and get ready for everything to change.

If you read this book and consistently apply its concepts, you will quickly:

- See the connection between your mindset and business performance
- Better assess your business challenges
- Find solutions and ideas faster
- Get more done in less time
- Strengthen your partnership with your franchisor
- Improve your customer service and build a loyal fan base
- Engage, inspire, and retain your employees
- Reduce your stress level
- Grow your business and build wealth more quickly
- Unload your mental junk, get out of your own way, and get down to the business of making money
- Become a wealthy franchisee

Let's get to work!

PART I

THE WEALTHY FRANCHISEE

When Edmund Hillary and Tenzing Norgay reached the peak of Mount Everest in 1953, they proved the climb was possible and blazed a path for others to follow. Now each year, hundreds of adventurers attempt to walk in their footsteps. With the same weather, the same gear, and the same resources, some make it and others don't. Some quit. Some fall ill. Some never leave the mountain. It's not enough to know the road to travel. You must also be the right kind of traveler. You need to get in shape. You need to prepare. You need to enjoy (or be willing to endure) the long, brutal experience that is summiting the world's highest peak.

Your franchisor has done for your business what Hillary and Norgay did for climbing Everest. They've proved success is possible and have mapped the path to the top. Yet many franchisees fail to reach the heights they could potentially achieve because they underestimate the effort it will take—or overestimate themselves.

I want you to achieve your goals. I want you to peak. But before you start your quest toward wealth, you need to know what you're getting into. You need to understand what the franchise journey really is so you can prepare yourself. An operations manual can't capture the franchise ownership experience any better than a map can describe what it feels like to travel there. To know—to be *ready*—you have to study the accounts of those who've done it.

Running a franchise isn't as harrowing as scaling a mountain, but it has just as many pitfalls. There are factors you can't control. Ignorance, ego, and haste only increase the danger. That's why you need to know about and respect the work.

I'm not trying to scare you away from franchising. It's thrilling! I did it and loved it. I just want you to understand what to expect. Perhaps you've already been running a franchise, but having experience is not the same thing as understanding it. You need to take a step back to have context. That comes from looking at many franchisees across multiple brands. Just as traveling helps you better appreciate where you come from, looking at the broader experience of the franchise world will reveal a lot about your own business. The years I've spent working with so many other franchises have given me a whole new perspective on the decade I spent running my Edible Arrangements stores. There's a lot I couldn't see while I was in the trenches. I wish I had known then what I know now. That's the purpose of Part I—studying the larger franchise experience to widen your knowledge of your own.

These first chapters will give you critical insight into wealthy franchisees. We're going to look at their lifestyle. We'll explore the reality behind who they are as well as the myths. You need to know the truth if you want to replicate the conditions, characteristics, and tactics that enable their success.

CHAPTER 1

Meet the
Wealthy Franchisee

Chapter Features

- A profile of wealthy franchisees
- The three elements of being "wealthy"
- The three levels of franchisees
- Myths about top franchisees and why they succeed

D avid answers my call on his Bluetooth-enabled helmet from atop an Aspen ski slope. I catch him just before he pushes off to descend this powdery, black diamond heaven. He doesn't need to take calls on vacation—he just likes being available. I assure him we can talk later. Certainly we can wait until he's reached the bottom.

David is one of the top franchisees in a brand of early childhood development centers. He has money, but equally important, he has *time*. He doesn't always have to be at work, and his wife never has to be there. She practices law. Together they bring in plenty of money to raise their family in a great neighborhood, travel, and ski. David runs his business. It doesn't run him.

David is a good example of the many wealthy franchisees I've met over the years. When researching the companies that bring me in to speak, I always ask to interview their superstars. And by that, I don't mean the franchisor's favorites. I'm talking about the ones with the highest profits and the best lifestyles. They are the wealthy franchisees.

Being a wealthy franchisee is a question of personality. Anyone can take on this personality. Anyone can embrace these high-performance habits and get the same results. Wealth is nothing but a byproduct of choices. You don't need talent, education, or brilliance. You don't even need an idea—you've already paid your franchisor for one. Now you just need to execute.

That concept is simple to understand, but often hard in practice. Most people don't execute as well as they should. They don't appreciate their role as a franchisee. They think they've bought a recipe for success. In a way, they have. Their franchisor tells them what ingredients to get and what to do with them. But the franchisor can't control how well they measure, slice, stir, or bake.

Your franchisor can't control how warmly you greet customers. They can't force you to inspire your employees. They can't shift your focus from minutia to the big picture. So many elements of the business are on you. You are the biggest variable, and your impact on your operation can't be overstated.

But that's great news. It means you're betting on yourself. You're in control. When you work for someone else, you're betting on *them*.

There's a perception of stability when you have a job. Don't believe it. In that situation, you can do everything right and still get burned.

Most businesses in your industry are underperforming. That works to your advantage. You're competing against mediocrity. Lead with excellence, and you win.

Excellence comes naturally for some franchisees. Others need to be more conscientious. But everyone has the potential to build franchise wealth.

A Day in the Life of a Wealthy Franchisee

Imagine you're having a good day as the owner of a successful retail franchise operation. You start early. Coffee tastes best before the sun comes up. While the rest of the world sleeps, you read a business book and make some notes. Then you close your eyes and take a few final moments to envision your day until you hear footsteps. Time to parent.

After getting the kids out the door for school, you open an app on your smartphone that shows what's happening in your store. The lights are already on, and your employees are scurrying around, prepping for the day. You'll check in there later. First you'll go to the gym.

After exercising and getting cleaned up, you stop at a discount warehouse to pick up some supplies and throw them in the back of your Lexus. (You really *do* use it for business.) When you get to your store, you decide to leave the supplies in the car for the moment. Today you want to enter through the front door, as a customer would.

The place feels pleasant and clean. You notice a balled-up gum wrapper on the floor and reach down to grab it. You straighten a few display items. The display looks great, but you want it *perfect*. A team member is helping customers. He gives you a warm nod as you head to the back.

Your manager greets you as you make your way to the office. She's busy but in good spirits. She mentions over her shoulder that she'd like to go over a few things when you have a moment.

You enter the office and sit at the desk. Next to the keyboard is a note from an employee asking for a day off to take her mom to a medical appointment. You leave that for your manager to handle. There's also an envelope with your name on the outside. It's a note from last night's shift leader. She apologizes that she can't explain why the register closed out with an extra $20, which she's clipped to the note (unaware you asked your manager to slip the extra money in the till yesterday to see what she'd do). You're proud of her and look forward to announcing her promotion to assistant manager. Your manager was right about her. She's a keeper.

You run some reports on the computer. This week's sales are slightly down, but month-to-date you're up 14 percent. You run a "how heard" report to see if your recent marketing initiatives are bringing in customers. There's also lots of email to deal with, mostly invoices and shipping notices from vendors. Your corporate office has sent their weekly update. You read about upcoming franchises they're opening and a new promotion rolling out next month. And there's a notice from Yelp that someone has left you a review. They gave you five stars and mentioned one of your employees by name. You remind yourself to get her a gift card.

You pay a few bills and then do your walk around. There're always adjustments to be made and work to be corrected, but you also acknowledge everything your team is doing right. You hand your car keys to one of your employees and ask him to unload the supplies. Then you make your way to the front to greet a few customers.

Later you sit down with your manager. There are a few repairs she needs you to approve. She updates you on employee performance. She herself would like to take a few days off to attend a friend's wedding. You discuss how sales have been this week and brainstorm ideas to raise ticket averages. Finally, you tell her how grateful you are for her hard work. She thanks you and rushes out to help with a flurry of customers who just walked in. Realizing you're probably in the way at this point, you remove yesterday's cash from the safe and exit through the back door.

You make a quick drop at the bank and then head to a weekly meeting with your networking group. You're eager to speak with one of your colleagues who's had a lot of success with some new digital marketing initiatives. She actually seeks you out first to see if you'd like to donate a prize and say a few words at a charity auction she's chairing. Four hundred people will be there. Yeah, you'll help her out.

You now have just enough time to get to the high school for your daughter's volleyball game. On the way, you call your manager to tell her about the auction. She suggests donating three items and requiring the winners to come into the store to claim them. You like her thinking.

You're greeted in the gymnasium by the school athletic director, who knows you well. So do all the parents. Every game they see your sponsorship banner hanging on the wall beneath the scoreboard. Many come to chat with you after the game. Your daughter grows impatient. "C'mon—I have homework!"

You smile at the other parents. "Her majesty beckons!"

No one feels like cooking tonight, so the family stops for Italian. You all debate about whether you should hit another national park this summer or go back to Maui. Better enjoy these kids while you can. For a moment, your mind drifts back to those stressful corporate days reporting to that miserable vice president. The money was good, but it was costing you your soul. Did you really spend 15 years there?

On the drive home, you pass a busy strip mall and notice a "For Lease" sign on an end cap. The location would be perfect for another store.

The life of a wealthy franchisee isn't without stress. You're going to have some rough days. Sales will slump. Stuff will break. Employees will quit. Things happen.

Still, it's a pretty good gig. And it's probably a lot better than your jobs in the past. You get to do things on your own terms. You're the boss. You no longer have to worry about how you're treated. As a wealthy franchisee, you live your life by your own design.

Wealthy franchisees get to do what they want, as much or as little as they want. And they make plenty of money. That doesn't mean trillions of dollars, but relative to what they've invested, they're getting a great return. Wealthy franchisees live well.

The Three Elements of Being Wealthy

"Wealthy" is a subjective and relative term. Many people say having $1 million in the bank makes them wealthy, but some only need $100,000 and some need $100 million. In some parts of the world, you're considered well-off if you have your own cow. It all depends on your desires, your expectations, and where you live. I live in Los Angeles, California, and my brother lives in Greensboro, North Carolina. My house is worth twice as much as his, but it's half the size. If I were smarter, I'd invest in real estate here and live there.

But even if you meet your financial expectations, you must also consider the cost of building your wealth. The most basic report in business accounting is the P&L. The top portion of the P&L lists all revenues. The total amount of revenues is meaningless until you subtract the bottom portion of the P&L, your expenses. The expenses tell us how much it cost to achieve the revenues. The difference between the two is your profit or loss.

But that bottom portion, the expenses, only tells us about the financial costs of the revenues. It doesn't tell us about the time that was invested. It doesn't tell us how much stress was endured. It doesn't tell us about the strain the business put on your health and your relationships.

If you're working seven days a week and sacrificing all quality of life to stockpile cash, I don't care how much money you have. You're not a wealthy franchisee. You can always make more money, but you'll never get more time. I don't want an ulcer or a divorce. I don't want to miss the opening of the newest Marvel movie. And if getting rich means missing my kids' games and recitals, count me out.

On the other hand, basketball shoes and ballet slippers cost money. So do car payments, gym memberships, and dog food. I want to be able to pay my kids' college tuition, buy more cool stuff, go out to dinner with my wife, and see the world. I want to give a lot more to charity and secure my retirement. Mostly, I don't want to worry about money.

When you buy a franchise, you're getting more than a business. You're acquiring a lifestyle. You'll have more responsibility, more liability, and more surprises than any job you've ever had. And unlike a job, you can't just quit. You're on the hook.

With a commitment like that, you'd better like what you'll be doing. You need to have a passion for frozen yogurt, or haircuts, or home care for seniors—or for some aspect of providing these products and services. You'd better be excited about how you're going to spend your time, because you're about to spend a lot of it.

But that's the reward! You actually *get* to spend time doing something you enjoy. You get to make money working for yourself. If you like what you do, then the time you spend on it won't be a sacrifice. And if you're smart, you'll have plenty of time to do everything else you want, too, even if that's working on another business.

For the purposes of this book, the term "wealthy" refers not to a dollar amount but to a lifestyle. Wealthy franchisees are those people who build businesses that 1) make money, 2) free up time, and 3) maximize quality of life.

Making Money

Without a doubt, there is a financial aspect to being wealthy. I'm not saying being rich is more important than being loved. I'm not suggesting that making money is more important than making a difference. You shape your own values.

But making money does allow you to have more choices. And if you balance this component with the other two (time and quality of life), you'll have *enjoyable* wealth.

So how much is "a lot of" money? That's subjective. I can't name a number to define financial wealth for you. You should have an idea of the kind of money you can make in your particular business.

Some might say they just want enough money to be happy. So how much is that? There's actually an answer to that question: $75,000.

Princeton University's renowned psychologist Angus Deaton and Nobel laureate psychologist Daniel Kahneman analyzed more than 450,000 responses to the Gallup-Healthways Well-Being Index. They discovered that $75,000 annual household income is the threshold for increases in emotional well-being, even among those who live in more expensive cities. The comforts afforded to those earning above that amount yielded little or no increases in happiness. Those who achieved higher degrees of emotional well-being got it from other sources.

Maybe you don't believe the experts. That's OK. Try it for yourself. There's a good chance you can make more than $75,000 from your franchise, although you may have to adjust the number for inflation. (The Princeton report was published in 2010. In 2020, the number is probably closer to $90,000.) Read this book and do the work, and then you'll know.

Prior to selling someone a franchise, franchisors are required to disclose everything about their company in their franchise disclosure document (FDD). Item 19 of the standard FDD provides details on the financial performance of a franchise. It may provide earnings ranges, historical performance, costs, and other relevant information to give prospects an idea of their potential ROI. But Item 19 is optional. Many franchisors are reluctant to share this data. This may be because the numbers are low (sometimes skewed down by the worst-performing franchisees).

For most franchises trading in U.S. greenbacks, top operators are pulling in around six figures of profit per unit on the high end. Many franchisees make millions of dollars by running multiple locations. Some of them are large corporate entities running hundreds of units, sometimes from multiple brands.

It's up to you to set your own financial goals. To keep it realistic, you may wish to aim for a percentile within your system, such as being in the top 10 percent of all franchisees in sales. Almost all the wealthy franchisees mentioned in this book fall into that category. You may also wish to include an annual rate of growth. Look to your franchise system and your industry to determine the average growth rate. (If you plan to use what you learn in this book, be sure to shoot for a few points higher!) Most important, set goals for profit. What matters most is what you take home.

Of course, in evaluating your revenue, you also need to consider how long it takes you to generate it.

Control of Your Time

I once asked an audience of franchisees to raise their hands if they'd be happy making $1 million from their business. Most raised their hands. "Let me finish my question," I cautioned. "How many of you would be happy making $1 million from your business *over the course of 25 years?*" Most hands went down. They were working way too hard to make only $40,000 a year for the next 25 years. I asked another question: "How many of you would be happy making $1 million in a year if it would cost you your family, your friends, and reduce your life span?" A few hands went up, but not many.

There's an important relationship between time and money. Making $70,000 by working part time may be a smarter model than making $100,000 working full time. This is especially true when the time you save is invested in a second business, whether it's an additional location or another business altogether.

Some franchise systems require franchisees to be full-time operators. I understand this policy. They don't want passive investors who aren't committed to building the business.

At the same time, the entire concept of franchising is to create replicable systems that aren't dependent on any one person. It's all about scaling. As they say in the industry, if you only buy one location and run it yourself, you haven't bought a business. You've bought yourself a job.

The best franchisees make themselves as unnecessary as possible for day-to-day operations. That's not neglect—quite the contrary. It's the ultimate form of leadership. Great leaders breed more leaders. They create an infrastructure that frees them to focus on more important things. They invest a lot of time upfront so they have more free time later. Smart financial investments yield more money. Smart time investments give you more time.

I opened my first Edible Arrangements franchise with the intention of not needing to constantly be in my store. I could have saved on labor and maybe increased my revenues by running the franchise myself every day. But my objective was to run it part time while maintaining a slightly reduced speaking schedule. The net result was a significant increase in my annual income from multiple revenue streams, one of which was a tangible asset that would increase in value.

To accomplish this, I had to work smart, create systems, develop my team members, use technology, and focus on what mattered most. My work had to make money *and* save time.

It worked well for us. Even though I wasn't always there, we still became one of the highest-volume locations in the state. We earned stellar reviews for customer service and became a training store for other franchisees. We opened a second location and built that up as well. A smart time investment doesn't necessarily mean full time. It means full *commitment*.

There is nothing more valuable than time. We can always make more money, but time is something we'll only have less of. It's precious. It's like a bank account from which we only make withdrawals. None of us knows our remaining balance. All we can do with time is choose how we spend it.

Like financial wealth, I can't determine how you should spend your time. Some people love family time while others want solitude. Some people want an active social life and others just really love to work. Only you know what makes you happy.

The important thing is that wealthy franchisees have options. They're in control of their time. They can work 80 hours a week on their business if they want, but they don't have to. They're happy with the money they make given the time they invest.

Quality of Life

Finally, we need to look at what your life is like with this business in it. Are you having fun, or are you stressed out? Do you feel proud of what you do? Does the business contribute to your life or take away from it? These are important questions to ask. And over time the answers might change.

Wealthy franchisees live well and their business helps them do it. They may really enjoy the work itself, or perhaps they love the things the business allows them to do.

Honestly, I wasn't passionate about fruit, but I really liked being in the special-occasion business. People just lit up whenever they saw our fruit arrangements. At parties, they would gather around a basket and moan with pleasure as they bit into a juicy chunk of pineapple. I felt deep pride on a busy day watching all the activity in my stores. Employees were buying clothing for their kids with money they made by working in my business. Customers would hide engagement rings in boxes of our chocolate-covered strawberries. And the more experience

I gained by owning and working in this franchise, the more material I had for my speaking business. The professions complemented each other.

I had bad days and plenty of problems as a franchisee. If you had caught me on the right day in the wrong mood, I would have handed you the keys for free. (I'd say the same thing about my kids.) Invariably, though, those moments passed. Most days were good. Generally speaking, having the business made my life better. (Also true of my kids.)

I reject the notion that work is something to be endured. Sure, we must all pay our dues. But there's a difference between hard work and suffering. When my son's basketball coach asks him to run five more "suicides," he's working, but he's not suffering. Running suicides is a pain he appreciates because it's part of the training process, and he feels great when he's done. But a receptionist who is verbally abused by her boss, feels her work is meaningless, and goes home each night in tears—she's suffering.

Remember, you're not just investing in a business. You're buying a lifestyle. Owning a franchise should make your life better. Wealthy franchisees are happy people living full, rich lives, and their business makes it possible.

To be wealthy is to balance money, time, and quality of life in a way that works for you. If you can remember this, you'll sustain your success a lot longer.

I've asked a lot of franchisors to tell me about their "top franchisees," and it's always interesting to hear their criteria for "top." Some mention the franchisee with the highest-volume unit. Others choose the operator with the most locations.

Multi-unit operators have sophisticated operations and generate a lot of revenue for the franchisor. That gets them a lot of attention, but it doesn't necessarily qualify them as wealthy franchisees.

I met one multi-unit franchisee who had one of the biggest enterprises in the company. His combined stores generated $6 million in sales annually. His franchisor loved him for that, touting him as an exemplary franchisee. But he confided to me that the profit of all his locations put together was less than what many good single-unit operators generate. He had much more responsibility and little to show for it. Some years, he actually lost money.

I recommend multi-unit operation. It's the best way to make big money. But it starts by performing well at the unit level, and that requires high-level thinking.

Three Levels of Franchisees

In his book *Above the Line: Lessons in Leadership and Life from a Championship Program* (Penguin, 2017), Ohio State's former championship-winning football coach Urban Meyer discusses his "10-80-10" principle. Ten percent of football players are elite—skilled, self-disciplined, and committed. Eighty percent are compliant: They're reliable, but they're not as driven to succeed as the elite players. The final 10 percent are resistant—they're just coasting, not interested in trying to succeed as long as they can skate by with little effort. Meyer and his coaching staff worked with the elite players, but most of their time was spent trying to elevate the compliant players into elite players. That was the team's biggest opportunity for improvement. He estimates that by the end of their 2014 championship season, 30 percent of their team qualified as elite.

Most franchisees also fall into three categories, which I call "wealthy," "typical," and "struggling." The franchisees I highlight in this book are all among the top sales performers within their systems. They also meet the criteria for "wealthy" I described above. Struggling franchisees rank lowest within their systems. Many in this group have succumbed to anger. They're also resistant. They've given up but haven't yet gotten out. They're just biding their time.

But the majority of franchisees are "typical." They're the 80 percent. They're paying the bills and maybe even making a decent living. But they often feel stuck somewhere between hopeful and discouraged. They really want to grow. They want to get wealthy. They want to be among the elite. They just can't seem to figure out how.

It's always fascinating to ask franchisees which of these three groups they think they're in. Most feel they're typical—including the wealthy franchisees. I sometimes facilitate workshops for top performers. When I describe the three groups, most of them identify with the typical franchisees, despite their high rankings. It turns out that humility and ambition are also part of the wealthy franchisee profile.

I talk with franchisees at all three levels before every presentation. I want to know their perspectives so I can speak directly to their experience. Not only have I learned what wealthy franchisees have in common, but I also see what typical and struggling franchisees have in common. Getting to know them has helped me further distinguish their high-performing counterparts.

Wealthy franchisees aren't extraordinary people. In fact, they're really no smarter or talented than their lower-performing colleagues. They just manage their thoughts as well as they manage their business, making them operationally superior. Their mind flow leads to cash flow. Fortunately, their mental habits can be replicated, and so can their success.

 WEALTHY FRANCHISEE SPOTLIGHT

JEFF TOREN

Kitchen Tune-Up

Malvern, Pennsylvania

- Number one in sales
- Doubled sales from previous year
- 2019 Dave Haglund Entrepreneur Award (for embodying the entrepreneurial spirit of the founder)
- 2016 National Rising Star Award (for best first-year franchisee sales ever)
- Project of the Month multiple times
- 2019 Project of the Year

Jeff Toren is all about "belief." That word came up several times in our conversation and is clearly the reason for his success. He shared a story of seeing the phrase "100% Growth" on a slide being presented by Kitchen Tune-Up CEO Heidi Morrissey. She was actually advocating for 100 percent of locations to grow, but Jeff wasn't paying attention and thought she meant all franchisees doubling sales. He was already number one in the system by far, doing $2 million in revenue. But when he saw her slide, he envisioned $4 million in annual sales. "OK, we can do that," he thought matter-of-factly, and got to work. As this book goes to press, he's on track to do it.

Jeff is humble, yet hungry. He's constantly reading books and listening to audiobooks and podcasts. That helps him take calculated risks. He's replaced himself four times, hiring more people to keep himself out of the weeds. It's been scary, but acting courageously has enabled him to focus on growth.

"Mindset is the key," he told me. "If you don't have that, everything else goes down to a lower level. You're not going to drive, you're not going to increase your marketing, and you're not going to hire that one more person to help you grow."

Jeff's Wealthy Franchisee Success Tips:

- Build a great team and inspire their passion.
- Stretch yourself, believe you can grow, and keep investing in the business.
- Slow down when you get scared. Revisit your beliefs in your success, but tackle problems head-on. Get help from someone else with an objective perspective.
- Constantly feed yourself with positivity, motivation, and healthy messages.
- Continuously learn and grow.
- Find your why, go after it, and believe in it.

Myths about Wealthy Franchisees

It's hard to reproduce someone else's success if we don't know how they achieved it. There are a lot of misconceptions out there, and a lot of guessing. Your observations about the wealthy franchisees in your system may be true. But what you observe may not be the reason for their success. It's easy to mix up cause and effect.

I meet a lot of franchisees. I ask the best ones why they're successful. I see who they are and what they do. Then I talk to the struggling franchisees and ask them what they believe their high-performing counterparts have going for them. Often there's a huge disconnect.

I also talk with the franchisors. They have a wider perspective, as they see the results over a wide field of franchisees running the same operations. They also tell me about the misperceptions many franchisees have about their top performers. Let's explore the most common ones.

They Have Winning Locations

A fellow franchisee once told me how lucky I was to have my store location. I was a little insulted. He knew nothing about our operation or our customer service. He only knew our address, which was close to Beverly Hills. In his mind, rich people were lining up with stacks of Benjamins to buy enormous fruit baskets. But that wasn't our customer base. Our prestigious territory came with little parking, constant traffic (making deliveries tough), and high rent. I wouldn't sign that lease today. Our high sales weren't because of where we were. They were because of what we did.

Location absolutely matters in franchising, especially for restaurants and retail. Demographics, population density, foot traffic—they make a difference. You've got to fish where the fish are. Your franchisor can help with this. They know their customer profile and should be able to analyze your territory—at least on paper—and assist with site selection. Sometimes a great location can compensate for lackluster operations. It can also make some franchisees feel a little more confident about their business acumen than they should.

But a great location may be hard to identify. It may be too expensive. Or it may just not be available. That's OK. Ultimately, it's the franchisee who will make or break the business. Franchisors all have stories of amazing operators tearing it up in locations where others failed. Their loyal customers travel longer distances to repeat a great experience. Their dedicated, well-treated employees work harder to create those experiences.

Just ask Burke Jones, who twice bought struggling locations of The UPS Store. One was in an average neighborhood without any demographic advantages. The other was four doors away from a FedEx Office store. But with his stellar customer service, he built each location (on separate occasions) into the number-one unit in the entire network of almost 5,000 stores.

Wealthy franchisees look for great locations but don't rely on them. For them, "good enough" is all it takes.

Give the top franchisees in your system more credit. Their excellent operations make locations look better and may be easier to replicate than their ZIP codes.

They're Workaholics

Wealthy franchisees work hard and put in the hours. So do many typical and struggling franchisees, of course. Hard work isn't the secret to success. It's the prerequisite. Lots of franchisees are sacrificing and sweating, but not all of them are getting results.

The high performers I meet aren't always putting in *more* hours; they're putting in *better* hours. They know the difference between activity and productivity. They work *on* their business, not just *in* their business. They develop leaders rather than manage employees and put the necessary infrastructure in place to ensure they don't have to do it all themselves. A franchisee who owns 20 locations has no more hours in the day than someone with just one. With the right people, training, and systems, their work yields more results. They're no busier than other franchisees; they're just more productive.

They Have Previous Experience

Yes, previous business experience can give you a head start. Financial literacy, customer service, leadership, sales, marketing—these are all skills you can bring with you to your franchise. The next time I open a business, I'd like to think my experience with Edible Arrangements will give me an enormous advantage.

But "business" is a broad word. You can develop skills in one endeavor that don't translate into another. Past success in one career is in no way a guarantee of success running your own business. Even in a busy, high-stakes corporate environment, there's structure, feedback, and a regular paycheck. There are bosses, expectations, and a lot of intensity.

Running a business is a different kind of intensity. No one's directly supervising your work or holding you accountable. There's no threat of getting fired, only of being unable to escape.

And business ownership is different from franchise ownership. Independent business owners can do whatever they want. Forging a partnership with a franchisor, hewing to company standards, having others out there representing the brand—it's miles apart. Some folks struggle with that distinction.

Franchisors complain to me that many new franchisees with a lot of outside experience have a difficult time embracing their systems. They come with knowledge and biases that make it hard to trust the company methods. They have a hard time unlearning old ways of doing things and believe they know better than the franchisor. They try to outsmart the model.

Most wealthy franchisees stick to the system. When I try to convey this concept onstage, it can make me sound like a corporate shill, but it's true. I don't meet franchisees who've gotten wealthy by defying brand practices.

But I do meet a lot of great franchisees who don't have extensive business experience. They come in fresh and open and curious. They trust the ops manual, bring the right mindset, and execute better than anyone else.

So yes, experience is advantageous—provided it doesn't conflict with proven systems or close your mind to new ways of doing things. And if you don't have experience, don't worry. Running a franchise is the perfect way to acquire it.

They're More Educated

I'm grateful for the higher education I was privileged to get. It made me a better, smarter, more informed person. But it didn't make me a better franchisee. Books and lectures can tell you a lot about swimming, but they can't make you a swimmer. If there was ever a discipline that needed to be learned in the field, it's running a franchise. I watched one of my neighboring Edible Arrangements franchisees drive his business into the ground. He had a master's in engineering. A less educated franchisee with more relevant skills bought the business and made it profitable.

Many franchising legends never went to college. Peter Cancro was only 17 when he bought Mike's Subs, eventually turning it into Jersey Mike's. Wendy's founder Dave Thomas dropped out of high school and didn't get his GED until he was 61. And these are franchisors. I've met countless successful franchisees who also got their education on their feet and in their stores.

To be a wealthy franchisee, you don't have to be a college graduate as much as an ongoing student. What you know is less important than what you're willing to learn.

They Love the Business

I've heard different opinions on this. While CEO of Naf Naf Grill, Paul Damico told me without question that his top performers had a passion for their food and the experience they provide. I heard similar sentiments from Erin Walter, director of marketing at Global Franchise Group. Their best franchisees also love delighting customers with their brands' comfort foods and treats. When I asked Tropical Smoothie Cafe's CEO Charles Watson what his top franchisees have in common, the first thing he said was "passion for the brand."

But Great Clips vice chair Rhoda Olsen disagreed. "'Do what you love' is BS," she said. "This is work! We don't believe people need to be passionate about hair. They need to be passionate about the elements that build their business."

My take is that what franchisees love about their business is less important than that they love *something*. Whether it's the product, the process, or the people, some element of their business should jump-start their heart. I had no great love for fruit or gift baskets, but I did love the way Edible Arrangements made people feel. I really enjoyed talking to customers about their special occasions and helping them find ways to celebrate. Running a franchise is tough. It's important to balance the challenges you face with something personally meaningful to make the difficult times worthwhile.

The Truth about Wealthy Franchisees

When you speak to enough superstar franchisees, as I have, you start to see what they have in common. If all the wealthy franchisees I've met had MBAs, I'd point that out. If they all spent twice as much as their peers on marketing, I'd write a book on franchise marketing. If they all operated in dense urban settings, this book would be about commercial real estate. These are factors, but they aren't the reasons.

What's important are the internal traits they share, and how those impact external results. They don't just have winning businesses—they have winning outlooks. Their mindset is an asset to their business, as much as a great location or a superior staff. The way they think makes the difference.

Some franchisees don't believe this. They think top franchisees have a great attitude because they lucked into a successful business. They don't understand that a high-performance mindset is not the *result* of franchise success. It's the *cause*.

Mindset drives operational performance. Marketing isn't just about promotion; it's about *patience*. Management isn't just about directing employees; it's about *engaging* them. Customer service isn't just about financial transactions; it's about *human connections*. With a better understanding of how these emotional qualities affect your operations, you will run your business a lot more effectively.

My point? You can do this! You can adjust your thinking and your behavior. You can have a better experience running your business. You can make money, save time, and improve your life. Wealthy franchisees are just ordinary people getting extraordinary results simply by working and living the concepts outlined in this book. Nothing is guaranteed. There's a lot you can't control. But if others are succeeding in your system, chances are you can, too.

But first, you need to know how to handle the wild ride of entrepreneurship.

CHAPTER 2

The Emotional Roller Coaster of Running a Franchise

Chapter Features

- What it feels like to run your own franchise
- The issues you're likely to face as a franchisee
- Determining if the franchise lifestyle is the best fit for you
- How you're a factor in the results you get

" f we're going to date, you have to promise you'll never ask me to go on a roller coaster."

My wife, Rachel, made it clear early in our relationship that she was prone to motion sickness. Whether it's on land, air, or sea, excess motion isn't good for her. We had to split up at amusement parks with friends and, eventually, our kids. Some of us hit the coasters while the others rode the carousel.

But when I bought a franchise, I broke my promise. I asked her to join me on something much more tumultuous than riding the Cyclone, taking her on a wild ride with ups, downs, and much more neither of us could anticipate or control.

Not everyone has the stomach for running their own business. While a traditional job can also be quite challenging, it's structured and predictable. You can plan your life around a regular paycheck. You feel (whether or not it's true) that you're part of a stable company with clearly defined rules and a climbable ladder.

And doing a job is different from maintaining a business. After my brother graduated medical school, he wanted to set up his own practice. He liked the idea of building something he could run himself. His close friend didn't share those aspirations. He just wanted to practice medicine. He's perfectly happy working for an HMO and letting others count the beans.

Some people need the freedom of business ownership. It's more of an adventure. There's risk, adversity, and the chance of enormous financial gains—or nothing at all. Running a franchise is a modern-day treasure hunt.

The question is, is that for you? You could do the same things wealthy franchisees do and get the same financial payoff. But if you don't enjoy the journey, you won't have the quality of life to meet our definition of "wealthy." It's not enough to evaluate a business before buying. You need to examine the *lifestyle*. If you don't like roller coasters, you may not like franchising.

My Journey as a Franchisee

Those who can, do, and for ten years, I did. I proudly owned the title "franchisee." That pride was as much from what I overcame as from what I accomplished. It was an intense time with ups, downs, and plenty going sideways.

I'm going to share with you the highlights of that wild decade. As I recount my journey, try to put yourself in my shoes and imagine having the same experience. I'll discuss what I went through as well as what it felt like. I'll pause periodically throughout my story to give you a chance to reflect how it would feel to you.

I Blame My Father

My father is a serial business owner. He's never had a career, just a long string of small businesses and a few jobs in between. He's owned a luggage store, a sandwich shop, and a handful of ice cream parlors. He also got involved with a number of franchises. At various points, he owned a Winchell's Donuts in Los Angeles, a Love's BBQ in Denver, a Papachino's Ristorante in San Diego, and several PoFolks restaurants throughout Southern California.

Some of his businesses were cash cows and others were money pits. Ups and downs. Good years and bad. Milkshakes and migraines. I grew up watching him navigate through it all. Fortunately, with the help of my working mom's patience, faith, and health insurance, he made more than he lost, enough to move us into a better house every few years, buy himself some nice stuff, and support us through college.

My father is still a bloodhound for new business ideas. It's not unusual at family gatherings for him to go on about some new concept he's heard about. But in 2005, when he showed me an airline magazine ad for a fruit basket franchise called "Edible Arrangements," he caught me at the perfect time.

I'd already been speaking professionally for 12 years and was looking for an additional stream of income. Speaking was going well, but my wife and I were starting a family and I wanted to begin spending more time at home.

I traveled to Connecticut to attend a Discovery Day at the Edible Arrangements corporate office. Their presentation knocked my socks off. We learned all about the operation, their plans for the future, and what the current opportunities were. We sampled the product. We visited their corporate store. We asked question after question. We met team members from operations, marketing, and franchise development. Everyone in the office was young, dynamic, and passionate. They knew they were part of something special.

My mind raced throughout the flight back to California. What a cool concept! What spectacular franchise partners! I took out paper and pen and brainstormed what I could do with the business. I had all kinds of ideas the corporate office hadn't even thought of.

I was excited at the prospect of owning an asset. I wasn't going to end my speaking business, but I needed to build something else that would generate its own revenue and increase in value. It would also be a great opportunity to test my leadership concepts in the field. So many speakers hadn't done anything other than speak. I wanted to walk my talk.

As soon as my plane touched down in Los Angeles, I called my father. I wanted to do this. He also wanted in. We agreed to each invest in our own Edible Arrangements franchises.

Reflection

What are your reasons for wanting your own business?
What emotions does the idea of business ownership stir up?
How are those emotions affecting your judgment?
How might having your own franchise impact your lifestyle?

Honey, Can We Talk?

The hardest part of putting the deal together was convincing my wife. Rachel and I had very different upbringings. Her father, Ron, is a world-renowned professor emeritus who had two jobs his entire career. He and my mother-in-law lived in the same house in Chicago until moving to Los Angeles for Ron's second professorship at UCLA, where he worked until retirement. They've always lived simply and invested conservatively. Ron was never profit-driven. His primary desire was to contribute to a body of knowledge.

My father-in-law is as loyal and content as my father is restless and ambitious. Whereas I was raised in the frenetic world of speculative entrepreneurship, my wife grew up in the stable world of tenured education. Investing money I didn't have in a business I knew nothing about was normal to me. To Rachel, it was utter folly.

Her resistance angered me. Couldn't she see the opportunity? Didn't she trust me? We can't improve our lifestyle if we succumb to fear. Life is about risk. Life IS risk!

"But Scott, how are we going to finance this?" she asked. "How long will it take to get our money back? What if the business doesn't do well? And who are these Edible Arrangements people, and why should we trust them?"

Every doubt-filled question further enraged me. It felt like she wasn't just questioning my idea; she was questioning my *judgment*.

But she did force me to answer questions I should have already been asking. I really hadn't thought this through or vetted the franchisor. My readiness to sign was purely an emotional decision, not a logical one. I finally realized that the only way we could make this choice together was by getting the facts. Maybe that would ease my impulsiveness and alleviate her fear. *We needed to control our emotions.*

So we did our homework. We crunched the numbers. We slowed down and let time work its magic on our feelings. Eventually we were able to take a more calculated risk, so with Rachel's blessing, I pushed the red button.

Reflection

Who else will your choices impact?
Who questions your choices and keeps you in check?
How open are you to being challenged by others?
Should you allow others to talk you out of your dream?
Do you do enough due diligence when making important decisions?

Fasten Your Seat Belts

Two days later, the papers arrived via FedEx. I read through every page, pretending to understand what I was agreeing to. Every signature further committed me. And boy, there were a lot of signatures. There was a franchise agreement, a loan agreement, a lease, a construction contract, and, of course, an endless supply of checks to write. All this before I could make a single sale.

Selecting my location was especially scary. Los Angeles is filled with overpriced strip malls and glamorous retail spaces that make turning a profit seem incomprehensible. Can that Chipotle really be selling enough burritos to pay that much rent? Everyone kept telling me a good location would yield higher sales. But at these rates, I'd have to sell a boatload of fruit to keep rent at the standard benchmark of 10 percent of revenue. That's the reality of doing business in a high-end territory. In the highest-profile markets, some of the big brands actually run retail outlets at a loss just to keep a presence there. This practice jacks up rents into the stratosphere.

After weeks of scouring the streets in my territory, I saw a "For Lease" sign go up in a closed Cingular Wireless store on the first floor of an office building on Beverly Boulevard. An hour later, as I waited outside for a walkthrough, I contemplated the pros and cons. There was tons of vehicular traffic, but not a lot of foot traffic. There was great street exposure, but limited parking. There was a lot of square footage, but the layout was awkward. It was available, but it wasn't ideal.

In the end, corporate approved the location and I made an offer. The longer I negotiated, the more invested in the location I felt. I wanted the search to be over. My eagerness didn't serve me well—I probably could have gotten some better terms and additional free rent—but ultimately I got a lease, and that felt good.

The buildout was hell. I brought out a contractor from Boston who'd built many Edible Arrangements stores but was new to Los Angeles. We needed inspections and permits for plumbing, electrical, building and safety, and health. Multiple times one inspector would contradict the directives laid out by the previous inspector. Subcontractors wouldn't show up. The IT company had DSL-related issues I couldn't solve with the phone company.

I'd already found employees who were eager to start work, but continuous construction delays pushed back our opening farther and farther, so half the people I'd hired moved on to other jobs. My contractor made promises and then made excuses. When the Edible Arrangements field trainer flew in from Connecticut for our grand opening, he arrived at a store that was weeks away from being ready.

Meanwhile, my sparkling new delivery van parked safely in the building's garage was hit by a car during the night. It had yet to make one delivery and it already had a dent in the side, right below our logo.

After many extra weeks and thousands of extra dollars, we finally completed construction. The health inspector signed off and the lights came on. We were open! The phone started to ring. Curious passersby (see, there *was* some foot traffic!) came in for samples and took brochures. Some even placed orders. I had income!

On day two, three employees didn't show up. The only one who bothered to call in said the job just wasn't for her. Later that day I bought the remaining staff pizza and pretended I knew what I was doing. Thank heavens for the corporate trainer.

The scariest time was the next week, after the trainer had left. We were on our own, stumbling our way through taking, making, and delivering orders. I panicked every time the phone rang, wondering if I'd be able to answer questions and input the order into our sophisticated point-of-sale system.

My father came to visit during this week and invited me to lunch. It was the first time I had left the store during business hours, and my investment was now in the hands of my 19-year-old employees. We had sandwiches at a diner just across the street. I sat facing the front window and kept looking over my dad's shoulder to make sure the store wasn't on fire. It reminded me of the first time we left our son with a babysitter. But I knew I would have to get used to this feeling—I had to leave soon for some out-of-town speeches.

Each day we got better. We made our mistakes, figured stuff out, and learned what we were doing. Soon we had answers to most of the questions customers asked us. More employees left and new ones came. Before too long, we settled into a routine. Orders continued to roll in. During the first month, I paid every bill on time. Two months in, the bills were paid again, and sales were up over the first month.

I'd done it. I'd built a growing business. And it was exhilarating.

Reflection

When do you feel in over your head?
How do you respond when things don't go as planned?
Can you set aside enough money to manage unexpected expenses?
How prepared are you to trust others to run your business?

Enjoying the Ride

My best customers were my in-laws. They ordered fruit baskets for every possible occasion. I told my employees to give them discounts and eventually to refuse payment from them altogether. That's when they stopped ordering—they wanted to support me, not mooch off me.

Friends ordered, too; some wanted to support me, while many others wanted to get discounts. It's amazing how many dinner parties you get invited to when you own a fruit arrangement business. That's OK. It felt great to be a big shot business owner, what my grandmother would have called in Yiddish, a "big *macher.*"

A speaking colleague came in to meet me for lunch. I was wearing a long-sleeve Edible Arrangements polo and matching baseball cap, and she said, "Oh, you look so cute in your uniform!" She was just condescending enough to embarrass me.

Every day was a new experience. We turned new customers into repeat customers. We signed up corporate accounts. We made many arrangements to be used as props in TV shows. I personally delivered five arrangements backstage to *The Price Is Right* to be used in the "Showcase Showdown." We played a role in countless dinner parties, thank-yous, and marriage proposals. We joined the chamber of commerce and our local chapter of Business Network International. We ranked second out of almost 100 Edible Arrangements locations in California. Then we got to number one. We also won the "Best Customer Service" award out of 1,000 Edible Arrangements franchises worldwide. I wasn't in it for recognition, but I admit it felt great.

I would leave town to speak. When I got back, there was more money in the checking account than when I'd left. That was awesome.

The highs were high, but the lows were low. Twice there were break-ins during the night. Several times our delivery drivers got into fender benders. Our insurance company settled with a lady who "fell" in our lobby. A home delivery grocer contracted with us to provide them with fruit salads and then stopped paying us. I took them to small claims court but lost because my manager had accidentally disposed of the pickup receipts, leaving me with insufficient proof of delivery.

For a while, managing employees was particularly tough. I'm not one of those people who complains about "kids these days" or how entitled Millennials are. Every generation has all-stars and flakes. But it seemed like we always had issues with staff. My phone would ring at all hours with questions, problems, and requests. Employees would show up late or stop showing up altogether. Some would work, but not as fast as we needed them to. One male employee offered a female co-worker a heart-shaped piece of pineapple from an arrangement, and she complained it was a sexual advance. I fired our first delivery driver for racking up $150 worth of personal calls on the company cell phone. I let another employee go for calling ahead when running late and asking co-workers to punch in for her. Twice I gave second chances to employees who succumbed to drug addiction, and both relapsed.

I put a lot into figuring out how to build a great team, and over time my staff went from being my greatest headache to my greatest asset. By the time I sold the business, most of them had been with me for years. Leaving them was the hardest part of my exit.

Reflection

How do you see your role in the community?
What accomplishments are you chasing?
How will you react when problems arise?
How prepared are you to manage employee issues?

No Day at Disneyland

While the business ultimately made me plenty of money, we did go through several periods of very low sales. Bills would sometimes pile higher than the cash. You really haven't experienced business ownership until you've had to triage your accounts payable and decide who you're going to leave hanging. Invariably, that's when the delivery van suddenly needed a new transmission.

But even the busy times could be very stressful. One holiday our fruit vendor failed to deliver enough strawberries. I had to drive to seemingly every grocery store in Los Angeles to get the fruit we needed to fill our orders.

On one Valentine's Day, I was in charge of dispatching deliveries, and I failed to properly track order status, resulting in mass confusion. We couldn't determine if orders were in the cooler, in transit, or already delivered. At 5:00 P.M., as intended gift recipients were leaving work, we still had scores of orders that hadn't been delivered. People throughout Los Angeles had watched their co-workers get flowers and gifts all day long and thought their own partners forgot about them. Our phone lines lit up with enraged customers. It got so bad we had to turn off the phones, lock the doors, and deal with one order at a time. After staying up all night prepping for Valentine's Day, we were hardly in the right condition to manage this kind of stress. I couldn't begin to imagine the financial hit I was about to take, let alone the social media one. It was three days before my manager, Jennifer, could restore a sense of normalcy.

In the first year, I went through three managers. The first left to get back into the movie business. The second moved to the suburbs and wanted to work closer to home. Jennifer had been my son's preschool teacher. She actually had experience working in the flower business and was great with my son. I figured if I could trust her with one of my babies, I could trust her with the other. Together we would forge a partnership that lasts well into the writing of this book. She would become the very first winner of the Edible Arrangements "Manager of the Year" award.

It was a good thing I didn't decide to go into business with my father. We could talk shop without the stress that comes with financial ties. He opened his first store a few weeks before mine, and it was great to share our experiences, much to the chagrin of Rachel and my mom, who eventually banned Edible Arrangements talk at family gatherings.

Four and a half years in, business was good, but the commercial real estate market wasn't, which meant I was in a great position to negotiate my lease renewal. I'd always felt I was paying too much. Fair market value? Bring it on. I squeezed the landlord tight and got a great reduction in rent.

(Five years after that, however, our neighborhood experienced a hot resurgence, and my landlord struck back. He had leverage: The thought of relocating overwhelmed me. It was a bloody negotiation. I got worked.)

Seven years in, I opened my second location, taking over an existing Edible Arrangements that was all but abandoned by the previous franchisee. Our corporate office told me the location was immediately available, but I'd have to commit right away. They wanted to get the store reopened as quickly as possible, so if I didn't give a prompt response, they'd offer it to another franchisee. It was now or never. These weren't the ideal conditions for a six-figure commitment, but I reluctantly agreed.

I thought it was a bargain, but just before I got the keys, the previous owner gutted the place during the night, literally taking everything *including* the kitchen sink. What he planned to do with an outdoor electric Edible Arrangements sign is beyond me, but that alone cost $10,000 to replace. I had to rebuild the business from scratch.

If your franchisor allows it, running multiple locations is a great idea. Not only can you make more money, but you also learn to maximize efficiency. You can't be in two places at once, so you're forced to develop solid, replicable systems and turn employees into leaders. It helped that the first location was doing so well, which offset the initial slow performance of the second store. The place was a rescue operation, starting with the one-star average Yelp reviews left over from the previous owner.

I proudly hung an "Under New Management" banner outside. We canvassed the neighborhood with fliers, gave away a ton of free product, and sponsored a Boys & Girls Club across the street. We clawed our way forward one customer at a time and slowly built sales. That place was the little business that could. (I admit, I loved going to our franchise convention and getting the blue "Multi-Unit Owner" ribbon to hang from my name tag. It was the most expensive ribbon I'd ever purchased, but I wore it with pride.)

Reflection

How effective are you at organizing and managing systems?
How well do you handle stress and unexpected problems?
How quickly can you (or should you) make big decisions?
How well do you operate in tough negotiations?

Exit Strategy

Getting into Edible Arrangements had been a great choice, but after ten years, I'd had enough. My speaking business was doing really well. Thanks to my firsthand franchising experience, I started booking a lot of keynotes for other franchise systems. Splitting my time wasn't good for either business. It had been a good ride, but it was time to get out.

But exiting wasn't easy. First, I had to find a way to put the word out without alarming my employees. I hated being secretive, but I needed the operation to remain stable. Then I had to find interested buyers. It helps when the business is turning a profit, but buyers and sellers don't typically see things eye to eye. I took lunches, kicked numbers around, and tried not to feel insulted by the lowballers. At one point I had five different interested parties. Then it was four, then three. By the time I sat down with the only buyer left, I was much more eager to get out than I could let on.

The negotiation dragged on for a few months. Both of us moved at a deliberately slow pace, each trying to keep the other interested while making him sweat. Don't get me wrong—our conversations stayed pleasant and respectful. But we were only human.

Finally, we reached an agreement. Papers were signed, hands were shaken, and tears were shed. My ten-year odyssey as a franchisee was a wild, stressful, and character-building journey. And now it was over. I had built, operated, and sold a successful franchise operation and lived to tell the tale.

Last week a friend of mine had surgery. I ordered an Edible Arrangement for her from her local store and paid full price.

Reflection

What's your exit plan?
Do you know what your business is actually worth?
Can you be patient enough to make a good deal?
How will it feel to leave?

Extraordinary Is Ordinary in Franchising

Some people who read the above account will be scared off. Some will be intrigued. Most current franchisees will be completely unimpressed.

What I went through really wasn't special. It's all the typical stuff that happens when you run a franchise. But just as different people running the same operation will get different results, different people having the same experience will have their own unique reactions. Everyone responds differently to the same circumstances. It's important to consider how these circumstances might make *you* feel. Only you can make the determination if business ownership is right for you.

I didn't just run a franchise operation. I *felt* it. From the moment I saw the airline ad to the day I handed over the keys to the new owner, that business stirred up something inside me. Those emotions, that psychology, that human side of the business was always there, permeating every decision I made. And I learned that our emotions aren't just responses. They're also triggers.

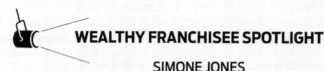

WEALTHY FRANCHISEE SPOTLIGHT

SIMONE JONES

Four Co-Branded Marble Slab Creamery/Great American Cookies locations

Greater Houston Area, Texas

- 2019 Franchisee of the Year
- Consistently ranked in top 10 locations for sales
- Marble Slab Creamery Ice Cream Council member
- Marketing committee member for Great American Cookies

Simone Jones and her husband, Alfred, are shooting stars in the treat business. In just a few years, they went from zero to eight franchise businesses in four cobranded locations. There's no sign they're slowing down, increasing both unit sales as well as the number of locations. What's her approach to success?

"I just think it's good old-fashioned hard work," she said.

Simone prefers to play an active role in operations. "I clean toilets, help customers, my husband makes ice cream—we're very hands-on. We try to be involved

---

WEALTHY FRANCHISEE SPOTLIGHT, continued

in all aspects of the business." With that level of commitment, they've been able to manage all four locations with only one assistant manager and a team of hourly shift leads.

I asked her how much the human factors matter to her business.

"One hundred percent!" she replied.

To her, that means creating moments people feel. Simone aspires to offer a lot more than treats.

"Customers must have a memorable time," she said. "We want to create an experience for them. Our goal is to make every customer feel special."

And they do. So much so that the majority of customers leave tips for her and Alfred (all of which she passes on to her team). But her experience of the business hasn't always been fun.

"In the beginning it was completely chaotic," she said. "We didn't anticipate such a huge response to our pre-opening marketing. We were up until 3:00 a.m. every night making cake orders. After a few weeks of that, we called our corporate office and told them we wanted to sell. It was too much!"

But inspired by her religious faith, she and Alfred persevered. "God wouldn't give us more than we can handle," she said.

Today, they enjoy running high-volume stores, participating in brand committees, and planning their next moves. "Now I feel like we can do anything!"

Simone's Wealthy Franchisee Success Tips

- Never expect anyone to put in what you wouldn't put in yourself. If you want 130 percent from your staff, you better give them 130 percent.

> **WEALTHY FRANCHISEE SPOTLIGHT,** continued
>
> ◆ Even when it's bleak and dark, don't give up. It'll get better.
>
> ◆ There will come a point when you know exactly what you're doing. Keep
>   learning and hang in there.

The Silent Struggle of Owning a Business

Sometimes, as part of my due diligence before speaking to a franchise, I survey the franchisees. I collect their responses anonymously so they can answer freely. Here are some actual comments from a variety of brands that reflect the answers I typically get to this question: "What has been your emotional experience of running this franchise?"

> *"The feeling is one that the whole enterprise is held together by 'string' and it requires an enormous effort by the user to hold together. Mentally, it is tiring."*

> *"Excited, anxious, nervous, and wondering if I will bankrupt my family before the business turns the corner of profitability."*

> *"Where do I begin? Way too much mental stress between managing staff and financial issues. Dealing with people, both members and employees, is a HUGE drain physically and emotionally. We expected if we worked hard, success was imminent. We are working our heads off and really barely making it."*

> *"I was told this business would cost me about $500,000 to get to break-even. It was nearly three times that amount. For quite some time, the worry about making the next payroll was oppressive."*

> *"Given our financial situation going into it, it has been much more challenging and stressful than I anticipated. The work combined with the financial stress has been very difficult to deal with at times."*

I also get responses from people who express excitement and gratitude. But everyone is feeling something. Deeply. If there's anything I've learned from working with franchisees and owning one myself, it's that running a franchise is an emotional experience. And these emotions directly impact the way business is handled.

When Edible Arrangements International started talking about running its first national television campaign, one of my fellow franchisees objected. That made no sense to me. We were still a new company, and most people had never even seen a floral arrangement made with fruit. We desperately needed more brand awareness, so I asked him why he was against it.

"There's already too many Edible Arrangements franchises in Southern California," he responded. "If we go on TV, it'll make even more people want to open franchises out here, and there'll be more competition."

His idea for marketing our brand was to keep it a secret. This was a highly intelligent guy with a graduate degree who owned multiple locations. His perspective wasn't based on data. It was based on fear.

I tried for several years to start a local marketing cooperative among franchisees in Southern California. We were the densest territory in the company, so logic dictated that we pool our marketing dollars. The company already had some functioning marketing co-ops, and they were working well. But too many people were scared to commit the money. One highly educated but struggling franchisee told me he couldn't afford to advertise. He didn't see marketing as an investment, just an expense. It didn't matter that he was smart. He was too afraid.

The Real Risks of Owning a Business

Statistics about small-business failure abound. Some sources will tell you that half of all businesses fail in the first year, while others say the failure rate is closer to 90 percent. Some stats cite the rate of SBA loan defaults: From 2006 to 2015, about 17 percent of SBA-backed loans defaulted. It's really hard to nail down the actual batting average of rookie small businesses, but all you really have to do is drive down the street and watch the changing storefronts to draw the conclusion that starting a new business is tough. That makes it an intensely emotional experience.

A franchise is a minefield of psychological dangers. It's so tempting to take your enterprise personally and associate your business performance with your self-worth. In one 2015 joint study by researchers at University of California, San Francisco; University of California, Berkeley; and Stanford University, 72 percent of entrepreneurs surveyed reported experiencing mental health concerns. In another 2019 study by the Canadian Mental Health Association, 62 percent of entrepreneurs reported feeling depressed at least once a week. It's not clear if the stress of owning a business causes depression, or if entrepreneurship attracts those who are predisposed to depression. But whatever the relationship, it's clear we business owners are total head cases!

I experienced a wide range of emotions as a franchisee. On the high end was exhilaration, and on the low end was total despair. There were times I felt completely trapped, hating the business but unable to escape it. I remember days when my expenses were rising so quickly it seemed like the walls were crashing in around me.

It would be helpful if more franchisees acknowledged these feelings. But emotion has always been taboo in business. Vulnerability is seen as a sign of weakness. There's no crying in baseball, and there's none in business, either. If anything, we practice the opposite, what psychologists call *impression management*. This is the process by which a person tries to influence other people's perceptions of their image. Think of someone wearing expensive clothes or driving a flashy car to project an air of success. Impression management is everything we do to make others think we're stronger, saner, and less human than we are.

There's no doubt people are attracted to perceived success. But the price we pay for that external image is internal neglect, and eventually it catches up to us.

Wealthy franchisees aren't immune to the emotional challenges of running a business—they've just learned to navigate through them. That's their advantage.

Fortunately, franchises are a little less mysterious than other new businesses. If a company is franchising, chances are they've had some success and know how to replicate it. They've done the market research and product development and negotiated with vendors. They've tried and erred and learned. A franchised business comes with a lot of data, and that makes it a safer bet.

But what the franchisor can't tell you is how *you* will run the business, just as an auto dealership doesn't know how you will drive and maintain their car. You're the X-factor. You are the most important variable that distinguishes your franchise location from all the others.

So maybe you *should* take your business performance personally. Maybe you're the source of your problems—or your prosperity. Whatever is happening in your business is on you.

Don't let the statistics about failing businesses scare you. Those businesses weren't run by *you*. If you invest in a proven concept and operate it intelligently, there's every reason to believe you're going to thrive. But you're going to have to manage your head as well as you manage your operation.

The Three Factors for Franchise Success

During the months between signing my franchise agreement and opening my store, I continued traveling and giving presentations. In every city that had an Edible Arrangements location, I stopped by, and I continued this practice even after we opened. I wanted to pick the brains of as many franchisees as possible. Once I was speaking in Jeddah, Saudi Arabia, and spotted an Edible Arrangements delivery van. I had my driver follow it back to the store so I could meet my Saudi counterparts.

Some of these franchisees were success stories, while others were cautionary tales. That's been the case with every franchise brand I've worked with: In the same system, running the same business, some people crush it, and others get crushed. Why?

It comes down to this formula:

$$C + O + H = R$$
(Circumstances + Operations + Humanity = Results)

These three factors—circumstances, operations, and humanity—combine to determine how successful you're going to be. Understanding how each of these factors impacts the rest of the equation is key to getting the results you want. Let's look at each of them in turn.

Circumstances

Your circumstances are all the external conditions affecting your business. These include factors such as the economy, the competition, government regulations, taxes, labor laws, and commercial real estate's "fair market value." Some businesses are impacted by the weather. I've worked with an ice cream franchise in Canada that slows down when temperatures drop and a soup franchise in Michigan that slows down when temperatures rise. One emergency restoration franchise I spoke with thrives after natural disasters.

I faced plenty of tough circumstances during my years as a franchisee, some minor and others major (and some that were somewhere in between). Two weeks before my first Valentine's Day at Edible Arrangements, torrential rains wreaked havoc on California's strawberry crops, impacting price and quality. When a new Edible Arrangements franchise opened nearby with a territory that overlapped mine, my numbers dropped. The same year, the economy collapsed. There were power outages, increased fuel prices, and ever-changing labor laws. For a while, a high-profile florist two blocks away started selling fruit arrangements. And on particularly hectic days, invariably the health inspector would show up for a surprise visit. I could go on.

But not all circumstances were bad. AIDS Walk Los Angeles decided to add our street to their course, routing thousands of hungry walkers right in front of my store. Just before building out our second location, I got a call about a closing restaurant looking to sell their walk-in cooler for pennies on the dollar. And that new competing Edible Arrangements I mentioned above? Right before the holidays, there was an explosion in their garage that shut them down for months. They were nice people and I felt bad for them, but it did redirect a lot of business to my location.

What's important to understand about circumstantial factors is that they're totally out of your control, so it's tempting to blame any problems you're having on them. I can't tell you how many people have said to me, "This economy is killing us," or "I'm doing everything I can, but there's too much competition." They blame the government, scapegoat their franchisor, and curse a "lazy" young generation of employees. Some even attribute their decline to a change in consumer taste: "They just don't like us anymore."

I appreciate the many real challenges franchisees face. I've faced them, too. But rarely do these circumstances tell the whole story of a business. It may be true that there's some new competition or an increase in minimum wage. But usually there's a lot more afflicting the business—and those are things struggling franchisees could control if they wanted to.

I'd like to suggest that if your business isn't doing well, it's probably your fault. I don't say that to insult you. It should excite you. You want your problems to be your fault, because if you're the problem, you can also be the solution.

Blame will not serve you. Taking responsibility will.

Wealthy franchisees know it's on them to find solutions to their challenges, and they'll look everywhere for them, including in the mirror. They rarely complain or blame. Instead, they open their mind, open their eyes, and get to work. Some franchisees feel entitled to good fortune. Wealthy franchisees feel entitled to nothing. They don't whine about the rain. They just grab umbrellas—or sell them.

Wealthy franchisees monitor their circumstances, but they don't use them to make excuses. They use them to make decisions. Their success is up to them. It won't come by accident, and they don't believe in luck.

It's true that some businesses are simply doomed. In the real world, there are such things as unbeatable competitors, losing locations, and unanticipated circumstances. But doom is rare. There are franchises in your company right now that are doing well despite fierce competition. There are plenty of poorly located operations that have found a way to make a profit right where they are. You're not a victim. You're a courageous business owner in partnership with a franchisor that wants you to succeed.

Circumstances matter. We need to keep an eye on them so we can respond appropriately where we do have control. Once we're clear about what's going on, we take action by focusing on the remaining two factors: operations and humanity.

Operations

This is everything related to work. This includes your systems, policies, and tactics. It's your recipe for great waffles, your formula for carpet cleaner, and your method for teaching foreign languages. It's your branding, marketing, and pricing. It's your scheduling, cost control, and accounting. Operations are the things you pay your franchisor to teach you. It's everything that keeps you busy.

Operations are the heart of a franchise. Their unique, replicable systems for serving customers profitably enable them to share the opportunity with franchisees. In most cases, you can come from an unrelated professional background and successfully implement the franchisor's systems.

The misconception in franchising is that fortune is born merely out of systems and sweat. So many franchisees buy into an incorrect, incomplete formula: Strategy + Effort = Success. They believe if they just follow corporate's manual, work hard, and work *long*, they will make money.

If only it were that simple.

I remember going through Edible Arrangements training in Connecticut with a large group of new franchisees. Many of them were also opening in the Southern California market. Over the course of five days, we all received the same training. We were given the same manual and taught identical procedures. Then we flew home and opened our businesses.

I visited many of my training buddies at their stores. The aesthetics of each location were identical. Our product line and pricing were the same, and we used the standard equipment. The locations varied a little in terms of exposure and demographics. But operationally, we all followed the same book.

Some of my fellow trainees thrived, while others struggled. Some expanded, and some disappeared. The differences were not subtle. Some locations outperformed others by hundreds of thousands of dollars per year—running the same operation. One by one, almost all the lower-performing locations were gobbled up and resurrected by better operators.

On the surface, it seemed like it had everything to do with location. But that wasn't really true. Some attributed their success to more marketing, since the top franchisees definitely invested in promoting their business. That made a difference, but it wasn't *the* difference.

Maybe the top performers were putting in the most hours? Nope. Many of my struggling colleagues worked feverishly to keep their businesses going.

Perhaps the top franchisees were the most innovative? It wasn't that either. People called them all the time looking for their secrets, only to hear they weren't really doing things that differently. Usually they were working the same systems as everyone else.

Top franchisees do have to work hard and constantly try new things to improve their business. But those aren't the only reasons they thrive. Hard work and good ideas are not the secrets to success. They're the basics.

The wealthy franchisees I meet definitely have superior operations. But it isn't so much because they're doing things differently. They just do them *better*, and they do it with the help of a third factor that most people dismiss or are too busy to bother with.

This third factor isn't tangible. You can't see it or quantify it. You can't deposit it in a bank. But it really is the distinguishing characteristic of wealthy franchisees. Look at the top people in your franchise, and you'll see this is the factor they have in common. If there's a secret to being a wealthy franchisee, it's this:

Humanity

Nothing influences our performance more than the way we manage the human elements that flow through every aspect of our business. That means psychological discipline, emotional control, and grit. It includes patience, empathy, and social skills. It's all those human characteristics that, for better or worse, distinguish us from computers.

Wealthy franchisees are masters of their humanity. They have a strong mindset that drives every business decision. It's what makes them great.

Let's put aside the human factor for franchisees for a moment and look instead at customers. Consumers make all kinds of decisions based on emotion. *Behavioral economics* is a whole discipline focused on just that idea. It studies the cross section of economics and psychology, and its guiding principle is that consumers behave irrationally. If computers were to make buying decisions, they'd simply assess their need and find the option with maximum quality and minimum cost.

People act differently. We make all kinds of illogical but emotionally satisfying decisions. It's common knowledge that tap water in most industrialized countries is continuously tested and safer than bottled water. But many people spend more per ounce on bottled water than they do on gasoline. We forgo bigger payoffs later to get smaller payoffs sooner. (This is known as *hyperbolic discounting.*) The threat of losing what we have motivates us more than the promise of gaining something new of equivalent value (known as *loss aversion*). And we all know that now-popular term "FOMO": "fear of missing out."

Understanding the psychology of consumer behavior helps businesses market and sell their services. One might argue the first known behavioral economist was Aristotle. In his treatise *Rhetoric*, written 2,400 years ago, he described the three key elements for influencing human behavior. These modes of persuasion, illustrated in Figure 3–1 on page 47, are still used today by companies, politicians, public speakers, and others trying to persuade people to take a specific action.

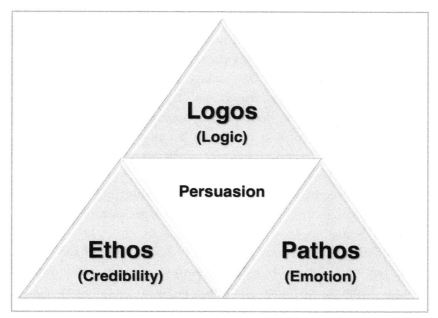

FIGURE 3–1. **The Rhetorical Triangle**

Logos

Logos means "logic." This is where we use information, reasoning, and data to make our case. For a politician, this might mean sharing statistics and a five-point plan to fix a problem. For a company, it's describing the benefits of its products and services. Imagine an automobile commercial listing the features of the car, such as the engine size, miles per gallon, or its voice-operated entertainment system.

Ethos

Ethos means "ethics," but more important, credibility. It's explaining why you're the expert, or why your company is most qualified to offer a solution. It could be a politician discussing their humble roots and legislative accomplishments, or a car manufacturer boasting about its J.D. Power and Associates awards and its number-one sales ranking in its class. If you're an established authority, you're worth believing.

Pathos

Pathos means "emotion." It's the human side. This is where we try to move people to action by getting them to feel something. Often this is done by telling a story or showing images that tug at your heartstrings. It's a politician describing a vision for what's possible or scaring people with what their country-destroying opponent might do. It could be a shot of the driver of that car getting attention as he pulls up to a fancy restaurant. Wouldn't it feel great if that were you? Or the woman in the crowded elevator with dandruff falling onto her black coat. Wouldn't it be embarrassing if that were you? Think of a public service announcement getting your attention with images of starving children. If you feel something, you're more likely to act.

Sometimes I survey my audiences and ask which of the three is most powerful. Invariably they say pathos. Humans are emotional beings. Tapping into their emotions is the most effective way to influence them.

So what does this mean for franchisees? Well, even though business owners are on the other side of the market as sellers rather than consumers, they can still be irrational. That doesn't mean they're weak or mentally ill. It just means their emotions still influence them. They're vulnerable to pathos. Their humanity is very much at play.

Wealthy franchisees don't deny their humanity. They just manage it. They control their pathos as much as possible so they can take action based on logos, their logic. Good business decisions are made with a cool head and clear data.

Some people are naturally level-headed. They default to calm, cool thinking. I have a friend who jumps out of bed in the morning ready to face the day. She's an eternal optimist who believes anything is possible. When she runs into a problem, she automatically rolls up her sleeves and looks for solutions. She doesn't have to try to be this way. It's in her DNA.

I have another friend with discipline flowing through his veins. When he decided he'd like to learn how to play the piano, he bought an electric keyboard and a book, and practiced two hours every day for a year until he mastered it. There was no deviation from the schedule.

That's also how he's written books and trained for a marathon. He decides to do something and doesn't stop until he's achieved it. When it comes to setting goals, the guy is all logos.

But my friends are not the norm. Most of us are prone to straying and more vulnerable to distraction and self-doubt. That doesn't mean we can't improve our mindset—we just have to be more deliberate about it. Some people have naturally big muscles, while others must go to the gym five days a week. But the end result is the same.

Our human condition matters because it determines 1) how we react to our circumstances, and 2) how we execute our operations.

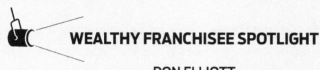

WEALTHY FRANCHISEE SPOTLIGHT

DON ELLIOTT

Great Clips

Knoxville, Tennessee

- Great Clips Hall of Fame inductee
- 56 locations; started with one and committed to master development
- Highest average customer count for all 20-plus unit enterprises
- Number-one customer count for Southeast Zone
- Opened first location in Knoxville with no brand presence—now one of the top markets in the system

As one of the top operators in a massive brand, Don Elliott hears from a lot of fellow franchisees who want to know his recipe for secret sauce. Often they're disappointed because Don doesn't have one.

Don is a great example of someone doing ordinary things extraordinarily well. He and his wife, Laura, have worked the system as prescribed by corporate, albeit with even higher standards. Whatever corporate's goal is for customer count, he sets it higher. Whatever their standard is for customer wait time, he wants it shorter.

He accomplishes this without any magic or deviation from Great Clips' proven system. He just focuses on the human elements that matter most. Don invests in building a great culture of team members, works to give customers a great experience, and executes.

"This business is easy," he said. "We just have to be better than everyone else."

Don is as humble as he is effective. He credits his team with his success. He spends a lot of time providing them with good training and coaching and makes sure they feel valued. "My team is always my top priority," he told me. That's paid off. They work hard enough to make running 56 locations possible.

"I definitely work less now than I had to before," Don said. "And I can focus more on what's most important."

Don's Wealthy Franchisee Success Tips

- Give your team the training, coaching, development, and mentoring they need to succeed.
- Your time is limited, so you need to identify the key drivers of your business and focus on those. Know which levers to pull.
- Create a culture of care.
- If someone else is doing it, so can you. You just have to stay diligent and keep at it.
- If your competition is doing it, work harder and do it better.
- Develop a network of people to reach out to for ideas and support.
- You don't have to be a people person to own a business, but you do need to be one to run one. If that's not you, hire someone else.

How Reactions Impact Business

In my presentations, I always try to speak to the specific issues franchisees are facing. I need to know their challenges in order to offer solutions. Take a look at the survey responses I got from one brand when I asked what they believe are the biggest factors impacting their business:

"My local concerns have to do with hiring good people and retaining them. Millennials like to job hop. We are also facing growth issues in our physical space."

"Receivables, finding new business partners, maintaining pace with the technology."

"Economics, employees, getting quality materials to produce final products."

"The economy and online competitors selling at bottom-dollar prices."

"Sales and marketing."

"Recent influx of new competitors, finding the time to generate new sales through prospecting/networking."

"Pricing, competition, staffing."

"I believe that as an owner, I need to ensure that I am prioritizing and staying positive."

"Corporate."

"The biggest factor to my success is how I make customers feel and how much time I spend selling."

"Adversarial relationship with franchisor."

"Price, price, price."

These responses are fairly typical. The franchisees are running identical operations, but their concerns vary considerably. This is understandable. Some locations have less square footage, while others face more competition. Not everything is equal from location to location.

If we were to list all the issues referenced in the above responses, they would be:

- hiring
- retention
- physical space
- bad economy
- supply chain
- sales and marketing
- competition
- time management
- pricing
- franchise culture
- owner attitude
- customer service

Some of these are circumstantial, some are operational, and some are human. Now let's look at Figure 3-2 on page 53 and compare the differences in how a struggling franchisee and a wealthy franchisee might approach these issues.

The struggling franchisee in this table is totally compliant with the system. They are working hard and addressing each issue in their own way. But their mindset is hindering their execution. Facing the same factors, the wealthy franchisee is far better equipped to excel.

Wealthy franchisees and struggling franchisees get different results because they react and execute differently. Their respective handling of the human elements is the important distinction. In Part III of this book, we'll look at exactly how and why that matters.

If you think of C + O + H = R (circumstances + operations + humanity = results) as a recipe, most franchisees don't consider how important the ingredient "H" is. They still have a human mindset, but it doesn't enhance their business. For wealthy franchisees, H is the key ingredient. It's why they do so much better.

It's not enough to duplicate the circumstances and operations of wealthy franchisees. If you want their results, you must also duplicate

Factors Impacting Business	Wealthy Franchisee	Struggling Franchisee
Hiring	Builds culture	Fills positions
Retention	Improves the employee experience	Complains about job jumpers, pays more to keep people
Physical space	Improves efficiency, invests in expansion	Limits production
Bad economy	Works harder, finds opportunities, markets more	Worries, complains, cuts back
Supply chain	Collaborates, sources, monitors inventory	Complains to supplier/ franchisor
Sales and marketing	Active, patient, constant	Passive, impatient, short-term
Competition	Feels motivated	Feels threatened
Time management	Trains, delegates, prioritizes, creates systems for efficiency	Struggles to do too much or too little
Pricing	Adds value and improves experience to drive repeat business	Discounts to drive business
Franchise culture	Collaborates and communicates with franchisor and assists fellow franchisees	Resents franchisor, insulates self or connects with other angry franchisees
Owner attitude	Clear, positive	Distorted, negative
Customer service	Creates meaningful experiences	Facilitates quick transactions

FIGURE 3–2. **Responding to Factors Impacting Business**

their human characteristics. You need the same mindset. Once you achieve that, you'll run a better business.

That doesn't mean you can neglect the other two factors, of course. You need to invest in a solid concept in a good territory and run it well. You need to market, you need to grow, and you need to *work*. Positivity is not a business plan.

But for most franchisees, the right mindset is the missing ingredient. And the best part is it's completely under your control. It's one BIG change you can make to improve your business and your experience of running it.

The Franchisor Factor

Franchisees aren't always clear about what their franchisor's role will be. Often their expectations exceed the scope of what's in the franchise agreement. It's important to understand your franchisor's function and limitations so you can plan accordingly. Let's break it down by the three factors we've already discussed.

Circumstances

It's reasonable to expect your franchisor to monitor everything impacting the business climate. They should stay current on legislation, the competition, and consumer tastes. But like you, they can't control circumstances. They can only respond, hopefully quickly and effectively. And sometimes even that's not possible.

At its peak in the early 1980s, Fotomat had more than 4,000 locations (company-owned and franchised) offering overnight film development in their iconic yellow kiosks. Then competitors entered the market with larger outlets that could offer one-hour service, and digital photos finally put the entire film processing industry out to pasture. Circumstances changed radically and rapidly. Fotomat didn't stand a chance.

Our franchisors can't stop innovation, control the weather, or reduce minimum wage. They don't control what the competition does. We should expect them to keep watch, work hard, and pivot as much as they can. But they're not fortunetellers or magicians. Stuff happens. We assume risk when we sign the franchise agreement. We can't pin it all on them.

That shouldn't scare you any more than going into business *without* a franchisor. At least in this model you have a team of people working on your behalf, who have information and contacts and resources. As they say in the franchise industry, "You're in business for yourself, but not by yourself." When circumstances turn against you, your odds are better when you're part of something larger. Just keep your expectations reasonable.

Operations

This is where your franchisor provides the most value. They've figured out a system, and they're handing you the manual. When they improve the system, they give you the updates. They're constantly trying new things and testing them. They're hiring marketing personnel to help you get the word out and negotiating with vendors to get you better pricing.

The whole idea of buying a franchise is to have access to a proven system. If you replicate a process that has worked many times in many places, it's reasonable to expect it will work for you, too.

But many franchisees can't resist tinkering with the system. They do things a little differently. They paid for the recipe but swap out an ingredient or two, thinking they'll get a better result. Once they do that, they've raised their risk factor.

I met Tim Davis, president of The UPS Store, who had an interesting take on this. He said, "One of the advantages of buying a franchise is to help mitigate risk. Your investment is safer when put into a proven system. When you deviate from that system, you expose yourself to the very risk you paid to avoid."

But sometimes it sure is tempting, especially for impassioned, proactive franchisees who are natural go-getters. "There are two sides to driven franchisees," Tim told me. "It's great that they're aggressive about their business, but sometimes that comes with a hunger to go beyond the system and start experimenting."

A good franchisor has a system for franchisees to submit ideas. Most franchisors will tell you some of their best ideas come from franchisees. Once you've really tried their system, it's good to make suggestions. But remember, the whole reason for buying into a franchise is to outsource innovation. Let your franchisor do the R&D. Let them experiment in their company-owned locations and figure it all out for you. The wealthy franchisees I've talked to thrive not from innovation but from execution. They strive to exceed brand standards but rarely deviate from them.

I had a great conversation about this with Rhoda Olsen, vice chair of Great Clips. This franchisor has been in the hair salon business for decades: experimenting, testing, measuring, making mistakes, and making discoveries. They have an enormous pool of talent at their corporate office and in the field and boast data from thousands of locations. They always listen to franchisees, but generally speaking, they know their business. They've built a system, and it works extremely well for those who follow it. Rhoda tells franchisees, with all due respect, "Your role is to do it. Our role is to think." They may as well. That's what they're paying for.

So are you. Your franchisor's main job is to create and hone the systems you need to run your business. Hopefully you examined those systems prior to joining the brand. They should train you on these systems, improve upon them, and support your execution. All you have to do is execute.

Humanity

Franchisors understand the need to master the human factors, but it's not part of their daily conversation with franchisees. Franchisors are not psychologists; they're experts in ice cream and home improvement. They know how to profitably sell sandwiches and oil changes. They're brilliant at tutoring and pest control. Franchisors specialize in developing reliable, replicable systems for selling specific products or services. Mindset enhancement is not part of the arrangement.

But this is what franchisees need most if they want to build their enterprise. Many franchisors have admitted to me they could do more in this area. Others have said they've tried to have these conversations, but some franchisees aren't open to it. (I guarantee those aren't the wealthy ones.)

Some franchisors do provide more of this kind of support and are reaping the benefits. Kitchen Tune-Up CEO Heidi Morrissey noticed a major acceleration in unit growth when she started her daily five-minute motivational *Stay Tuned* podcast, which 98 percent of her franchisees listen to. "Growth is not just about doing more jobs," Heidi said. "Growth starts with you being able to decide that you can do more jobs."

Anytime Fitness founders Chuck Runyon and Dave Mortensen captured their balanced approach to work and franchise support in their book *Love Work* (Beached Whale Press, 2017). Their philosophy for supporting franchisees centers on the four elements of "people, purpose, profit, play." They sent me the book before my first presentation for them to ensure I would support this philosophy. They don't just want to train their franchise partners. They want to inspire them.

Anytime Fitness is so big on the human components of their operation that they actually named their parent company Self-Esteem Brands, with a corporate mission of "Improving the self-esteem of the world." That starts with their franchisees, and they clearly feel it. The result is more than a love fest—Anytime Fitness is now the largest fitness chain on the planet.

One of the real masters of franchisee mindset is Jersey Mike's founder and CEO, Peter Cancro. Though very much a franchisor, Peter has had the wealthy operator mindset since he purchased the original Mike's Subs as a teenager. Peter shared his philosophy with me over breakfast in Laguna Beach.

He said, "I always knew we had so much more than a sandwich shop. We had an opportunity to touch people's lives. That's our mission, 'making a difference in someone's life.'"

And they do, through great customer experiences, support for franchisees and team members, and community involvement. With that focus, Peter's one original shop has grown to thousands of locations that have generated billions of dollars in revenue and tens of millions of dollars for charity and ownership opportunities for deserving store managers. Peter has proved that you can make money while making a difference.

Peter personally vets every franchise candidate to ensure they're a cultural fit for Jersey Mike's. Ninety-five percent don't cut the mustard (my pun, not his). Those who do are treated like family.

"I tell my area directors, 'When you show up at a store, don't be a policeman. Be a fireman. Come with care, not a clipboard,'" he said.

These franchisors aren't just cheerleaders. They have rock-solid operations, crunch numbers, and hold their franchisees accountable. But they also realize that their franchisees experience their businesses emotionally as well as financially, and they want to build their confidence along with their competence.

This is what franchisees need. Not just knowledge of how to remodel a kitchen, market a fitness center, or reduce food waste. They also need to learn how to manage their emotions and think at a higher level.

Ideally your franchisor will provide both operational and motivational support. But if I had to choose, I'd still choose a franchisor that excels at operational support. You need systems, branding, and a good product or service. You can find plenty of other resources to help you manage the human elements impacting your performance. Just remember to nourish your head as much as your body.

Our best time is spent on the factors we can control. There's not much we can do about external circumstances. Operations, of course, is the core of the business. But the internal human factors determine how well we execute those external operations. So let's move on to Part II and start exploring the internal behaviors you need to level up your business and start building wealth.

MASTERING THE WEALTHY FRANCHISEE MINDSET

You are incredibly powerful.

So much is possible for you. You have everything you need to build a great business. You can make money. You can make an impact. You can create something that will change your lifestyle dramatically. And while there are many uncontrollable forces that could affect your results, you are by far the biggest determinant of what happens.

But is that a good thing?

For some it is and for others it isn't. The answer depends on what you bring to your operation. Some make it better; some make it worse. Some create growth, others stifle it—all running the same franchise. It all depends on your level of *emotional intelligence*.

This term, also referred to as "EQ," first appeared in the 1960s but became popular in the 1990s with the book *Emotional Intelligence: Why It Can Matter More Than IQ* by Daniel Goleman (Bantam Books, 1995). EQ refers to an individual's ability to understand and manage their emotions and those of others. Increasingly companies are recognizing the importance of EQ and promoting it within their organizations.

So should franchisees. You must be willing to look inward and reflect to ensure you're making a positive impact on your business.

The reason we're discussing these issues before addressing operations is because I see so many franchisees struggle in these areas, many without realizing it. Franchisors notice it, too. As a franchisee, I experienced these issues firsthand. These are the mental factors that will determine how well you execute the operational practices we'll discuss in Part III.

Wealthy franchisees are masters at managing the internal dynamics described in these chapters. Some are wired to do it naturally, which is a huge advantage. Others have to be more deliberate about their mindset, continuously working to improve themselves to ensure they're operating at their best. Their self-work is ongoing because they know that, like everyone, they have good days and bad days. But their franchise needs the best they have to offer, every day. Succumbing to their human vulnerabilities, even subconsciously, is bad for business, so they make self-improvement a priority.

Many franchisees believe they're better equipped mentally for business than they really are. Complacency, ego, lack of self-awareness—these things blind people to ways they need to grow. Those people will only skim this section of the book because they don't think it applies to them. That lack of self-awareness will limit their performance. If you feel an urge to skip these chapters, recognize that may be a sign that you need this information. If nothing else, you need to understand these ideas to effectively lead team members who may struggle in these areas. They're humans, too, and it's your job to manage them.

To optimize your mindset for franchise success, we're going to explore what I call *The Quintuple-Double C*. These are five areas of distinction that separate wealthy franchisees from everyone else. They're the difference makers. These areas are:

- Clarity and Calm

- Controlling Your Critic

- Cool Confidence

- Combating Complacency

- Constructive Comparison

You think you're powerful now? Wait until you master *this* stuff! You'll be operating at a whole new level. Supercharged with these skills, you'll be much better equipped to use the operational tools we'll discuss in Part III.

Keep an open mind in this section and reflect on how these issues impact you and your team members. Doing this work will align you more closely with wealthy franchisees and increase your chances of getting the same results.

CHAPTER 4

Clarity
and Calm

Chapter Features

- The "Trigger to Trouble" process
- Identifying your triggers
- How to restore your sense of calm when faced with adversity
- The most effective approaches for managing problems

'm writing this book on my laptop. This machine is completely obedient. When I push down on the trackpad and slide my finger over some text, it selects it. When I hit "Command-X," it cuts the text from the document. When I move the cursor and hit "Command-V," it pastes the text in the new location, every time, without hesitation.

What my computer *doesn't* do is second-guess itself. It doesn't doubt its ability, compare itself to other computers with faster processors, dwell on past crashes, or stress about remaining battery life. It doesn't emote—it just performs. It is perfectly efficient.

The human brain is much more sophisticated and a lot more vulnerable. When we receive input, our brain interprets it. The trigger might be an event, a problem, or an offhand comment by a colleague. Instantly our brain decides whether this input is good or bad, pleasant or painful, fair or unjust. We recall similar input in the past and envision what it might mean for the future. We take our objective analysis of the event captured by our physical senses, develop a *subjective* perspective, and experience an emotional response. Only then do we take action. All this happens in a fraction of a second. And the more subjective we are, the farther from the truth we get. That makes it harder to make good decisions. I call this process *trigger to trouble,* which you can see in Figure 4–1 below.

William Shakespeare understood this process: In *Hamlet,* the title character describes Denmark as a "prison" to his old friends Rosencrantz and Guildenstern. They protest that it's great, to which Hamlet famously replies, "There is nothing either good or bad, but thinking makes it so." Now replace "Denmark" with, say, a smoothie franchise. Is the opportunity good or bad? Depends on your thoughts.

Many franchisees evaluate circumstances based on how they feel, looking at just a few data points and interpreting them through an emotional prism. Rarely do these feelings yield accurate information about what's really happening.

One franchisee from General Nutrition Centers (GNC) complained to his director of franchise operations that corporate had opened a mini location inside a nearby Rite Aid drugstore, causing his sales to drop. But when his DFO pulled the numbers, the data told a different story. It was true that the franchisee's gross sales were down since the mini location opened, but his transactions were up by 15 percent. More

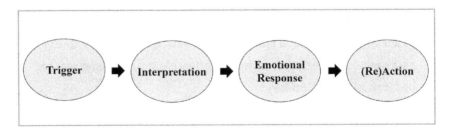

FIGURE 4–1. **Trigger to Trouble**

customers were coming in, but his average ticket had decreased. The drop had nothing to do with the Rite Aid location. It was caused by the franchisee and his staff selling poorly. His anger at corporate had distracted him from the real problem. He apologized and confessed that the lower balance in his bank account had caused him to freak out and rush to judgment.

Most corporate field representatives working directly with franchisees will tell you that much of their job is psychology. Their mandate is to ensure compliance with company standards and help franchisees build sales and profit. But the best among them know there are days when the franchisee is not in a good place to go through the operational checklist. Sometimes they need a different kind of help.

However, we can't always rely on our corporate team for mental support. We have to manage our own mind as much as we have to manage our own business. This mental discipline is essential for good leadership. It's also the key to becoming a wealthy franchisee.

You're going to *feel* your business, but you need to understand that your emotions are often a reflection of your state of mind, not the state of your business. That's why you must be self-aware.

Metacognition

Metacognition is the practice of building awareness of how your mind works. Simply put, it means thinking about how you think. It's not a perspective many franchisees consider. Most are too busy—they just want to work. But being more aware of your thoughts will allow you to take control of them.

Wealthy franchisees are human, and they too experience the triggers, interpretations, and emotional responses shown in the first three steps of Figure 4–1 on page 64. But their self-awareness allows them to disrupt the process before they react, shown in step four. As illustrated in Figure 4–2 on page 66, they insert an additional step between step three and step four: reflection. They pause, calm down, and reclaim their objectivity before reacting, which leads to more constructive responses.

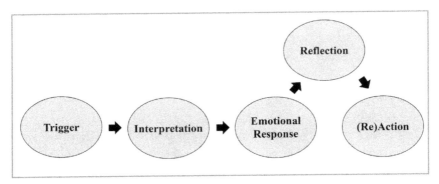

FIGURE 4–2. **Disrupting Trigger to Trouble**

When you feel a strong emotion, think of it as an alarm. Stop what you're doing and stop what you're *thinking*. Take a quick moment to reflect on where your head is and regain control of your thoughts, because that space between your emotional response and your reaction is where wealth is built or lost.

Cognitive Distortions

Metacognition makes it easier to identify the inaccurate thought patterns that may be clouding your reality. Psychologists call these patterns *cognitive distortions*. These are the subjective ideas that lead you away from truth. Cognitive distortions infect your brain as viruses do computers. They stop you from operating correctly. When you unload your mind of this stuff, you start to see things as they really are, allowing you to make better decisions. But you can't manage them if you don't acknowledge them.

Deliberate Thinking

The hardest part of controlling your thoughts is stopping them altogether. Great practitioners of meditation can empty their minds. By concentrating on one focal point, such as a sound, a mantra, or their breathing, they completely clear their heads, allowing them to be fully present in the moment. This is difficult. Most people who meditate spend lots of time having to refocus their wandering mind.

Meditation may sound like New Age nonsense, especially in a book about business. But make no mistake—all franchisees meditate constantly without even realizing it. They just have different focal points. Some focus entirely on improving their business. Others obsess over the competition. Many can't get their mind off the bills. If you have a franchise, I'll guarantee you spend more time thinking about your business than a monk does about his breathing.

The idea is to be deliberate about your concentration to ensure maximum productivity. Learn to control your thoughts, because thoughts lead to feelings, which lead to behaviors, which lead to wealth—or bankruptcy.

Clarity vs. Positivity

Clearing your head doesn't mean being optimistic. A positive attitude is not a business plan—and neither is a bad attitude. Positivity and negativity are just two extremes on the denial spectrum.

I'm not about positivity or negativity. I'm about *clarity*—seeing things as they are. That's the most useful perspective in business. That doesn't mean I don't expect good things to happen—but when I do, I have data to back up my prediction.

Feelings matter in business and in life. Emotion is what distinguishes us from machines. Pathos defines and connects humanity. It's what makes all this business and *busyness* worthwhile. Later, when we talk about customer service, we'll focus on creating experiences with emotional resonance, something a computer could never do. The cold, logical Mr. Spock was a great science officer, but you wouldn't want him greeting your customers.

Clarity is about taking in information with as few filters as possible. We need to get an objective lay of the land. Only then can we take meaningful action.

Leading with Courage

Courage doesn't mean you never feel fear. It means you're afraid but do what you have to do anyway. It's a choice, and wealthy franchisees make that choice. In a way, all franchisees do at some point. I can't tell you how many of my friends have expressed an interest in franchising but were too scared to pull the trigger. Opening a business is a risk. If you've decided to buy a franchise, you've already demonstrated more courage than most. That willingness to move through the fear and step toward the risk is the key to greatness.

One good example of franchise courage is Maurice Levine, former master franchisee of Anytime Fitness Asia. I met Maurice at the Anytime Fitness headquarters in Minnesota, where I was brought in to work with all the brand's international masters. The company has a solid network of international operators, but none of the others could rival Maurice. He was bigger than the rest in every way. He was tall, energetic, and rarely seen in public without his purple Anytime Fitness cape. He oversaw hundreds of Anytime Fitness gyms in nine countries. His franchise network was the largest gym system in Asia. But opening his 300th gym didn't take the same courage as opening his first.

The fitness market in Asia has developed more slowly than in other regions. When Maurice set out to open his first gym in 2013, it was practically nonexistent. Given his plans to expand the brand over multiple countries, his inaugural flagship location in Singapore had to be a winner.

Real estate consultants pushed him to open his first location on the prestigious Orchard Road, the heart of Singapore's upscale shopping district. He looked at all kinds of massive, expensive spaces. Signing a lease for any of those would unquestionably take courage.

But Maurice had an even riskier plan that shocked his advisors. He wanted to open his gym *away* from the action, closer to where people lived. He chose Woodlands, a perfectly nice but much more suburban setting. And he chose a space with a much smaller footprint. He recounted to me how his consultants thought he was crazy. "They asked me 'How in the world can you create a flagship Anytime Fitness in no-man's land?!!'"

What they didn't understand was that Maurice's top priority was to prove the model could work. He wanted to demonstrate that you don't have to spend a fortune to run a profitable gym. His theory—proved in

North America but up to that point untested in Asia—was that Anytime Fitness could thrive in suburban districts, closer to where people lived.

"It was against anything anyone would ever say about location," he said. "It was the highest-risk opening for Anytime Fitness, as far as first locations are concerned, because if it failed, as a consequence of that, we would not have been able to penetrate the market at the speed that we did."

All eyes were on him, especially his competitors', who looked forward to seeing Anytime Fitness crash and burn in their first location in the region. He felt the pressure.

Maurice confided in me, "I was crapping my pants, man. I was scared!"

But he believed in the model and trusted his instincts, and his gamble paid off. The gym was cash-flow positive within its first three months and became one of the most profitable gyms in Asia—even while it was one of the smallest. Having proved his model worked, Maurice would go on to build a regional operation larger than most franchise systems.

After just a few years, he was positioned to sell his enterprise for a massive, life-changing profit. A diagnosis of deep vein thrombosis made frequent travel risky, so the timing was right.

Then came the COVID-19 pandemic, and all his gyms shut down. Business deals and negotiations suddenly ceased worldwide. Maurice found himself in charge of a company with 70 employees, no revenue, and a sale that was all but dead.

He pushed forward, investing everything he had to keep things running while scrambling to close the deal. Miraculously, in one of the worst economies in recent world history, he got the deal done. And having sold to his operational partners (he turned down better offers from private equity firms), he was able to exit knowing his franchisees would be in good hands.

A lot of people with the same information, resources, and capital would not have gotten the same results—not unless they also had the same fearless approach to business.

Another example is senior placement franchise CarePatrol, which recognizes franchisees for courageous success with their "Sexy Buffalo

Award." The award is given to franchisees who bravely acquire struggling locations and convert them into winners. It's an amusing name with a powerful meaning, as described by company founder and CEO Chuck Bongiovanni.

He said, "The word 'sexy' represents the confidence these franchisees have. They believe in themselves as well as the business. The 'buffalo' references their courage and willingness to face adversity head-on."

Chuck explained that while other herd animals run from a storm, buffalo charge in the opposite direction, heading directly into the storm. They know it's the quickest way to get through it, and that where the storm has already passed through, the grass has gotten greener from the rain.

Sometimes, a fear of failure is overpowered by enthusiasm. What inspires many people to buy a franchise is their belief in what's possible. They envision the positive aspects of having their own business and jump in. That's courage, and that's great. It's the first step toward success. Where franchisees really need courage, however, is when things don't go as planned.

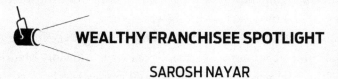 **WEALTHY FRANCHISEE SPOTLIGHT**

SAROSH NAYAR

Fastsigns

Dallas, Texas

- Number-two franchise in the system for 2019
- 2016 franchisee of the year
- CEO Circle Award
- Sales achievement awards
- Franchisee Advisor Committee member
- Public Ecommerce Committee member

After 15 years in corporate America, working for companies like PepsiCo, Philip Morris, and American Express, Sarosh Nayar was looking for something

---

WEALTHY FRANCHISEE SPOTLIGHT, continued

different. "I wanted something that was more relationship-based than numbers-based," he said.

His search led him to an existing Fastsigns territory in Dallas. By the time the sale closed in 2009, the U.S. economy was in a bad way. Building a business in that climate meant being scrappy, learning quickly, and serving customers better than anyone else. It wasn't easy, but it was the best environment to cut his teeth.

Sarosh said, "What we did then was the foundation for our success."

Many of those early customers still work with him today. Since he took over the territory, his sales have quintupled.

Sarosh attributes much of his success to two things. The first is embracing a wider vision for how Fastsigns can help customers. "I want to be more than a sign company," he said. "We're more of a marketing agency." That means serving customers at a much higher level. Sarosh helps his customers innovate solutions, rather than just acting as a retail sign shop. It's a different mindset that's served him well.

He also credits the investment he's made in his team. I actually learned about this aspect of the business from his partner, Joey Carrasco. Joey and I met after a presentation I made for a different franchise. He was exhibiting at their vendor fair and led a roundtable discussion, and I assumed he worked for Fastsigns corporate. But no—he's one of many team members Sarosh has coached to success. Today, he's a partner in the business. The two work hard on developing their team. "We treat our employees like family," Joey told me. "We're there for them, and they'll go the extra mile for us."

Sarosh's Wealthy Franchisee Success Tips

- Think of your team as a family.

WEALTHY FRANCHISEE SPOTLIGHT, continued

‣ Hire for attitude.

‣ This is not for everyone. You need to be pretty even-keeled to own your own business.

‣ Don't be afraid of the "downs." There will be good times and bad times. Be prepared to ride them out.

‣ Make sure you're doing something you really like and with the right attitude.

‣ Put your team first and they'll work for you.

‣ Give your team the tools and direction, and then let them go out and succeed, fail, or learn.

‣ Don't nickel-and-dime at the expense of people, ideas, and capital improvements.

‣ Share the rewards. Make sure your team does well when you do well.

Catastrophizing

Seventh grade was the most stressful year of my life. I was taking pre-algebra, and it felt as though my entire future depended on getting a good grade. My junior high only had one eighth-grade algebra class. Poor marks in pre-algebra meant I wouldn't get in, which would pull me off-track to take geometry, algebra 2, pre-calculus, and calculus in high school. And as everyone knows, if you don't take calculus in high school, you can't go to a good college (or so I thought). That would render me forever unemployable and homeless (also not true, as it turned out).

In my mind, pre-algebra wasn't an opportunity. I wasn't working toward a goal—I was fighting off failure. I was in a constant state of crisis. When I got a C on my first chapter test, I didn't sleep for a week. At only 12 years old, I had already failed at life.

Catastrophizing is the act of exaggerating adversity. It's when we take our problems and infuse them with our fear, stress, and imagination.

We blow them way out of proportion. We create the darkest possible perception of our circumstances, making our problems seem bigger and more meaningful.

Typically, catastrophizing happens in two ways. The first is to make a problem seem much worse than it is. The second is to make a dire prediction about where your circumstances will lead. Either way, it's a major distortion of the facts.

There's a good reason behind the human mind's tendency toward catastrophizing: It's a survival mechanism. In each hemisphere of our brain is an almond-shaped structure called the *amygdala*, which is associated with emotion, fear, and self-preservation. It becomes most active when we perceive imminent danger. Think of it as the brain's fire alarm. When triggered, it begins to release a flood of adrenalin, cortisol, and other stress hormones into our body, heightening our alertness, triggering our "fight or flight response," and helping to keep us alive. If you hear a loud bang, your brain doesn't want your first response to be curiosity. It wants you to duck. Safety first, then understanding.

But activity in the amygdala also blocks the neural pathway to our *prefrontal cortex*, which disrupts executive function, decision making, planning, logic, and other important cognitive functions. In other words, it disables the part of the brain we need to calm down and solve our problem. It's like having a fire block the path to the fire extinguisher.

These days, most of us are rarely in physical danger. Instead, we react to the mental dangers all around us. The threats we imagine are far worse than the real ones. Few children have been attacked by a monster in their closet. It's the monster in their mind that keeps them awake.

Unexpected events in our business can activate our amygdala and cause us to feel threatened. These events may include:

- Falling sales
- Losing key employees
- Legal problems
- Negative press/reviews
- New competition
- Pandemics

Depending on their significance and your emotional response, these things can create a lot of stress. They sure did for me.

For three consecutive days one summer, I experienced an unexplained drop in business. I don't mean a decline. I mean our customers virtually disappeared. It was as if the city had been abandoned and our phone lines had been cut.

It caused me to panic. Something must be wrong. I went to the Edible Arrangements website and placed an order with my own location to ensure the system wasn't malfunctioning. I called my store from my cell phone to make sure the lines weren't down.

I reached out to our corporate office for an explanation, called my neighboring franchisees, and checked the web for any news about the company or the fruit industry. I racked my brain trying to figure out what was happening. How could business just stop overnight?

Finally, I realized what must have happened: My business was dead. People had had enough of us. It was the end of Edible Arrangements (at least for me). No amount of marketing would make a difference. I had bills to pay, a lease to honor, a loan to pay off, and no money to meet these obligations. I was in serious trouble.

I would have to remortgage my house. No, I'd have to sell it and move my family into an apartment. I'd have to pull my son from his club basketball team and take my daughter out of ballet. We'd have to give our dog away. I took out a notepad and started brainstorming other possible cutbacks.

Friends and family were going to judge me. My wife would say "I told you so." I might have to borrow money from my in-laws. Worst of all, I'd have to get a job—there's no way people would book me as a speaker when I had failed at my own business. (You might have thought motivational speakers were immune to this kind of thinking. Think again.)

On the fourth day, I came in to a stack of new orders. The phone was ringing, the usual flow of traffic resumed, and business returned to its usual levels. I took my first breath in 72 hours. Somehow, the bills got paid that month.

So what was behind the three-day dead zone? To this day, I have no idea. What I can say is that in the middle of it, it didn't seem like a temporary lull; it felt like the end of the business. It felt like the end of the *world*.

Because I didn't know what was happening, I imagined the worst-case scenario. It was a stress like nothing I'd ever felt before. I might have been just a few days away from making some desperate, terrible decisions.

I can't tell you how many business owners I've talked to who've expressed feelings of hopelessness. In one of my surveys, I asked franchisees to describe the emotional side of running their business. One responded, "Stress and anxiety. It actually keeps me up at night and interferes with running the day-to-day business."

It's easy to understand why franchisees would be on edge. They've dipped into their life savings and refinanced their homes. They've left stable jobs, taken on debt, and put everything on the line. It's an investment in their own work that will reflect on them personally. They're not just risking money—they're risking self-esteem. When the stakes feel this high, everything gets amplified, and it becomes easy to think in hyperbole.

The more experience you have, though, the less likely you are to overreact. You learn which performance indicators are meaningful and which are inconsequential. What once felt like a crisis will soon feel like a Wednesday.

My father's businesses caused him tremendous stress. I remember times he was so overwhelmed with dread that he'd alert the family that we were on the brink of disaster. "Don't expect much for the holidays this year," he'd warn us. "And don't get too used to this house." He'd go on and on about our impending financial ruin. When he finished, my mom would roll her eyes and fetch him a bowl of ice cream.

Invariably, he'd climb out of the pit and do what needed to be done. Most of the time, his problems weren't nearly as cataclysmic as he thought. A few times they were serious, and he had to close some of his businesses. But no matter how bad things got, he always, *always* got through it. Then he'd start another business and make a ton of money. Peaks and valleys.

During *my* valleys, my first phone call was always to my father. "That's the life of an entrepreneur," he'd tell me. He'd been there. He knew what it felt like. And while he couldn't always advise me how to fix my business, just knowing he'd survived similar circumstances was usually enough to keep me going.

My mom knows my dad well and can maintain a clear head even when he's stressed. Rachel does the same for me. Your family or your employees may not be able to. Stress is contagious, and those who depend on you will follow your lead. If you tell them the sky is falling, they may panic. So we're not just talking about *your* well-being. We're also talking about your family and your team. When great leaders can't manage their anxiety, they at least hide it from the people who depend on them. "Fake it till you make it," as they say.

Lots of franchisees catastrophize. That doesn't make them weak— it makes them human. Anyone can overreact when a high-stakes investment is threatened.

But just because it's normal doesn't mean it's OK. Catastrophizing isn't good for business. It leads to impulsive decisions and can make you do what feels best rather than what *is* best. You can't allow your need to relieve stress to influence your actions.

There's a lot you can do to regain your perspective when things get tough. It always starts with reflection and clarity. Disrupt the trigger to trouble pattern, and then take action. The next section will cover a few ideas for how to do that.

Manage Stress Before Problems

Your inclination may be to act immediately to relieve your stress, but knee-jerk reactions lead to bad decisions. Your choices should be driven by the desire to grow your business, not your need to feel better. Stress will cloud your judgment and distort your understanding of what's really happening. No matter how bad things seem, always start with your head and work your way outward toward your problems.

This isn't just about emotions—it's also about brain function. You want to calm your amygdala and engage your prefrontal cortex as quickly as you can. A calm brain is an efficient brain.

Clear Your Head

It's hard to get perspective on all those irrational thoughts swimming around your noggin. Anything you can do to get them out of your head will make things easier to manage.

One way is to write down your worries. Pen and paper are powerful tools for purging your mind. You could do it journal-style, recording every detail about your situation and your feelings. (Make sure to include the latter.) Or, if you're like me, make lists. Whenever I feel like everything is going wrong, I list "everything" on paper. Usually it's just a few issues coalescing into a perfect storm.

The act of writing can be cathartic enough to re-center you. It's also easier to find solutions on paper. I like to list my concerns in a column. Next to each one, I'll add a few more columns to make notes that help me regain my perspective. My page might look something like the one in Figure 4–3, on page 78.

You'll notice I left some boxes blank. Sometimes the answers come and sometimes they don't. But my immediate priority isn't finding solutions—it's clearing my head. Organizing my thoughts on paper helps me do that.

You can also try talking through your thoughts with someone else. That might mean getting professional help or just calling a friend, a franchise colleague, or your field support representative. Discussing your feelings out loud will help you hear when they are irrational and allow others to give you additional information and/or a fresh perspective. Remember, if you're catastrophizing, you're probably experiencing cognitive distortion, and it might be better to trust an outside perspective rather than your own.

Avoid Hyperbole

This is easier when you write down your thoughts. Notice where you use exaggerated language. Look for words such as "everyone" vs. "some people" and "always" or "never" vs. "sometimes." If you're speaking in absolutes or drawing big conclusions, chances are your thoughts are distorted.

Problem	My Interpretation	Alternative Thoughts	In My Control?	Action to Take
Drop in sales	Business is failing	This is recent and could be temporary. I've had drops in the past. Other locations are also down. I haven't been marketing enough. There's more I can be doing.	Yes	Run reports to better understand the drop. Brainstorm ways to increase transactions. Brainstorm ways to increase ticket average. Do more marketing. See what other locations are doing.
New competition	Sales will drop	Sales haven't dropped yet. We control our level of service. There's competition because it's such a good idea.	No	Do more marketing. Improve quality. See how other locations are competing.

FIGURE 4–3. **Journaling for Perspective**

Problem	My Interpretation	Alternative Thoughts	In My Control?	Action to Take
New competition	Sales will drop	Other locations are thriving even with competition. There are plenty of customers out there. They should be threatened by us!		
Can't find good employees	No one wants to work here.			Place ad for new employees. Revisit our compensation package. Revisit my management style. Ask current employees for referrals to friends. See what other locations are doing.

FIGURE 4–3. **Journaling for Perspective,** continued

Notice Feelings But Focus on Facts

Facts provide better insight on your circumstances than emotion. Get the data and study the measurables. Do you think your business is failing? Prove it. The data will back up your conclusion if it's true. Your franchisor knows what metrics to look at and can provide context based on their global perspective. Have them run reports and help you interpret the data. If things are better than you think, they can help you see this. If not, they can intervene and help you turn things around.

Practice Meditation

Countless CEOs and heads of industry meditate as part of their daily routine. Research indicates it's not just good for their health, but also good for business. It enhances creativity, boosts emotional intelligence, helps us focus, and strengthens relationships. We know that business problems cause cognitive distortion. Improving your ability to center yourself will help you counteract that.

Having said that, I'm not good at meditation. It works for some people, but I find myself spending too much time noticing that I'm not concentrating. If you find that it doesn't work for you either, there are other relaxation methods you can try.

Take a Walk

I can't focus well on my breathing when I try to meditate, but I can concentrate on the flowers, the trees, the buildings, and the life going on all around me when I take a walk. Walking among them charges my brain and distracts me from my fears. I can't tell you how much material for speeches I've written while taking the dog around the block. Philosopher Friedrich Nietzsche once wrote, "Only thoughts that come by walking have any value." He was describing what Stanford University researchers Marily Oppezzo and Daniel L. Schwartz would conclude 125 years later in their 2014 paper "Give Your Ideas Some Legs: The Positive Effect of Walking on Creative Thinking." They wrote that the physical act of walking actually increases creativity, both during the stroll and even for some time afterward. The perspective you need might be found outside. To get out of your head, try getting out of your business.

Wait

Sometimes your attempts at calming down just don't work. In that case, do nothing and let time work its magic. Being patient is different from being passive. While you're waiting to calm down, more information and solutions may present themselves. You want to act, not *react*.

Focus on the Here and Now

Part of catastrophizing is making dark predictions about the future. While you need to prepare for tomorrow, you can't let it distract from today. Today is tangible. It's right here, and it's real. You can handle that, but you don't know what will happen tomorrow. And there are a lot of tomorrows—trying to think about all of them is overwhelming.

The best way to prepare for the future is to make the most of today and give it all you've got. Solve the problems in front of you. Serve your customers, inspire your employees, and pay any bills that are due. Try to learn something that you can bring to your work the following day.

You can't predict what the future will look like, but it's safe to assume it will be different. New things will happen. Many of them will be good.

Just get through today. Then do it again tomorrow.

Anticipate Adversity

This doesn't mean you should expect the worst. But the path to wealth is riddled with potholes, and you're going to face some unexpected challenges. That's part of what you signed up for. Knowing this in advance will make them less shocking when you encounter them.

Prepare for Adversity

Don't make predictions, but do make plans. Real catastrophes are easier to deal with when you have made contingency plans. Don't wait until your house is on fire to figure out your safety plan: What will you take with you, and how will you get out? Your business should also have a "fire plan." What if business drops off or your company fails to grow? What if another pandemic shuts you down or quarantines your customers? What will you need to survive, and how will you adjust? How much capital can you save up to get you through the tough times? Figure all this out before you're in the middle of a crisis. Not only will this give you a smart operational and financial backup plan, but it'll also protect you emotionally.

Help Others Who Are Catastrophizing

Just as you must learn to regulate your emotional reactions in business, you need to teach your team to navigate through their own stress. I used to get phone calls all the time from panicked employees at my Edible Arrangements franchise, reporting on a crisis: The delivery van broke down. The lights went out. A customer was upset. I appreciated their concern, but I wanted them to handle the problem. That was their job.

I had a rule for my manager, Jennifer, that I didn't tell her about for many years. When she'd call, I wouldn't answer my phone. Instead, I'd listen to the message she left. If it was a small issue that could wait, I'd get back to her when it was convenient. If it was a bigger problem, I still waited 90 minutes to call her back. Nine times out of ten, that was enough time for her to calm down and solve the problem herself. I wasn't shirking my responsibilities—I was trying to foster her independence. It's easy to ask for help when it's readily available, but I wanted my team to help themselves as much as possible. Allowing them to figure it out on their own was better than simply telling them what to do.

The best way to keep your team calm and functional when there's a problem is to appear calm yourself. The expression isn't "Never sweat." It's "Never let 'em *see you* sweat." Your employees take their cues from you. If you remain composed and confident, it will give them a sense of stability.

Never tell anyone to "calm down" or "take a deep breath." As good as this advice is, saying it when someone's upset will only anger them. Instead, model calm behavior and validate their feelings. If appropriate, make a joke. Confidently express your certainty that the situation is manageable—even if you're not actually feeling it in that moment.

Calm minds have clear perspectives. You'll build wealth more easily when your decisions are based on data. Catch yourself when you feel yourself giving into your emotions. Reject any dark predictions inspired by fear or unreasonable expectations based purely on excitement. You're running your business to shape your future. That will work best when you have an objective handle on what's really happening right now.

By the way, I did get into eighth-grade algebra and stayed on the math track until my senior year, when I decided to skip calculus altogether and take a year of French. I still got into the college of my choice, though no employer or client has ever seemed to care that I went there. C'est la vie.

CHAPTER 5

Controlling Your Critic

Chapter Features

+ Recognizing your mental critic and what it says

+ How insecurity impacts employee performance

+ How self-doubt impacts your customers' choices

+ How to minimize your critic's influence

"Nice shirt!"

The sarcastic comment came from an inebriated college kid sitting with his friends inside a well-known Hollywood comedy club. The comic onstage had paused between jokes just long enough for the obnoxious drunk to fill the silence. The comedian didn't respond, but you could tell the insult had thrown off his timing. His next joke bombed.

To stand-up comedians, "hecklers" are the enemy. Some try to ignore them and push through their routine. Others respond with clever comebacks. This is normal in stand-up comedy.

It's also normal in franchising. We, too, face a stream of criticism that throws us off our game. But unlike stand-up comedians, who can simply leave the stage, there's no escape for franchisees because our hecklers live inside us.

Each of us has our own private inner critic. I call it the *mental heckler*. It's not your conscience or your usual stream of thoughts. It's that specific self-critical voice whispering in your ear. You've heard it. It's the voice that tells you:

- "You're unqualified."
- "It's not going to work."
- "You're going to fail."
- "You made a complete idiot of yourself."
- "You're inferior."

You don't have to be a franchisee to have these thoughts, but owning a franchise can make you more susceptible to them. After all, when you open a new business, you're going out on a limb. There's a whole lot in that situation to get your mental heckler going. There sure was for me.

After I signed the lease for my first location, a friend who lived nearby offered some "helpful" feedback: "OK, you know there's not a lot of foot traffic there, right?"

It was an offhand comment made in casual conversation. She had no data, just an impression of the area, and thought her observation would be useful. Instead, it sent me into a mental tailspin:

What have you done? No one's going to walk into the store. They'll just drive by without even noticing the storefront. You should have taken more time before committing. There are probably much better locations. You're never going to cover your rent.

My mental heckler also accompanied me to Connecticut for the Edible Arrangements owners' training. I remember walking into the corporate kitchen and seeing posters with pictures of the product line. *Look how many arrangements there are. There's no way you're going to remember all this!* I watched the other new franchisees making fruit baskets. *Their arrangements look so much better than yours.* The trainers showed us their sophisticated business management software. *This technology is so over your head.* At night, I had drinks with some of the other franchisees. *These people have run more businesses than you have. You're not qualified to be doing this.*

I didn't always have these thoughts, but they popped up just often enough to distract and depress me, which made learning the business harder.

Ultimately, I still got what I needed from the training. I learned the whole product line, figured out the point-of-sale system, and got plenty of walk-in business at my store. So much of what my mental heckler said was wrong.

The mental heckler is quite wily, and for some reason, it's easy to believe. It has tremendous credibility. If someone else talked to you that way, you'd walk away. But when the heckler speaks, you listen.

With experience comes knowledge and context. Things don't freak you out as much. You have the facts, and you know better. That's when the heckler starts losing its power over you. It's not that you don't still have negative thoughts; they just don't haunt you as much. The trick is to manage the mental heckler long enough to get to this point.

I love discussing the mental heckler with franchisees. When I ask who among them hears that negative inner voice, most of their hands go up. Many volunteer to confess their insecurities out loud:

- "You really don't know what you're doing."
- "You're never going to turn this business around."
- "Other franchisees are making more money."
- "You're only successful because you lucked into a good location."

I get similar responses even when I speak to high performers. The real estate franchisor RE/MAX brought me in to speak to their top 500 agents in Texas. This was a group of high achievers, but they, too, shared all kinds of self-doubt, telling me their inner hecklers made them believe things like:

- "You're not working hard enough."
- "You just got lucky this year."
- "You're a bad parent."

Sometimes I'll invite franchisees in a large audience to text me their mental hecklers during my presentation, and then I read them from the stage. Take a look at these screenshots in Figure 5-1 below, showing texts (with names redacted) I received during one presentation:

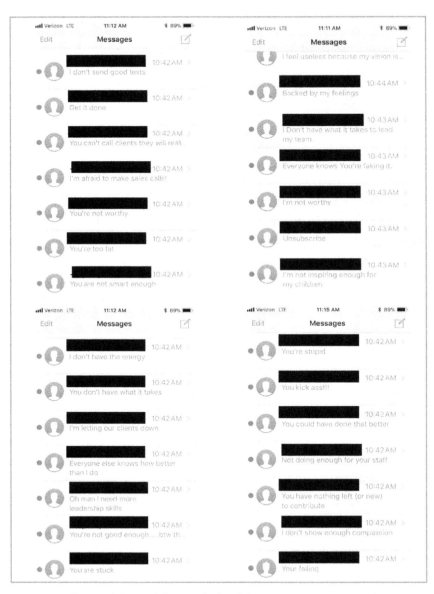

FIGURE 5-1. **Franchisee Mental Heckles**

You'll notice some of what they shared were personal insecurities. The mental heckler makes no distinction between personal and professional time. Often self-doubt in one area spills over into others.

(You'll also notice one person texted me saying "Unsubscribe." I hadn't even signed this person up for anything and already he was opting out! I read this to the crowd and got a laugh. I got a second laugh when I confessed the text triggered my own mental heckler.)

Insecurity is not something franchisees expect to discuss at their meetings, but it's very powerful when they do. It helps them realize they're not alone with these thoughts, and it's a reminder that we're all human.

I once had a woman ask me if the mental heckler was the devil. Considering how evil it feels when it's whispering in your ear, I can understand her question. But what's truly tragic is that it isn't an outside influence—instead, we do it to ourselves.

We are our own mental hecklers, our saboteurs, our worst critics. We're the ones behind the curtain generating the heckler's comments. And consequently, we might be the ones screwing up our businesses.

Sometimes I meet ultra-confident people who claim to never hear self-criticism, saying things like "I never doubt myself," or "I can do anything I put my mind to!" It's hard to know whether they really believe this or if they're parroting back the motivational podcasts they listen to. What I can tell you is that I've spoken to groups ranging from teenagers to CEOs, and in every case, people have admitted to having a brutal inner voice. It's normal to have a mental heckler.

Your Employees Have Mental Hecklers

Maybe—*maybe*—you never doubt yourself. But your employees do. I've met many confident people who are terrible leaders because they expect the same level of confidence from their teams. They're clueless about the inner experience of their employees, and since they're unable to sympathize, they don't know how to support them.

Angela, one of our employees, was great at customer service but terrible at selling. During her first month on the job, her average ticket was well below our staff average. We repeatedly explained to her the importance of boosting sales and retrained her on what to suggest, such as extra fruit, chocolate dipping, or balloons. We gave her all the information and help we could, but her sales remained stagnant.

I recently heard a management-training expert tell a crowd that when employees underperform, it's because they either don't have the know-how or the desire. I totally disagree. Certainly these can be factors, but I've met many well-trained employees who want to succeed but don't. There's more to human performance than information and attitude.

I asked Angela why she believed her sales were low. She dropped her head. "I'm afraid I might make someone angry," she said, and went into detail about her fear of offending customers with suggestive selling. As she spoke, I could clearly hear her mental heckler, feeding her lines like a cynical Cyrano de Bergerac. She said things like "They're going to say no," and "They might yell at me or complain I'm being too pushy." And finally, she offered the most predictable mental heckle: "I'm just not good at selling."

Angela's problem wasn't a lack of know-how, desire, or ability. She just had some incorrect messages coming from her brain that made her job harder. She didn't need more training, a pep talk, or a warning. What she needed was help clearing these distorted thoughts from her mind.

It's important for employers to understand this. If we misdiagnose our employees' challenges, we can't help them. All that retraining and motivating will just intensify their discouragement and our frustration.

When you train someone on a procedure, remember there's a voice other than yours talking to them at the same time. Here's what they might be hearing:

You say: "To take an order, click on 'New Order.' Then click on this menu and scroll down to 'Item List.' Then . . ."

Wait, where's "New Order"? This is so confusing.

". . . type in the SKU number, confirm it's the right product, and request the recipient's ZIP code."

You're lost already. This makes no sense. Is the "recipient" the customer? Just nod your head. You're going to look so stupid if you already have to ask a question.

"Now, on this screen, there are additional options to suggest to the customer. Describe each one and explain how it will enhance their order. Highlight to select and then click 'Add.'"

You're terrible at selling! The customers are going to get annoyed. They won't want these things. You're going to fail at this.

You can't train a human the way you program a computer. It's not enough to provide input. You need to support them through the self-doubt, the fear, and all the other issues that come with a new experience. It's not that they can't work through these mental challenges on their own. It's just that it'll take more time, and some will shut down before that happens. You want them to get past their issues quickly.

Train with compassion. Don't just check for mastery. Instead, gauge their confidence, acknowledge their fears, and offer encouragement. Make it clear that it's OK if they feel confused. Warn them that it's normal to feel self-doubt and praise them when they get something right. Remember that you're competing against their mental heckler, but if you offer your employees a positive alternative to that voice whispering in their ear, it'll go a long way toward making it a better experience for both of you.

We helped Angela recognize how her thoughts were holding her back, acknowledged her mental heckler, and took her through the "Fact vs. Feeling" exercise (see Figure 5-2 on page 99). That conversation was more productive than peppering her with vague motivational phrases like "You can do it" or "You need to try harder." We coached her through her mental heckles, which raised her ticket average and boosted her confidence at the same time.

Your Customers also Have Mental Hecklers

Customers' inner dialogue impacts their purchasing decisions. Sometimes it drives them to buy something (*You have yellow teeth. Better get that whitening toothpaste*) and sometimes it scares them away (*You're too fat for those pants*). Consider all the self-critical thoughts that might be going through the mind of an Edible Arrangements customer wanting to send a romantic gift to his girlfriend:

If you don't do something special, she's not going to like you anymore.

You can't afford this.

Maybe this isn't her taste.

You're coming on too strong.

Your message on the card is too corny.

There's a lot going on during the transaction that has little or nothing to do with our product. If I can identify where his insecurity is, I can then better serve the customer and help him decide.

My employees understood they needed to build more than sales; they needed to build the confidence of our guests. I wanted our customers to walk away feeling a little taller and excited about their purchase. This was our value proposition and was part of the experience we were selling. That meant breaking through their mental barriers to purchasing.

Along with ideas and information, we validated their purchase and expressed our enthusiasm and confidence in their choice. We assured them (in defiance of whatever their mental heckler said) that their fruit basket was about to blow some minds. It wasn't about flattery. It was about helping them build a spectacular order and celebrating that with them. All franchisees are in the people business, and part of doing business with people is helping them overcome the traps their mind sets for them. Do that, and you'll enjoy much greater success.

If you want to effectively communicate with others, you need to acknowledge the mental heckler and understand how it influences performance.

Where Does the Mental Heckler Come From?

Our culture breeds insecurity. Each day we're exposed to thousands of messages about how we're supposed to live. We're surrounded by beauty magazines, fast cars, and fancy houses. We celebrate celebrities, adore athletes, and worship the wealthy without having any idea how happy they really are. We mimic their hairstyles, buy their perfumes, and wear their signature sneakers.

Closer to home, we monitor our franchise colleagues, notice how they're doing, and then compare our accomplishments to theirs. One franchisee is clearing six figures from his store. *You barely make half that.* Another franchisee just opened her third location. *You still only have one.* Before long, everything good we see in others turns into self-criticism. Franchisors mean well when they celebrate top performers onstage at their conventions. They're hoping these high performers will inspire everyone else, but for many, seeing others succeed has the opposite effect. (We'll discuss this more in Chapter 8.)

The mental heckler also echoes criticism we've received from real people. Every insult makes its mark. Sticks and stones will break our bones, but words do permanent damage. This is especially true when they come from people who matter to us. Our parents, our coaches, our teachers—they may have the best intentions, but often their "help" cuts deep. I'll never forget my high school geometry teacher telling me I could never get into Stanford. He may have been right, but I'll never know—thanks to him, I didn't even apply.

But in the end, we are responsible for our own insecurities. We choose to play the game and set our own goals and standards for success. We decide whether to honor our own values or those we see on TV. We choose whether to listen to the opinions of others. And when we look outward to measure our progress, we hear the feedback of that critical inner voice.

The mental heckler points out the gap between who we are and who we think we should be. For some, this is motivating, but for most of us, it's horribly discouraging. We believe the heckler's criticism and don't attempt to prove it wrong.

But what if it is wrong? What opportunities have we missed out on? How much unnecessary pain have we felt? And how much is our business suffering as a result?

Most of the time, the mental heckler misses the mark. Its opinions are completely without merit. Why should it be credible? It's no more educated or experienced than we are, and it has no more information than we do.

Silencing Your Inner Critic

I wish I knew how to quiet my mental heckler for good. I've spent decades helping people overcome this stuff, but my own inner cynic still occasionally speaks up. Sometimes I'll see someone in my audience with a sour look on their face, and the mental heckler starts chipping away at my confidence. Often, when I'm done, those people are the first ones in line to buy my book. Intellectually, I know I can't accurately read an audience member. But intellect can't compete with feeling.

While promoting the movie *The Hours* in 2003, Oscar-winning actresses Julianne Moore, Nicole Kidman, and Meryl Streep confessed their insecurities to Oprah Winfrey during an interview. All three admitted to trying to back out of parts they'd been offered, and Oprah asked Meryl Streep why.

"Because I say to myself, 'I don't know how to act—and why does anybody want to look at me on-screen anymore?'" she said.

Julianne Moore and Nicole Kidman echoed similar feelings. Here were three of Hollywood's most accomplished actresses, admitting they still worry that each movie will be their last, as if the world is going to realize they've been faking this whole time. No number of Academy Awards could compete with their mental hecklers. Maybe their success is a result not just of having talent, but of having the grit to do their work in spite of their insecurity.

That's why I respect all franchisees. Lots of people would love to open a new business, but few actually do. It takes guts to defy your self-doubt. That's the true meaning of courage—to feel fear but go for it anyway. That leap of faith is an enormous step toward wealth.

The Mental Heckler Cares

One exercise I do with franchisees is a role-playing scenario in which I ask them to play the part of their own mental heckler. I speak directly to it and ask why it so brutally discourages the franchisee. After a little discussion, invariably it comes down to this: *The mental heckler cares.* It worries about the franchisee and wants to protect them from failure.

Often the mental heckler will admit it's doing more harm than good and agree to disengage.

It's just a game, but for the franchisee, it can be an empowering shift in perspective. It's easier to coexist with a concerned friend than an enemy. Think of C-3PO in *Star Wars*, or Ron Weasley in the Harry Potter books. They're not negative—they're cautious. They're the first to suggest retreating. They can be annoying at times, but they mean well.

You can decide how you'd like to perceive your heckler. Hate it, hug it—whatever makes you feel powerful. Just don't let it hold you back.

WEALTHY FRANCHISEE SPOTLIGHT

BURKE JONES

The UPS Store

San Diego, California

- Purchased, built, and/or sold seven stores—currently owns two
- Twice he's acquired struggling locations and made them number one in the network
- Four times ranked number one in annual state sales
- Peak Season Performance Award (high growth year over year)
- Terrible student in high school and kicked out of college

The UPS Store franchisee Burke Jones is plain-spoken and down-to-earth. "I'm rarely the smartest guy in the room," he told me, which is clearly untrue. He's plenty smart where it matters.

When Burke first considered buying into The UPS Store, he started visiting some of the top franchisees in the system to see what they were doing and pick their brains. He realized he didn't see anything he couldn't replicate, but he was going to do it with an obsessive emphasis on customer service. That obsession has earned him top marks on Yelp and top rankings in The UPS Store network.

Like many other wealthy franchisees, Burke's really into personal development. "I'm a big reader and listen to a lot of personal growth recordings," he said. "Zig Ziglar was one of my heroes." This has resulted in what his wife described as "toxic positivity." Burke leans heavily toward optimism, expecting things to go well if he puts in the work.

Burke told me there's no operational secret to succeeding in The UPS Store. You just have to build great connections with customers. And he sells to everyone. "I can't imagine why you wouldn't want to do business with me!" he said, not out of ego, but fully aware how committed he is to helping people. And he's happy to charge them for it.

"My customers pay more and are happier about it because they're getting a better experience," he said.

Burke's Wealthy Franchisee Success Tips

- Teach your customers to be your salespeople.
- Look at each customer as a lifelong relationship, not just as a transaction.
- You bought a franchise for a reason. You need to be all in. Commit!
- Figure out a way to love what you're doing, or at least some part of it.
- Some days suck. Everyone has them. Don't quit. Keep moving forward.
- The worst stuff happens between our ears. We've got to keep putting good stuff in our heads to get through the bad times.
- Everyone is a lead.

Managing Your Mental Heckler

Some people are motivated by their insecurity. They respond to these thoughts as a challenge. For example, I once waited at a marathon finish line to greet my brother. As I watched tens of thousands of people complete their 26.2-mile journey, I felt like an out-of-shape loser. That moment inspired me to train for and complete a marathon the following year.

When your mental heckler brings out your best (like it did for me at that finish line), you can go along with it. But when it paralyzes you, you need to manage it.

For some, the mental heckler is totally debilitating. For most of us, it's just an annoying distraction that makes work harder. I don't know how to stop it, but I do know how to make sure it doesn't stop you. By managing it, you can free up your brainpower for more important tasks.

Here are some effective tips to help you do that.

Expel the Heckler from Your Head

Like a shark that never stops swimming, the mental heckler is always ready to strike. But a shark is only dangerous in the water. Get it out of the water, and it flops helplessly. The mental heckler does its damage in your head. Get it out of there, and it, too, loses its power. There are a few ways to do this.

First, try writing down what it says. Just as you would with catastrophizing (as you read in Chapter 4), get all your thoughts onto a piece of paper or write them in a journal. Just as you would with catastrophizing (as you read in Chapter 4), get all your thoughts onto a piece of paper, in a journal, or in the first column in Figure 5–2 on page 99.

You might also try sharing your mental heckles with someone else: a friend, a colleague, a therapist, or anyone else you trust. Speaking your insecurities aloud allows you to hear them outside your head. Here, too, they can sound silly. Discussing them with someone else also allows you to get an outsider's perspective, which can often be more accurate than your own.

Acknowledging these thoughts is an important part of overcoming them. Write them down. Say them out loud. Just don't sit around obsessing over them.

Use the Fact vs. Feeling Test

One woman I coached had a relentless mental heckler. She was a graduate student only three writing assignments away from completing a required course. But that might as well have been 10 years at hard labor, because her heckler told her she couldn't write. Her mental block was so strong that she couldn't even sit down at the computer. She finished with an incomplete, and eventually she received a letter from the dean advising her to leave the program.

When I asked her why she couldn't get her work done, she said there were a million reasons. When I told her to list them all, it turned out there were only eight. These reasons included:

- "My ideas are too crazy."
- "I'm not smart enough."
- "I don't have what it takes."
- "Everyone can do it but me."
- "I don't have enough to say."
- "I'll have to neglect my family."

Here's an intelligent woman at a prestigious university, completely paralyzed by her insecurity. Her friends told her she was crazy to think such things since her talent was so obvious. But her friends couldn't outtalk her mental heckler.

To coach her through this block, I used a technique I call *Fact. vs. Feeling,* a simple method for determining if your mental heckles have merit. See Figure 5–2 on page 99 for a sample worksheet.

Whenever you feel inadequate, unqualified, or in trouble, ask yourself if your conclusion is based on a fact or just a feeling. A fact is something that can be objectively verified. Its existence can be demonstrated to the point where there can be no debate. It just is. A feeling, on the other hand, is subjective. It's an interpretation of reality

Problems, Insecurities, and Mental Heckles	Fact	Feeling
1.		
2.		
3.		
4.		
5.		
6.		
7.		
8.		
9.		
10.		

FIGURE 5–2. **Fact vs. Feeling: My Problems, Insecurities, and Mental Heckles**

based on a perception that may or may not be accurate. Compared to a fact, it's unreliable.

For each of the mental heckles you listed in the left-hand column in Figure 5–2 above, determine whether it's based on facts or just your feelings. In other words, are you objectively stating what the situation is, or are you throwing in your own interpretation?

Example #1: Your business is losing money. You owe three years of back taxes. You have no savings, and the bank is foreclosing on your home. So you think, "I have money problems."

This conclusion is based on facts. No one would argue with you—there's a set of real financial problems here you need to address. You probably have some feelings to go with these facts, but the facts themselves are undeniable.

Example #2: Business is slow, and you have a lot of debt. You still have to get your kids through college. You think to yourself, "I'll never be able to afford retirement."

This conclusion is based on feelings. It might turn out to be true, but without a crystal ball, there's no way to know how your circumstances might change. Many people have overcome their financial problems and prospered. Your conclusion *could* be correct, but so far there are no facts to suggest it's *necessarily* true.

If your problems are based on facts, they're real and require your attention. This is actually good news. Real problems can be looked at objectively and have tangible solutions. For example, debt can be overcome by consolidation, negotiation, and increased income.

But chances are most of your problems are based on feelings because the mental heckler is giving you an incorrect self-assessment. In a court of law, you're innocent until proven guilty. In your life, you're doing well until proven otherwise. If the mental heckler argues that something's wrong, demand proof. Get the facts and then make an informed assessment of your situation. You'll probably find you're doing better than you realized.

After my graduate student client listed her conclusions, she realized that every one of them was based on feelings. There were no factual circumstances stacked against her. Her problem was pure, unfounded insecurity. This realization alone encouraged her, but she still felt her ideas were too crazy. I explained that this might be true, but we needed some facts before we could know for sure. So I gave her permission to go ahead and write a crazy paper. "Don't assign judgment," I told her. "Just write and let it be whatever it is, brilliant or bizarre." This, she said, she could do with no problem. She completed her first assignment in one sitting and turned it in the next day. The professor gave her top marks and raved about her "innovative ideas."

I could have argued with my client, saying things like, "Of course you can write!" or "Stop being so hard on yourself!" Her friends had already tried this approach, with no success. Instead, I just asked her a few questions and let her draw her own conclusions.

The Fact vs. Feeling test is a great tool you can use for yourself or when coaching employees. It's also useful when you receive criticism from someone else. If there aren't any facts to back up their feedback, their heckles are just as unreliable as your inner critic.

Join a Group

Whether it's a goal group, a mastermind group, or a support group, there's tremendous value in working through this stuff with others. Many franchise brands actually help enroll their franchisees into performance groups with colleagues from around the system. Not only can you get outside perspectives on your issues, but you can also listen to *their* unfounded insecurities and begin to recognize the patterns of mental heckler thinking.

I was in such a group in college, and I remember noticing how obvious the solutions were to everyone's problems but my own. Somehow I didn't have the same clarity when it came to my own life. But others assured me I was no different from the rest of the group, which was comforting. I began to perceive how my issues sounded like everyone else's. When everyone was complaining about the same mental heckles, we could laugh at them for what they were—common insecurities. These conversations validated our feelings while stripping them of power. Once it's exposed to other intelligent people, your mental heckler doesn't stand a chance.

I've given several presentations for the Young Presidents' Organization (YPO). YPO is a prestigious networking organization for some of the world's top business leaders. Many of its members have shared with me that the most valuable benefit of membership is joining a "forum": a small, intimate group of members who meet regularly in confidence to support one another in personal and professional growth. Even at their high level, they need a safe space to work through mental roadblocks.

Do what top-performing people do and join a group to connect with others who can provide objective feedback and perspective.

Restate Subjective Feelings as Objective Facts

Often our feelings are judgmental interpretations of the facts. Think about weight, for example. Scientifically speaking, our weight is an objective measurement of the gravitational pull of the Earth on our body. When you step on a scale, it gives you a number without judgment. It doesn't say "fat" or "skinny." It simply provides data. But when you interpret that data and assign an opinion about it, that's when your emotions kick in. You might feel elated that you've reached the weight you believe is attractive or depressed about some added poundage. Maybe you'll feel guilty about eating that extra bear claw for breakfast.

The mental heckler notices information and then interprets it to generate feelings. These feelings are distractions. They're counterproductive. We need to undo them by distilling our thoughts back to the objective information.

Notice the difference between the following pairs of statements:

- "My business is failing" versus "My business is down 15 percent."
- "There's no way I can learn this computer system" versus "I need to learn this software."
- "There's nothing I can do" versus "I don't know what to do."

While the second statement in each pair might generate some emotion, it's still more useful. It accurately describes what's happening or what needs to happen. The first statements are absolutes. They're unhelpful and probably wrong.

That's why writing down your thoughts is so useful. It makes it easier to see where you're infusing them with judgement and clouding your perspective. Get back to the facts and nudge your mind back to objective thinking.

If you sometimes doubt yourself or feel abnormal, it means you're normal. It means you're just like the rest of us. And you're just like wealthy franchisees. But wealthy franchisees manage their heads well. They don't let negative self-talk stop them from taking the action needed to grow their business. Feel your feelings, but continue to do the work. Don't let your inner critic stop you.

It takes humility to admit you have an inner critic. Denying it won't do you any good. Of course, humility itself is another component of the wealthy franchisee mindset that's worthy of discussion.

Cool Confidence

When I'm speaking at a conference, it's common for me to go onstage immediately after a CEO's state-of-the-company address, so I've heard a lot of them. Sometimes they're inspiring; sometimes they're not. Some are entertaining, and others are monochromatic PowerPoint presentations. Most of them are informative. But one really stands out in my memory:

"I've worked hard to build my company."

"The other members of my CEO forum suggested I take a different approach, but I did what I always do— ignored them and did it anyway."

105

"So here's my plan moving forward."

I. Me. My. You'd think he was the only person in the company. He didn't mention his corporate team or talk about the efforts of the franchisees. He never spoke in terms of "we" or "us." He could only see the company as a glowing reflection of himself. He did share a bit about upcoming branding changes and how the industry was developing. But the primary message of his presentation was clear: He was awesome.

Many franchisees told me afterward that gushing about "his" company was of no use to them. They wanted help, ideas, and direction. They wanted praise and encouragement. They wanted to know how he was working to help them succeed. It's what they were paying for.

The CEO never acknowledged his franchisees' dissatisfaction or addressed the mixed online reviews of the company. There were some serious problems in this franchise, but listening to him, you'd never know it. He seemed so out of touch. No doubt he's enjoyed some success as a CEO, but as a guy who profits when his franchisees thrive, he wasn't accomplishing all he could.

Ego is the enemy of service. It puts the focus on the wrong person, makes it hard to listen and hard to learn, and is really annoying to be around.

For all their success, the wealthy franchisees I meet are self-assured but not arrogant. They believe in themselves and have faith in what's possible. But they're not trying to impress anyone. They maintain the perfect balance of confidence and modesty, what I call "cool confidence." That duality is a major component of their high-performance mindset.

Checking Your Ego

The most cursed franchisees are those burdened with a need for affirmation. Rather than focusing on building their business, these poor souls constantly seek validation, recognition, and respect. They confuse business performance with self-worth, putting themselves at the center of their operation, and their business suffers for it.

Ego messes with your business acumen in many ways. It closes your mind to new ideas and constructive criticism, gives you a false sense of security, and deprives you of empathy for others. It makes it harder to resolve conflict (and often causes it), alienates your employees and your customers, and stops you from recognizing others' contributions. Mostly it makes you a jerk with whom no one wants to do business.

Not that there's a shortage of accomplished narcissists. You can probably rattle off a long list of politicians, rock stars, and heads of industry who will be the first to tell you how great they are. Their insatiable need to demonstrate superiority might be the very thing that drives their success, but often that success is only on the surface. They may have money and power, but they could also be wildly unhappy. Remember, emotional well-being stops increasing after $75,000 per year. Some of these people might be stressed, depressed, or in a constant state of self-loathing. The greatness they brag about may have come at the cost of their integrity, their relationships, or their physical health. They chase success at any price, only to find it kindles an endless need for more. They feed their ego, but not their soul. The miserable millionaire is a common cliché.

Our definition of "wealthy" is three-pronged for a reason. It's about balancing financial payoff with a deliberate use of your time and a high quality of life. It means being able to enjoy your success.

Most of the wealthy franchisees I meet are humble, not arrogant. At a welcome reception for Buffalo Wings & Rings franchisees, my client waved me over to meet someone: "Scott, I want to introduce you to one of our top franchisees, Al. He's amazing!" Al shook my hand and smiled. "Well, I don't know about that," he said. "But definitely the luckiest!"

He shared a little about his operation, and I asked about his success in as many ways as I could think of: "What's your secret?" "What have you done differently to drive sales?" "Why do you think you've done so well?" I really wanted to know. But no matter how I worded the question, his answer remained the same: "Our people." They hire great people. They treat them well. They're like a family. "They do it all," he insisted. He took no credit, not even for assembling the team.

Al is smart. Really smart. So's his wife, Mary. They know the business and work hard. They've won awards and made money. If there's anyone who should feel good about themselves, it's these two. But neither let success go to their head. Instead, they let it go to their pocketbook.

Al and Mary perfectly fit the profile of the wealthy franchisee. They appreciate what they have, but they don't flaunt it. They redirect praise to their teams. They have an insatiable desire to grow and learn, but they're not trying to impress anyone. They simply like what they do and strive to get better at it. And at the core, they're just nice people.

Arrogance is different from confidence. Arrogant people brag about themselves to others; confident people believe in themselves, but they have nothing to prove. Arrogance is also different from pride. If you're proud of your business, you feel gratified about the work you've done and the difference you've made.

Arrogance is about feeling important and needing to express that importance. I used to work at a hotel for a guy who always introduced himself as the "general manager and part owner." Telling guests he was the manager was just good customer service. It let them know they should go to him if they had concerns. But why tell them he was "part owner"? Did he think it would impress them? You could argue that it made the guests feel important to meet the owner, but I never sensed he was trying to elevate *them*. He needed admiration.

It's easy to spot the egotistical people at franchise conventions. They talk more than they listen and boast too much about their numbers. They're not there to improve their business—they're there to prove themselves.

For example, I visited one owner of a franchise who refused to go to his company's convention because he was feuding with the franchisor. He had shared a recipe he'd concocted with the corporate office, and they turned it into a regular product. In other words, he was angry that they took a good idea from the field and replicated it for other franchisees (as is common in franchising). He felt he wasn't getting enough recognition. His ego was driving his actions (and reactions).

In my case, one of the hurdles I had to overcome when selling my stores was the sensitivity of my buyer. We did an installment sale, which meant he would pay me over time rather than getting an outside loan. I agreed to this arrangement but wanted guarantees and collateral to keep the transaction secure. I asked for a lot, but it was less than a bank would require. My terms had nothing to do with this buyer in particular. I would have insisted on these conditions with anyone paying me over time. It was just good business.

But the buyer found my requests offensive. He thought I didn't trust him and believed my terms were insults to his character. It almost killed the sale. To make the deal, I had to assure him of my personal respect.

As we discussed earlier, ego is also the enemy of customer service. I know a florist who "records all calls for quality service." He's really recording the calls in case customers accuse him of promising deliveries by a certain time, which he never did. If an angry customer said they were promised delivery by 3:00 p.m., he would play the call back for them to prove them wrong. I always wondered what he said after that. "I told you so"? With this kind of service, you'll win lots of arguments and lose lots of customers.

My wife and I used to have dinner every Sunday night at our favorite Italian restaurant: fantastic food, festive environment, and impeccable service. They knew our favorite table and our favorite drinks, and the server used the most enticing language. Instead of saying "May I take your order?" he'd say, "So what can our chef prepare for you tonight?" He wouldn't offer "dessert." He'd suggest "Italian treats." Every week we'd have wine, dinner, and sometimes Italian treats. Often we'd bring friends. I once added it up and estimated that between us and the friends we brought, we were easily generating $2,000 a year in revenue for the restaurant.

One night we came with another couple and decided to use a coupon from the *Entertainment* book: buy one entree, get one free. Three of us ordered pasta dishes, but Rachel just ordered a small side salad.

When the bill came, they didn't remove an entree; they removed the side salad. I pointed out the error to the waiter, who said that's their policy. That seemed weird to me. An entree is an entree. We ordered three. I asked to speak to the manager, who coldly repeated what the server said. "Sorry, but if that's all she ate, then that's her entree. That's our policy." And then he walked away. We had told our friends what great service the restaurant provided, so I was angry and embarrassed.

Reading this, you may agree with the manager. But allow me to finish the story.

The next day, I was still upset. This wasn't just some random restaurant. This was our Sunday night home away from home. We were good, loyal customers. So that afternoon—between lunch and dinner—I returned to the restaurant and requested an audience with the manager, who seemed annoyed to see me. I reminded him of the previous night's issue and let him know I was still upset. He insisted that the *Entertainment* book actually said an entree is any meal, no matter how small. I had brought the book with me and asked him to show me where it said that.

He grabbed it and flipped through the pages. Finally, he said angrily, "I really don't have time for this."

You don't have time for this? For a couple that comes every week for dinner? I said, "Well, you'd better make time for this, or you'll never see my wife and me again."

I realize this might sound crazy—taking time out of my day to argue about a free side salad vs. a free pasta dish. The difference in price was about $8. But for me, it was about feeling valued as a customer. Even if the manager didn't care about us, it's simple math: $8 vs. $2,000 a year.

And honestly, he could have made us happy for even less than $8. He could have offered us a free tiramisu or a round of drinks for the inconvenience. A few dollars for him, but a meaningful gesture for us.

Instead he handed back the book, said, "OK, see ya," and walked back into the kitchen.

He let his ego—his need to be right—stop him from doing the smart thing. He won the argument and lost the customer.

As a business owner, I appreciated complaints. At least those customers gave me a chance to make things right. In my experience, if you validate their feelings and appease them, they become customers for life. That could have happened here, but instead, we never returned. The restaurant has since closed.

Too many franchisees get defensive and argue with customers. The customer is not always right, but the customer is always the customer. Right or wrong is irrelevant. All that matters is that the customer comes back and brings others with them. I'm not suggesting you sacrifice your principles. Your ego, however? That's got to go.

Lose the Need to Win

Your attempts to save face can hurt your relationships. That's what happens when you get defensive. You can feel as though you're under attack, triggering your amygdala (which you read about in Chapter 4). The brain produces stress chemicals, setting off the "fight" part of the fight-or-flight response. In that moment, you're not using your prefrontal cortex to solve problems. You're governed by emotion rather than logic, making it hard to listen, reflect, empathize, or have a constructive conversation. Instead, you engage in a variety of behaviors that only make things worse: redirecting the blame, making excuses, countering with an unrelated accusation, barking at the person for how they're speaking to you, or pointing out their hypocrisy ("Last week you did the exact same thing!"). And when you do these things, how do they respond?

Often the reply is, "Stop being so defensive," which only makes you feel angrier and even more defensive.

In most disagreements, the parties involved are coming from different perspectives. They don't see the same things, or they see them in a different way. To each of them, their outlook makes sense, and the other person's doesn't. Clashing logic leads to conflict and debate. And humans like to win!

Why is that? What's the motive? What's the advantage?

Healthy relationships shouldn't be competitive. In an argument, for someone to win, someone else must lose. That doesn't promote harmony. Winning an argument with my wife has never improved my marriage. It's hard to enjoy victory while sleeping on the couch.

Likewise, winning an argument with a customer never improved my business. Many franchisees struggle with angry customers because their ego gets in the way. I recently interviewed a franchisee from a home services business who shared a story of how he got rid of a rude customer. He took great satisfaction in telling the guy off. But I didn't get the impression the franchisee ever really understood the customer's concerns. He just didn't like the way the customer spoke to him. I get that, but people aren't themselves when they're angry. We all have a different threshold for stress, and it's easier to reduce tension in confrontations when we don't take things so personally. Tim Davis, president of The UPS Store, shared with me a good thought on this:

"You can do everything right, but you can't control the mood of that customer who walks in. You don't know what's going on in their life and why they might be acting a certain way. You need thick skin—to control your emotions—to ensure they don't get to you and to make sure you give them the service they expect from the brand."

None of us should accept abuse. But when you can put your ego aside, pull yourself out of the equation, and try to understand the customer's point of view, they may not sound so abusive. You'll figure out how to help them more quickly and quite likely earn their apology. More important, you'll hang onto their business. You shouldn't punish yourself financially because the customer has poor communication skills.

Instead of out-arguing someone, your goal should be to resolve the conflict and have both parties walk away feeling good. That only happens when you stop competing and start understanding. Resist the urge to be right and replace it with curiosity. What's the other person's perspective? Why do they see things that way? How would you feel if you saw things the same way? Even if their perspective is factually incorrect, it's still the subjective reality in which they're forming their opinion. Understanding that is the basis for empathy.

It's OK to be wrong. In many ways it's better. When you're wrong, you have an opportunity to learn something, change, or improve. That's something you can control. Convincing someone else they're wrong is much harder, but apologizing is a great way to reduce tension. People calm down when you take responsibility for a problem, and that makes it easier for them to meet you halfway and own up to their mistakes. They'll also respect you more. Respect doesn't come from always being right—it comes from being a kind person who's open to all perspectives.

When other people accuse you of something, try not to process it emotionally. Take a second to cool off and breathe. Chill your amygdala, and replace defensiveness with compassion. Remember that your accuser sees things through their unique prism. Their accusation reveals as much about them, their needs, and their perspective as it does your behavior. Be interested in their point of view. Clarify that first. Maybe they're right about the facts, in which case you can apologize and do what you can to make things right. They'll appreciate that. If they're wrong about the facts, they're still right about their feelings. Make sure you respect those feelings.

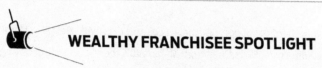

WEALTHY FRANCHISEE SPOTLIGHT

KEN DEARY

The UPS Store

United Kingdom

- Right at Home Master Licensee
- Former McDonald's Franchisee
- McDonald's Golden Arch Award (top 30 franchisees in the world)
- British Franchise Association Franchisee of the Year
- BFA Emerging Franchisor of the Year
- WorkBuzz Best Franchise Award—Management Sector three years in a row (and counting)
- One of only four franchisors in UK to have seven years of back-to-back five-star franchisee satisfaction (90 percent or more)

I met Ken when I led a half-day workshop for Right at Home's international licensees. He was smart, serious, and not afraid to ask challenging questions. Ken knows the franchise world well, having spent years as an award-winning multi-unit McDonald's franchisee and now as a franchisor of Right at Home in the UK.

WEALTHY FRANCHISEE SPOTLIGHT, continued

Ken admitted to being a little overwhelmed when he started with McDonald's.

"In the beginning, the business drove me," he said. "As I matured in franchising, I realized I wanted to drive the business. I wanted to go from firefighting to being in control with a great team around me. That's the key—building a great team."

That realization enabled Ken to expand to four locations (the most McDonald's would allow at the time), while maintaining operational excellence and quality of life.

Today Ken works hard to support his franchisees and to provide the UK with the best possible home care. He learned from McDonald's the importance of having solid systems and then sticking to them.

Ken's Wealthy Franchisee Success Tips

- Expect to work hard, especially in the first few years.
- Be willing to invest in your own self-development.
- Beware of knee-jerk decisions.
- Work with intensity. Do everything at the highest standards. Be better than everyone else.
- Look after your staff. Then they'll look after your clients.
- Be positive about your franchisor. Respect what they've built and stick to the system.
- Get into the community so locals know who you are.
- To be influential, you need to make rational decisions, think things through, and build good relationships.
- Your mindset is massively important! You need resilience to stay at the top. Ability without the right mindset is a waste. Work with courage and believe in yourself.

Proving Yourself vs. *Improving* Yourself

Stanford University psychologist Carol Dweck outlined in her book *Mindset: The New Psychology of Success* (Ballantine Books, 2008) the difference between what she calls a "fixed mindset" and a "growth mindset." People with a fixed mindset believe that ability is innate. You either have it or you don't. These people spend their time trying to prove (or appear) that they're among the talented. Often this leads to jealousy, resistance to feedback, and fear of failure, none of which is good for business.

Those with a growth mindset believe they're a work in progress. They focus on learning and welcome feedback. They don't like failing, but they don't beat themselves up about it or blame others. Instead they embrace the lessons failure offers. They fail forward. This mindset enables them to live with less stress and improve.

Wealthy franchisees don't focus on how great they are—they focus on getting greater. Then even greater than that. They're forever students of their business.

Few people care about your ranking, your car, or how clever you are. If you win an award at a convention, they'll applaud politely and maybe shake your hand. Then they move on with their own lives. They really don't care that much about your success. How invested are you in anyone else's? No one will judge you too harshly for failing, either.

What people do care about is your impact on *them*. They'll remember how you treat them and how you serve them. The real legacy of wealthy franchisees is their contributions to others. That's how they attract people—and money.

Employer Arrogance

Some franchisees like to flex their muscles with their staff. They like to bark orders and make their team tremble. In Niccolò Machiavelli's 16th-century treatise on power, *The Prince*, he wrote, "It is far safer to be feared than loved."

But Machiavelli never had to work with 21st-century employees. He would've been a terrible franchisee. He certainly wouldn't have been a wealthy one. Feared? Loved? Who cares? It's not about you!

I didn't worry about how my employees felt about me. I wanted them to focus on the customers. I told them they didn't work for me;

they worked for the people who were coming in and spending money. That's who was funding their paycheck, and that's who they needed to please. If they were ever in a situation with a customer that they weren't sure how to handle, they were trained not to ask what would make Scott happy, but what would make the customer happy. What would it take to ensure this customer returns? As long as those questions guided their decisions, I'd always support them.

When I was a teenager, I worked for a mean boss who intimidated me whenever he came in. Everyone shuddered in his presence. He knew it, and I think he liked it because it made him feel big.

But when I became a boss, I didn't like it when my employees got nervous around me. If I intimidated them, I couldn't be helpful. I hoped that when I showed up, their first response was, "Oh good, Scott's here." That way they could ask questions and reach out for what they needed.

Owning a franchise isn't about being feared, loved, admired, or respected. It's about getting wealthy. If you want to be loved, be lovable. If you want to be respected, be respectable. But if you want to make money, take yourself out of the equation altogether. Lose the ego and let your customers and team be the stars of the show. Be what management research expert Robert Greenleaf called a "servant-leader" in a famous 1970 essay by focusing on your employees' growth and well-being. Being a servant doesn't mean being subservient. It means actively enhancing the lives of others, which promotes performance and attracts wealth. (We'll talk more about building high-performance teams in Part III.)

There's another practical reason why you shouldn't try to set yourself up as the hero of your business. Your franchise is an asset, and one day you may want to sell it. If you've told the world you're the reason your business is successful, then how much value will it have without you? If you want your payday on the back end, focus on building something much bigger than you.

The Power of Humility

Cool confidence is important for franchisees. Being aware of your abilities increases your motivation and decreases your fear. It makes you stronger when things get tough and inspires those who look to you for leadership. It's an attractive quality that gets people's attention.

Overconfidence kills leadership, though. It decreases others' esteem of you and themselves, weakening your influence.

Confidence becomes arrogance when your appreciation for yourself diminishes your appreciation for others. When you believe you're better than those around you, it's easy to stop listening and learning. As a result, you fail to acknowledge your mistakes or recognize others' contributions, making you less effective.

Humility can regulate your confidence, allowing you to recognize your strengths as well as what others have to offer. When I ask wealthy franchisees why they're successful, by far the most common response is to talk about their team:

- "My employees do it all."
- "I have great managers."
- "We have a great culture."
- "I couldn't do it without my employees."

They're not self-deprecating or insecure. They don't deny that they've hired and trained and built their team. They just don't focus on themselves. I've never heard a great franchisee attribute their success to their own brilliance or their magic touch. Instead, they see themselves as part of a greater whole. That selfless focus makes a huge difference.

Franchise success comes from building something great that's bigger than any one person. It should be so big that it can continue in perpetuity without you. That will make it more valuable when you're ready to exit the business.

Building Your Confidence

For many franchisees, the problem isn't an abundance of confidence but a shortage. The spectrum ranges from shyness and minor self-doubt to social anxiety and major self-loathing. The mental heckles I shared in Chapter 5 shed light on what's going on beneath the surface for many franchisees (and people in other industries as well).

A little insecurity is normal. For most people it's an unpleasant inconvenience, but when it starts to impede your life and work, it becomes a problem. You need to believe in your ability in order to realize it. To develop that resolve, we'll focus on three areas that require your attention: mind, body, and environment.

Your Mind

By now you should understand how important your thoughts are to your business. Optimizing your mind will not only make you more effective at running your franchise, but it'll also allow you to enjoy being who you are. So monitor your thoughts. Notice which ones weaken you and learn to replace them with positive affirmations. They're truer and more useful. Be as forgiving of your own faults as you are of your loved ones'. Don't beat yourself up for what you can't do or don't know. There's room for error. You're so great in so many ways that your strengths will compensate for any shortcomings. At the same time, keep working to improve. Never stop learning. Most powerfully, practice gratitude. That means wanting what you have and loving who you are, rather than getting what you want and changing into someone you're not.

Your Body

Your body and mind are connected. When you're sad, you cry. When you're stressed, you ache. Fear, excitement, and arousal all manifest in physical ways. Our brain creates hormones and chemicals based on thoughts and feelings, and vice versa. Changes in our physiology directly impact your thoughts and feelings. In other words, physical health boosts your mental state. So exercise, eat well, and take care of your appearance, which includes grooming and dressing for success. When you look good, you feel good. A lot of franchisees neglect their health—it's easy to do when you get busy. But I've observed that wealthy franchisees tend to make it a priority.

Your Environment

Your environment is the world around you, and it affects how you feel about yourself. Physically, keep your spaces tidy and organized. Keep

Dirty? *My* store? That couldn't be. My employees were far too attentive to let that happen.

I came in the next day and looked around. Actually, the store *was* looking a little neglected. It was subtle enough that no one would complain, but there was a smudge here and chipped paint there. A brochure holder on the front counter was empty, one of the lightbulbs in the walk-in cooler had burned out, and there was a red light on the phone indicating unchecked voice mail.

I looked a little closer at everything. It turned out our average ticket amount for the past few months had slightly decreased, and our labor costs had slightly increased. Our driver was making deliveries with a Dodgers cap on instead of an Edible Arrangements one. (To make matters worse, I'm a Padres fan.)

No one on my team was purposely slacking off. But they were getting too comfortable. Even Jennifer, my loyal manager of the year, was operating a bit on autopilot. I had disengaged, and they followed my lead.

While some franchisees become complacent with success, others disengage due to a lack of it. I've met many business owners who are just tired of trying. They've worked and fought and experimented until they hit the wall. It's as if they've accepted defeat.

One example is Janet, a neighboring franchisee who wanted me to buy her store. Months earlier she'd fallen out with her business partner and was now operating alone, and it wasn't going well. Sales were sluggish, and she was behind on rent.

Long before we discussed a purchase, I tried to help her turn things around. We talked about working things out with her landlord and plugging the holes in her business. But I could tell she wasn't interested. She actually got a job somewhere and let her employees run the business. She was completely checked out of the operation.

When I went to visit her store, I was shocked at the neglect. There were used napkins balled up on the front counter, the displays were disheveled, and the only employee there was talking on her cell phone and ignoring an order that came in on the computer while I was there. The place was being managed with complete indifference. I didn't know if this was the result of their poor sales or the cause.

The timing wasn't right for me to buy the franchise, but the woman who did quickly turned it around and made it a winner.

Another example is Michael, who was addicted to making deals. He loved to build and acquire new businesses, but he hated running them. He left things like daily operations and training employees to his managers. Michael's interest was in expansion.

Consequently, his neglected franchises plagued him with constant problems. He was sued for sexual harassment allegedly perpetrated by a manager. His former employees banded together and sued him for failing to provide proper breaks and overtime. Government agencies fined him for unknowingly hiring undocumented workers for seasonal help. Michael himself didn't do any of this—it was his young, inexperienced managers. But as the owner, he was held accountable for it.

"My managers have no common sense!" he complained to me. "Why won't these people just do their jobs?" Maybe because he didn't do his.

Other franchisees I've met have decided it's time to slow down, but they don't want to let go. "I don't need to grow the company at this point. I just want it to run itself and provide me a modest salary," they've told me. If you're using your business as a retirement fund, you're in grave danger. It won't run itself—and it might die before you do.

Your franchise is not a passive investment. It's a living, breathing child that needs nurturing. That doesn't mean you must always be there. But you need to give it adequate attention and stay involved.

Business Entropy

The second law of thermodynamics states that all isolated systems will become increasingly chaotic. This gradual decline from order to disorder is known as *entropy*. Entropy is the reason no system is perfectly efficient. There's always a loss of energy. Think about heating your house on a cold day. Once you hit your ideal temperature, you can't just shut off the heat, or your house will cool back down. To keep things cozy, you must continuously add more heat. The only way to counter entropy is by constantly introducing new energy. Nothing can sustain itself. Your franchise is the same way—it needs constant attention to stay up and running.

Great businesses are vulnerable to their own form of entropy. There's always a loss of energy that needs to be replaced. Your customers begin craving something new. Your employees are getting bored. Things need fixing.

And outside your doors, there are always new developments you must deal with. Laws and regulations change, suppliers increase their prices, and the competition creeps ever closer. The marketplace is a dynamic, unreliable arena that remains in continuous flux. What worked yesterday may not work tomorrow. We live in the age of disruption.

This means you, as the franchisee, must remain engaged. You need to keep new energy flowing into your operation. Continuously remind your customers you're there to serve them and offer them fresh incentives to keep them coming back. Actively motivate and retrain your employees. Update your offerings. And always keep your eyes peeled for new opportunities and threats. Your business needs constant attention and new input, or it will gradually become more chaotic and less profitable. The fire will burn out if you don't add more fuel.

A slow leak in your business is dangerous because it so easily goes unnoticed. It's like being in the sun without sunblock. By the time you realize your skin is burning, it's too late. That's why the directions on the sunblock bottle tell you to consistently reapply.

Franchise success is not something you achieve once; it's something you must actively sustain. And the way to do that is by pushing harder. Focus on growing, work on getting better, and then do even better than that. Again, it's not that you should feel dissatisfied with what you've achieved. It's just that moving forward is the only way to avoid slipping backwards.

Think of a bell curve (seen in Figure 7–1 on page 126). The most vulnerable point is at the top of the curve. That's when things fall and business declines. To avoid this, don't wait until you reach the peak. You must act before you get there and growth slows down.

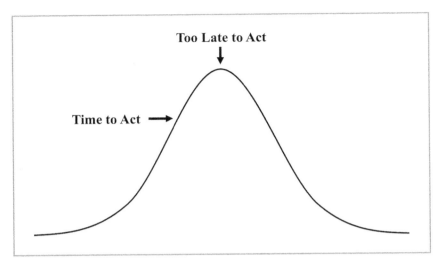

FIGURE 7–1. **Bell Curve**

This bell curve doesn't just describe business growth. It also represents customer loyalty and employee motivation. It warns that momentum will only carry you so far, and eventually it will change directions. Your job is to keep things moving upward without ever peaking. Because "good enough" won't be for long.

Embracing Change

Franchisors are very familiar with the bell curve shown in Figure 7–1, above. It's always on their minds, and rightly so, since their business model is vulnerable to changes in the marketplace. Even if they do everything right, there's bound to be disruptions. It could be a new competitor (consider what Netflix did to Blockbuster), a new technology (consider what cell phones did to pay phones), or a new way of delivering products (consider what Amazon has done to everyone). Economies can change dramatically due to world events (as they did in 1927, 2007, and 2020). Franchisors are also aware that consumers gravitate toward new things, so they need to provide that novelty before their competitors do.

Franchisors also want to boost efficiency and reduce costs. That might mean a new point-of-sale system, new goods, new procedures, or new vendors. And if new leadership comes onboard, you can expect them to implement their own ideas.

With new ideas comes debate. That's not just true for franchising—that's human nature. People tend to fear anything that threatens what they're comfortable with. If they're used to doing things a certain way, disrupting that triggers the amygdala. Often there's pushback before they will even consider new ideas, even when there are potential benefits to switching things up.

Change is an extremely sensitive topic in the franchise world, especially when it's required, and even more so when it costs money. Most franchisees don't like being told what to do, and certainly not what to spend, although they will welcome new ideas when the benefits are obvious. Sometimes franchisees request changes to the model and complain that corporate is dragging their feet. But when they're unsure about a change, they can be reluctant to accept it.

I was certainly guilty of that. Edible Arrangements had an active R&D department that came out with new products often. Some I embraced and others I resisted, although my resistance was based more on gut feelings than data.

One of the products I disliked on sight was chocolate-covered bananas. Bananas are a mushy fruit. I couldn't imagine how a small slice would stay on a skewer without being frozen. The process for dipping the slices in both dark and white chocolate was difficult and time-consuming. They were a headache that would complicate our operation without any meaningful impact on revenue. Why not just focus on how to better sell our current product line? It seemed like innovation just for the sake of change.

I couldn't have been more wrong. The bananas were an instant hit. People loved them and they sold like crazy.

On another occasion, corporate introduced pears, and I was skeptical. This time I was right. They didn't sell well at all.

When I disagreed with our corporate office, I was right about 30 percent of the time. I eventually realized, however, that if I was willing to fail with them 30 percent of the time, I could succeed with them the other 70 percent. That's a pretty good record. It's probably better than I could have done on my own. That's exactly why I bought a franchise—to be guided by people who knew better than I did.

Failure is a necessary ingredient in the recipe of success. You have to try things to create *great* things. The popular Post-It note is the result of an adhesive that failed to tightly bond. Thomas Edison conducted thousands of experiments in order to create his alkaline storage battery (often misattributed to the development of his lightbulb). And that spray in your garage is called "WD-40" and not "WD-1" because it took them 40 tries to get it right. It's worth having a few bad pears to get to the chocolate-covered bananas.

Of course, trying out pears wasn't too risky. Sometimes, as a franchisee, you may be expected to embrace an idea with a lot more on the line. You might be asked to contribute another point to a national ad run or told to remodel. There could be a major shift in the product line that redefines the brand. Sometimes you're asked to do these things without enough evidence that they're going to work.

Do franchisors occasionally roll out bad ideas? Absolutely. When it's a high-stakes bad idea, tensions build. Better companies work through this, but when they don't, franchisees fight back. That's usually what inspires the formation of franchisee associations. It's unfortunate, but sometimes it's necessary. You have to protect your investment.

If this were a chronic problem in our industry, I'd steer clear of franchising altogether. But franchisors pushing bad ideas is nowhere near as common as franchisees resisting good ones. That's a dynamic I see all the time. It's one of the biggest issues franchisors bring up when they call on me to deliver a keynote: The people they want to help don't want their help.

It's not my place to endorse or reject my clients' proposed changes. I'm not an expert in their operation or product line, so it wouldn't be appropriate for me to chime in. What does interest me are the social dynamics within a franchise system when it comes to change and innovation. Are decisions being made with facts instead of feelings? Is healthy communication flowing? Is there trust between the franchisor and their franchisees, and if not, why not?

Earlier in the book, I explained that I would be focusing on what you, a franchisee, can do for your business. If I were instead advising franchisors about implementing change, I'd talk about testing and collecting data from their company-owned locations and from volunteer franchisees. I'd encourage them to consult their franchise advisory council (FAC) and involve franchisees in their decisions. I'd advise them to communicate constantly and explain their reasons for the change. I'd remind them they're gambling with people's livelihoods, so they must proceed carefully.

But when speaking to my franchisee brothers and sisters, the message I want to deliver is this: When it comes to change, we need to lean in. As risky as change might be, *not* changing is deadly. As a collective, we can't rely on the status quo. We must ask questions but keep an open mind and trust the people with the track record and the data. We need to allow for a certain margin of error to encourage ongoing innovation.

Mostly, we need to follow the lead of wealthy franchisees. They have good instincts and clear heads, and they're engaged with the franchisor. There's a good chance they were involved in creating the new idea. Wealthy franchisees are excited to be at the forefront of innovation and frequently volunteer to be trial stores.

Diffusion of Innovations

Social scientists have studied the way members of a population embrace change. Some of the most interesting work came from Bryce Ryan and Neal Gross, rural sociologists at Iowa State University. In their 1950 report, titled "Acceptance and diffusion of hybrid corn seed in two Iowa communities," they examined the rate at which farmers in Iowa adopted the use of hybrid corn seed. Later, in his book *Diffusion of Innovations* (Free Press of Glencoe, 1962), communications professor Everett Rogers expanded the discussion to other industries. He classified people within a population into five different groups based on how rapidly they embrace an innovation. Figure 7–2 on page 130 breaks these groups into percentages of the population:

- *Innovators* are the risk takers who jump onboard as soon as something's available. These are the folks who spend the night

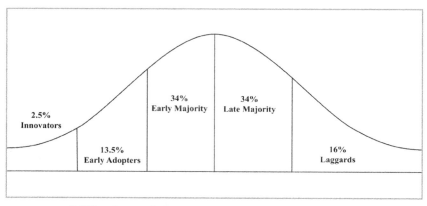

FIGURE 7–2 . **Diffusion of Innovations**

in front of a store so they can be the first to own the latest cell phone or gaming console.

- *Early Adopters* are among the most influential people in society when it comes to accepting innovations. They notice what the innovators do and take a slightly more calculated risk. They still come onboard before most people, but they want a little information first. This group has a lot of influence over the rest of the population.

- The *Early Majority* joins in once the innovation is proven. They follow the leadership of the early adopters.

- The *Late Majority* comes in behind the curve. They're skeptical about change but realize they probably don't have much choice if they don't want to get left behind.

- *Laggards* are the last to get onboard. They cling to tradition and only change when they absolutely must. That's my grandmother, buying a touchtone phone only after it was no longer possible to use her rotary dial telephone.

Like all models, it's not an exact science. It does, however, provide a pretty good general idea of how groups of people adopt new ideas.

Wealthy franchisees are generally among the innovators and early adopters. Their desire to keep getting better opens their minds to experimentation. They also speak up assertively (but respectfully) when the change seems flawed. As top performers, they have influence with corporate. Often they're especially quick to embrace new ideas because they're the ones who came up with them.

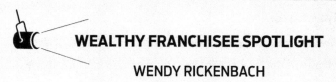

WEALTHY FRANCHISEE SPOTLIGHT

WENDY RICKENBACH

CarePatrol

Sarasota, Florida

- Number one in sales four years in a row
- 2018 Franchisee of the Year
- 2020 Mentor Award

Wendy Rickenbach is a clear standout franchisee in the CarePatrol system. Ninety-eight percent of her fellow franchisees voted for her to receive the Mentor Award, which is given to the franchisee considered most helpful to their peers. Wendy took on 12 franchisees, all of whom went on to win Rising Star Awards, given to franchisees who experience 350 percent to 650 percent growth in one year. She did this while maintaining her own number-one sales ranking in the system. Wendy knows what she's doing and wants others to know they can duplicate her success.

Other franchisees describe Wendy as passionate, enthusiastic, driven, and energetic. This was obvious from our first conversation. She goes nonstop! But she doesn't think these traits are unique.

"I believe all people have these qualities in them, too, but don't always know how to tap into them," she said.

Wendy puts in the hours, but it's her mindset that makes these hours productive and fruitful.

WEALTHY FRANCHISEE SPOTLIGHT, continued

Wendy's Wealthy Franchisee Success Tips

- Always hang onto the one thing that inspires and gets you up every day. Find your purpose.

- You're going to have to put in some sweat, blood, and tears. Of all three, the emotion is the toughest, so find someone to call to help with the tears.

- Put in the long hours until you figure out how to work the smart hours.

- People do business with people. Personal connection trumps expertise.

Continuous Improvement

Top franchisees are constantly looking for ways to enhance their business, which includes setting newer and higher goals. They relentlessly look to raise the bar.

There's always more your business can accomplish. Sales and profit are only the start. Try improving your online reviews, boosting your team's skills, improving employee retention, or doing more for the community. Maybe the business has already met your personal needs—in that case, you can use it to help others. Remember, this isn't just out of altruism. It's also about preventing backward movement. Stay ambitious to ensure you stay engaged.

We've already discussed the importance of inner reflection to ensure you're thinking productively. Wealthy franchisees also take time regularly to assess, adjust, and optimize their operations. There's an easy, well-established process to do this: a SWOT analysis.

Conducting a SWOT Analysis

One of the most useful tools often overlooked by small business owners is a *SWOT analysis.* "SWOT" stands for "strengths," "weaknesses," "opportunities," and "threats." This is a basic strategic planning method many companies use regularly to assess where the business stands and what their next steps should be. You can conduct the analysis alone or with a group.

Start by reviewing your goals. What are you trying to accomplish? How have you progressed since your last analysis? Then begin the brainstorming process.

Determining your strengths and weaknesses requires looking inside your business, while defining your opportunities and threats requires you to look outward. Make a list of all four. If you're doing this as a group exercise, I recommend recording your lists on a flip chart or a whiteboard so everyone can see them.

Under "Strengths," you might list things like your credit line, your skill set, or your strong relationship with your franchisor. You could also add something about your employees, such as their team culture. In the "Weaknesses" column, you might list a shortage of cash, your fear, or any dysfunction within your team. You get the idea. You're basically brainstorming four lists to assess the current state of your business. Don't forget to include your mindset and other human factors.

Some would argue that feelings of fear, impatience, or mistrust aren't weaknesses, but essential survival tools. That's for you to decide. If these things are leading to measurable improvements in your business, then include them under "Strengths." But if they're distorting your perspective or hindering operations, they belong in the second column.

On the other hand, maybe you don't have to label these things as strengths or weaknesses—just notice that they're there, along with all the other factors. There are no hard and fast rules here. You just need to stay aware and focused on what's happening.

Your SWOT analysis might look like the example in Figure 7–3 on page 134.

Your combined analysis should culminate in a final list of action items. You want to leave with things to do.

A great way to generate this final list is by answering three more questions, in light of your brainstorming. To achieve your goals, ask yourself:

INTERNAL ANALYSIS		EXTERNAL ANALYSIS	
Strengths	Weaknesses	Opportunities	Threats
Business location	Lack of marketing	Radio advertising	New competition
Reputation/ reviews	Too much debt	Expansion	New labor laws
Great product/ service	Understaffed	New products	Supplier price hikes
Helpful franchisor	My stress level	Another location up for sale	Others wanting available location

FIGURE 7–3. **Sample SWOT Analysis**

1. What must we CONTINUE doing?
2. What must we START doing?
3. What must we STOP doing?

A SWOT analysis is only one of many ways to evaluate your business. There are other approaches. Figure out what works for you. But whatever you choose, do it regularly. Ask lots of questions about your business, and decide what action you need to take. Repeat the same process a month later, because some of the answers will change, and those changes will point you to places where you can improve your business.

Places to Improve

There are certain parts of the business franchisees sometimes neglect. Each of these areas needs constant attention if you want to get wealthy. While reading the sections below, consider where you could use some improvement.

Marketing

Operationally, marketing may be the area where franchisees differ the most. Some are aggressive, actively advertising and going out into the community. Others just run an occasional ad and wait.

Many franchisees neglect marketing because they think it's enough to pay into their franchisor's advertising fund and resent being told to spend even more. "What are you doing with my marketing dollars?" they complain. "Why don't we have more TV commercials?" Or they see the national ads but don't experience a resulting increase in business activity in their market.

Marketing at a national level is not the same thing as marketing in your neighborhood. Your franchisor can create large-scale brand awareness, attract customers to the brand, and facilitate a few of the six to eight touches needed to influence consumers to buy.

But they can't drive customers to your storefront, build relationships in your community, or target their message to your specific demographic. All that's on you. You and your franchisor are marketing partners. They do their part, and you do yours. Don't think for a second that a national advertising contribution will be enough.

It's tempting to cut your marketing budget when sales are down, especially when you don't see an immediate response to your efforts. Your desk may be stacked with bills for payroll, supplies, and utilities. Why not skip advertising for a few months and save a few bucks?

But ceasing marketing when sales are down is like a farmer trying to save money by not planting crops. It may solve your immediate needs, but you'll have trouble down the line.

You are a farmer growing a customer base. You must plant seeds and consistently nurture them, even when they don't sprout immediately. That requires foresight, patience, and faith. And, of course, it requires money. Don't think of marketing as an expense; it's an investment. It's the only way to keep your doors open. No one has ever saved their business by decreasing their exposure in the marketplace.

So how much should you invest? The SBA recommends spending 7 to 8 percent of gross revenue on marketing. This assumes your margins are in the 10 to 12 percent range after all costs, including marketing. If

THE **WEALTHY** FRANCHISEE

you're less profitable, you should probably allocate more. What you don't want to do is pay all other expenses and then market with whatever's left over. To use another analogy, marketing for your business is like fuel for your car. You're not going to get too far without it.

Wealthy franchisees don't wait for customers or rely on their franchisor to supply them. They're out in the community, reminding people they exist. They advertise. They promote. They pull customers in. They don't stand at the shoreline waiting for the fish to bite—they jump in the water and grab them.

The Numbers

I once interviewed a licensee from a brand of nutritional supplement stores and asked, "So, how's business?"

"Pretty good," he replied. "You know how they say most businesses close within a year? Well, we're still here!"

This guy had no idea how he was doing. He saw customers and some money in the register. His business was alive over a period of time, so he assumed that meant he was successful.

The only way to evaluate the state of your business is to look at the numbers. Activity isn't solvency, and sales aren't profits. You must look at everything, including sales and expenses, the reduction or increase in debt, and sales trends. Numbers tell the truth, and accounting software and good data entry habits make accessing your numbers easy.

I'm shocked by how many franchisees ignore this. One franchisee who came to me for business coaching took a month to generate a (supposedly) accurate P&L report for us to review. Like so many franchisees, she just had too much to do to worry about bookkeeping. She measured her performance by how busy she was.

Holidays were huge at my Edible Arrangements locations. On Valentine's Day and Mother's Day, we received a month's worth of orders in one day. Phones rang off the hook, and customers lined up out the doors to buy fruit arrangements. Often we'd reach capacity and would have to turn away customers. Our goal each year was to improve our operation so we could take more orders. Usually we succeeded, so I assumed we were doing better.

But a close look at the numbers told a different story. One holiday we increased the number of orders by 15 percent over the previous year, but customers were buying cheaper arrangements, resulting in a net decrease in total sales. Other times sales were up, but so were expenses. Once we hit a certain number of orders, we had to take on new fixed costs, such as additional refrigeration. We couldn't just fill more orders to cover these expenses—we had to fill *a lot* more. Increasing sales but decreasing profit is not a success; neither is providing mediocre service to customers because you're so swamped with business.

Your goal as a business owner is not to be busy or to maximize sales. Your goal is to maximize profit, and the only way to do this is to look at the numbers all the time. Your numbers will show you trends and help you identify problems and opportunities.

Cost Control

Your franchisor may require you to purchase from specific vendors. Hopefully they've negotiated good pricing. You probably have control over some expenses, and those need to be watched and periodically reviewed. The cost of goods can quietly gobble up more and more profit without you noticing.

Cheap is not always best. Quality and reliability also matter. So does anything that saves you time. Still, you need to be conscious of how much you're spending.

High pricing isn't the only way your expenses increase. There's also waste, which means you must buy more. A lot of franchisees will look at their invoices but won't track how their goods are being used. Even when employees aren't negligent with your supplies, they can still be overly generous with them. I can't tell you how many times I've been given straws or coffee refills I really didn't want. Someone's paying for that stuff.

For example, we carefully tracked how many melon balls we could extract from a cantaloupe. We counted how many strawberries went into an arrangement. We monitored the consistency of our melted dipping chocolate. It wasn't just about saving pennies—it was also about engaging employees in a profit mindset. We were already training them to increase sales—we also wanted them to help control costs. In both cases, it required constant oversight.

Watch where your money goes. Talk to other franchisees about what they're spending and which suppliers they're using. Go over your P&L and look at every expense. Your franchisor should be able to recommend benchmarks to help you determine what percentage of sales should be going into every item. For example, a quick-service restaurant chain might make the following recommendations:

Expense	Percent of Sales
Food and Paper	28%
Labor	25%
Rent	10%
Marketing	8%
Utilities	3%
Franchise Royalty	5%
Other Expenses	10%

A restaurant operating at the above numbers is making an 11 percent pretax profit. A reduction in these numbers means as much to your bottom line as an increase in sales. And since you're probably paying a percentage of gross sales to your franchisor, a penny saved is actually worth more than a penny earned.

Many franchisees rarely track their expenses. Some look at them at the end of a financial period to see how they did, like it's a report card. Wealthy franchisees study these numbers incessantly. When an expense line item goes up, they immediately investigate to figure out why, and they scour their businesses looking for ways to reduce these numbers. Because wealth is built one fraction of a percent at a time.

Study your costs regularly. Just as you set sales goals, also set spending goals. Remember, pennies matter. Profit is in the details.

Employees

If you give employees 100 percent of the pay you promised, they should give you 100 percent of their effort, right? That sounds fair—but it's not realistic.

Compensation isn't motivation. Employees need something more. As their manager, you must work continuously to keep them engaged—that's management's primary function. That means providing encouragement and feedback, as well as giving reminders, reviews, praise, and reprimands on a regular basis. Struggling franchisees often feel burdened by this: "Why can't my people just do their jobs?"

But wealthy franchisees understand that motivating employees is *their* job. People need to be led. Good employees must be pushed to greatness, and great employees must be kept that way. Neither will happen without consistent, ongoing management. The time you put into your employees is an investment that pays off. You'll spend less time motivating yours than struggling franchisees spend "dealing" with theirs.

Never think of your employees as a burden. They're your greatest asset. They can serve and sell and do all the other work that needs doing, but only if they're regularly reengaged in the business. That's on you. They don't need much, but what they do need matters. Never take them for granted. If they're worth keeping around, other employers will happily steal them away from you. Trust me—I'm one of them.

(There's much more on managing employees coming up in Chapter 11.)

Physical Condition of the Business

The Toys "R" Us in my neighborhood must have looked great when it opened. Its bright colors must have stirred the imagination, and its clean white floors must have sparkled like a sea of diamonds. The first kids to visit probably had their minds blown by this ginormous toy heaven.

But even years before they closed for good, I noticed that most of the lights in its dilapidated street sign were out. The building had become old and run-down, with graffiti scrawled across its side. It looked nothing like a place that once professed to be "The World's Greatest Toy Store." In a time when street retailers are fighting for their lives against the internet, nothing about its physical appearance invited passersby to stop in.

Capital improvements are painful. It's not like marketing, where you feel your investment will increase traffic. Remodeling and repairs require a major cash outlay with no immediate ROI. But is that true? One 2014 study in Australia found that retailers experienced a post-remodel sales spike of almost 50 percent. *Franchise Times* reported a 10 percent sales bump at remodeled restaurants for Fazoli's after the chain renovated nine company-owned locations in 2017. For Long John Silver's the bump was as high as 16.5 percent. There are many similar stories out there to suggest that remodels get customers' attention—and drive a corresponding increase in sales.

I can't say that was my experience when I remodeled my first store, however. I was given similar statistics, but I was suspicious. My feelings were borne out in the end: The remodel didn't lead to a measurable jump in revenue.

But as a consumer, I'm turned off by tired-looking stores. When the paint starts chipping and the signage looks faded, I lose interest in shopping there. And when something new and shiny opens in the neighborhood, I'm more likely to try it out.

Sometimes franchisees must do things that aren't about increasing sales, but protecting them. A business that loses its luster will also lose customers. Keeping your location looking clean and new is an important way to maintain what you have achieved.

Interestingly, when we remodeled our store, it reinvigorated *my* enthusiasm for the business. I had the same feeling you get when you paint a room in your house or wear a new outfit. I felt a pride in my store that recommitted me to the business. Aesthetics impact our mindset, and our mindset impacts our bottom line.

The appearance of your business sends a message to customers and employees about your standards. Keep it impeccably clean, up-to-date, and irresistibly attractive.

Operations

When you do something long enough to become a habit, you stop thinking about how you're doing it. There are thousands of things you do reflexively every day, and many of them are opportunities to improve. Most of them are little things that might not even look like they need to be fixed unless someone points it out.

For example, I'm right-handed. At Edible Arrangements, I used to cut fruit wedges by hand and place them on a tray to my left. I did this for three years before a new employee (who had a fresh perspective) pointed out that if I put the tray on my right side, I wouldn't have to stretch across my body with my right hand to reach it every time. It was obvious, but it had never occurred to me.

Any time we took a step back and looked, we'd find tweaks that enhanced operations. Moving a table to another location. Storing strawberries on a different side of the walk-in cooler. Replacing phone handsets with headsets. Downloading bank transactions rather than manually entering them. Every little improvement saved time and money, reduced backaches, and increased profit.

Some people love to say, "If it ain't broke, don't fix it." Like hell. Don't wait for things to break, employees to get bored, or a more efficient competitor to pass you up. Keep getting better at what you do, and never stop tinkering with your operations.

Your Own Personal Development

It's interesting that so many people stop trying to improve themselves. You are the biggest factor impacting your business, so you need to stay sharp. Getting too busy to be your best can easily lead you to being your worst.

Carve out a portion of your day for your own development. Read books, listen to podcasts, or watch TED Talks.

For learning things specifically related to your business, go to your franchise convention. It's not just about getting new ideas—it's also about recharging your batteries. You need an infusion of fresh energy to fight off your own entropy. It's also important to connect with colleagues and strengthen those relationships. Wealthy franchisees always go to conventions. If you want to be among them, be *among* them.

Impassioned franchisees are excited to do the things described in this chapter. Others are totally over it. That's OK, too, but you need to respond accordingly. If you're burned out, sell the business. The fresh energy your franchise needs might be a new owner. You should be an asset to the business, not a liability.

Guard your business with love, ambition, and a little paranoia. If you keep taking care of it, it's a lot more likely to keep taking care of you.

CHAPTER 8

Constructive Comparison

Chapter Features

- The difference between constructive and destructive comparisons

- Choosing the best reference points by which to measure your performance

- Using "upward targets" to improve your business

- Playing "The Perspective Game" to generate new ideas

- The metrics that really matter for evaluating your business

Hundreds of Edible Arrangements franchisees roamed the halls of the Gaylord Palms Resort & Convention Center in Kissimmee, Florida. It was my first franchise convention, and I felt like a freshman on the first day of high school. Everyone was shaking hands and exchanging hugs. Multiple colored ribbons hung from their name tags, indicating all the ways they were special. Mine had one lonely green ribbon that said "Franchisee." I felt totally inadequate.

Some ribbon-bearers were truly wealthy franchisees, while others were just peacocks. It was hard to tell the difference. Many of them freely shared their best practices, some boasted about how many orders they filled on Mother's Day, and others talked about their expansion. There were a whole lot of people doing what I was doing, many of them at a very large scale. I wanted to learn from them, but as a newbie, I was a bit intimidated.

I felt the same way as a boy, watching the other kids at baseball tryouts. As an adult, I've felt it in the weight room at the gym. I've experienced it watching other speakers give presentations. In comparing myself to others, it hasn't always felt good.

Studies have shown that frequent comparison of yourself to other people can lead to feelings of guilt, envy, regret, blame, defensiveness, and other destructive emotions. Normal human experience tells us the same thing—we all know how measuring ourselves against others bums us out. Still, it's one of our most common behaviors.

Comparison is also a standard practice in franchising. There's a good reason for this: It's one of the key indicators of business performance. It tells you, the franchise owner, who's doing well and hopefully why. But left unchecked, comparison can be a debilitating mind trap that can mess up your business, so you have to watch out for it.

While progress should be measured against your goals, in a franchise system, it's also measured against other locations. This seems logical—knowing your ranking relative to other franchises provides context for how you're doing. A slow month for just your business means something very different from a slow month for the entire company. If the whole company's down, there's a macro problem. But if just your location is down, there's an issue unique to your business. It's important to know the difference so you can figure out what to do.

However, you don't always have enough data to make fair comparisons, leading to inaccurate conclusions. That can also mess with your head and cause you to have poor judgment.

Comparison starts early and continues for the rest of your life. Our pediatrician tracks our growth as a percentile of kids our age. We're graded on a curve. We see who gets into what college. We notice who has the prestigious jobs, the nicest houses, and the flattest abs. None of us really knows how we're supposed to live, so we look to those around us for clues. This is a double-edged sword—it can help, but it can also be harmful.

Constructive Comparison vs. Destructive Comparison

Comparison is helpful when it reveals truth about performance. If one business is doing 20 percent more in sales than another and the only difference is that the first one does more marketing, it's easy to draw an accurate conclusion. If stores located in colder climates are outperforming warmer locations, that's also useful information. Comparison is great when it helps you understand what's happening. A scientific experiment relies on comparing your results when you change only one thing, while keeping everything else the same. That's how you get objective data—and it's how you learn the truth.

But when you don't have all the information you need, comparison can distort the truth. Too often, you guess what's going on and fill in the blanks. Through this subjective process, it's easy to reach wrong conclusions. That's when comparison becomes destructive rather than constructive.

At Edible Arrangements, I could see my weekly and year-to-date rankings in gross sales at the local, state, and national levels. I'm a numbers guy, so I watched these rankings closely.

The problem was that I really didn't know how to interpret them. What did they actually mean? It's easy to assume that highly ranked locations are better businesses, but gross sales alone don't tell the whole story.

One top-ranked franchisee in a printing franchise shared with me that 70 percent of his business comes from just two corporate clients. I give him credit for earning those accounts, but it wouldn't be accurate to say he's built a great business. His number-one ranking doesn't reflect his vulnerability—if he loses even one of those clients, his business will tank.

I know another multi-unit franchisee who redirected business from two of his locations to the third just to drive up his ranking. For one week, he could brag that he had the number-one store in the state (while his other two plummeted in the rankings).

I'm not saying gross sales aren't an important metric—they're vital for telling you who's getting the most traffic and revenue. Hopefully they'll also explain why. It's helpful to know what methods (and mindsets) are driving sales. If looking at other people's businesses gives you replicable ideas to improve yours, then by all means do it. That's constructive. But if comparison is distorting the truth or causing you to feel bad, it's destructive.

Filling in the Blanks—Incorrectly

There are many reasons another franchise location might outperform yours. When you don't know why, it's tempting to guess. Here are some possible interpretations you might have:

- "They're luckier than I am."
- "They're better than I am."
- "I don't know what I'm doing."
- "Our franchisor favors them."
- "They have a better location."
- "I'm not working as hard as they are."
- "They're marketing more."
- "They have more money to invest."
- "They provide better customer service."
- "I'm facing more competition."

Some of the above conclusions are about circumstances, some are about behavior, and others are about ability. The truth might be all, some, one, or none of the above. It's important to find out which. You can't learn from someone unless you can correctly identify the key factors influencing their performance.

Earlier I mentioned an Edible Arrangements colleague who expressed envy over my first location. He wasn't the only one. As we rose in the rankings, many attributed our success to pure geography. "I wish

I had a location like yours," they would say. Our location *was* good, but there were plenty of other factors they failed to consider, such as our customer service, our marketing, and our stellar online reviews.

Often our interpretations of comparative data reflect the way we see ourselves. If you feel you're an unlucky person, you're more inclined to draw conclusions that reinforce that belief. If you're insecure about your business acumen, you're more likely to blame that for your inferior performance. Frustrations about your location might cause you to measure all other businesses by their geography. The stories you tell about yourself will inform how you see the world.

If you hope to learn from comparison, you must rein in your subjectivity, cut through the cognitive distortions, and narrow your observations to objective data and provable explanations.

Making It About You

"Their business is doing better than mine, so they must be better than me."

Far worse than having a failing business is the belief that you're a failure. Comparison can make you feel that way if you draw conclusions about *yourself* rather than about your business.

I've met many franchisees who raise the stakes of business performance by taking it personally. When they get outperformed, they fill in the blanks with self-criticism:

- "I'm not as smart as they are."
- "I don't know business as well as they do."
- "I've made some bad choices."
- "I'm in over my head."
- "I'm a failure."
- "They're better than me."

There are so many factors affecting your business that have little or nothing to do with you. And the ones that do are only a result of your actions, not your identity. This is an important distinction because you can change your actions.

What matters isn't who you are but what you do. Drawing blanket conclusions about yourself is counterproductive. Instead, use your comparisons to other franchisees to inspire yourself to act.

Let's try reframing the above self-disparaging conclusions into action statements:

Insecurity	Reframe
"I'm not as smart as they are."	"I'm going to learn more."
"I don't know business as well as they do."	"I'm going to learn from them."
"I've made some bad choices."	"I'm going to make some different choices."
"I'm in over my head."	"I'm getting help."
"I'm a failure."	"I'm still working toward my goals."
"They're better than me."	"It's possible to do better. I'm figuring out how."

The purpose of reframing these statements isn't to contradict your insecurities as much as to convert them into productive thoughts. If a comparison makes you feel bad, acknowledge the feeling and then follow it up with the question, "So what can I do to improve?" Wealthy franchisees focus on action and look to other high performers for ideas.

Choosing Your Reference Points

Is your home big or small? It depends on the homes you compare it to. A moderately sized house on a block of mansions will seem small. The same house in a row of two-bedroom ranch homes might seem huge. Size is relative.

Without objective measures for performance, you might look to other franchisees to gauge how you're doing. But which franchisees make for the most useful comparison? Do you look to the ones operating in a similar territory? Those in business for the same length of time? Or do you just look at the top sales leaders in the system? Your choice impacts how you perceive your performance.

In his multivolume work *The American Soldier* (Princeton University Press, 1949), sociologist Samuel A. Stouffer compiled data he collected from surveying hundreds of thousands of American soldiers during World War II. His research developed the concept of *relative deprivation*, a feeling of discontent that occurs when we are denied something we feel entitled to. People generally set their expectations by comparing what they have to social norms. For example, Stouffer observed that in the Air Force, where promotion occurred rapidly, privates felt more deprived than those in the same rank in the Military Police, where promotion was much slower. The Air Force personnel had higher expectations and felt more discontented because of it.

Stouffer also noted that black soldiers stationed in the South, where discrimination was worse, nonetheless had higher morale than those stationed in northern states, where black civilians generally fared better. The theory was that these soldiers compared their lifestyles to their civilian counterparts. Southern soldiers saw black civilians struggling, and therefore felt better about their own circumstances. The northern soldiers who observed more prosperous black civilians had lower morale. Relative deprivation suggests an inverse relationship between our perception of other people's circumstances and how we feel about our own.

There's also the concept of what psychologists call *counterfactual thinking*. This is when we compare our actual circumstances to what might have been. Multiple studies have shown that Olympic bronze medalists are happier on the podium than silver medalists, as both measure their success in comparison to what could have happened. Often silver winners compare themselves to the gold medalist, thinking, "I was *this* close." The bronze winners compare themselves to all the athletes who won nothing. "I was *this* close," they think gratefully. They placed lower than the silver medalists but feel happier, because they are thinking about how they could have done worse, not better.

A franchisee doing $400,000 in sales may feel bad when they compare their business to one doing $900,000. But they could just as easily make the comparison to a location doing $250,000 in sales. If you feel entitled to make $900,000 or believe that's the standard for your franchise, of course you're going to feel bad.

The franchisees we compare ourselves to are called *targets*. *Upward targets* are people we perceive as superior or more fortunate. *Downward targets* are those we see as inferior or less fortunate. The $900,000 franchisee is an upward target, and the $250,000 franchisee is the downward target. Both have an effect on our psyche.

Downward targets can make us feel better about our circumstances. "Wow, at least I'm doing better than him." These comparisons increase our gratitude. If we're feeling empathetic, however, they can also make us feel sad for the downward target.

Our responses to upward targets are a bit more complicated. Sometimes they inspire us. This is especially the case when it's someone we can relate to: "If she can do it, so can I." Seeing one of our own accomplish something confirms it's possible for us, too. That makes them great role models.

Some franchisees miss out on the inspiration by focusing only on the *differences* between themselves and their upward target:

"I don't have the location they do."

"I'm not like him."

"She just got lucky."

These conclusions, which are often inaccurate, only reinforce their self-doubt. And if they compare *themselves* to the upward target rather than focusing on behavior, they're bound to drop deeper into the darkness.

Actually, no matter how upward targets make you feel, comparing yourself to them can be harmful if you don't have all the information. Many of them are false idols. Your perception of them may be completely off, in which case following their lead could be dangerous. That franchisee grossing $900,000 might be spending $1 million on marketing or paying much higher rent. Maybe they're working themselves to death and their personal life is in shambles. Unless we know the true costs of their gross sales, we really can't measure their success. Your upward target may not be "wealthy" at all. The franchisees in your system with the highest profit, the most time, and the best lifestyles (remember, it takes a good balance of all three) may be doing it quietly, way down in the rankings. It's hard to know who's really thriving just from looking at the gross sales numbers.

Using Upward Targets to Improve

Olympic silver medalists may sometimes look at gold medalists and feel bad. But that comparison can also be productive, depending on what they focus on. Instead of simply envying the final results, they can study the gold medalists' training regimen and see what might help them improve their own performance for next time.

Studying the true high performers in your franchise system can be immensely helpful. The key to benefiting from this upward target comparison is to focus on ideas, not on identity. Who they are is less important than what they do. That includes their action steps and their mindset. We want to see what they're doing and how they're thinking. Those are things we can replicate.

WEALTHY FRANCHISEE SPOTLIGHT

SHERRI GILLETTE

Caring Transitions

Tucson, Arizona

- Number one in system sales several years in a row and twice as much as the next highest franchisee
- Multiple Franchisee of the Year and Top Sales Awards
- Pioneer Spirit Award

Sherri Gillette is serious, competitive, and focused on the big picture. In 2010 she left a corporate job to open a Caring Transitions franchise in Tucson. The brand helps seniors with relocation, estate sales, and other services. Her market is

---

WEALTHY FRANCHISEE SPOTLIGHT, continued

smaller than many others in her system, but some fellow franchisees still attribute her success to the number of seniors who live in her area.

"People say, 'You're in Tucson,'" she said. "I'm like, 'You're in Florida!'"

Sherri started operating with two family members and today oversees ten managers and dozens of employees, who handle a territory that many of her colleagues would serve with just four or five people. She purposely created her infrastructure to serve as many clients as possible and attributes her success to the team she's built externally and the mindset she has internally. "You have to believe that you can do this and not let anything stop you," she said.

When I asked what keeps her up at night, she said it's worrying about her clients when things go wrong: "It's emotionally wrenching." She places a lot of emphasis on building the right culture, constantly reminding her team at every meeting and party that their work is special and important. "We're passionate about compassion."

Sherri's Wealthy Franchisee Success Tips

- The customer experience is the only thing that really matters.
- Cultivate a team of compassionate people.
- Thinking hard is more important than working hard.
- Let the numbers tell you the story, not your feelings.
- Ask for the order. Ask for the opportunity to serve!
- Don't let money get in the way of you making a difference in someone's life.

Don't dwell on their circumstances. You'll always find another franchisee who seems better off, with a superior territory, fewer competitors, or better weather. It's easy to assume that's why they're outperforming you (assuming they actually are). It does no good to focus on factors that are out of your control. Other franchisees' advantages are irrelevant to your business when you can't replicate them. So don't even try. Play the hand you've been dealt, cook with the ingredients in your pantry, and run *your* operation. If you make the most out of what you've got, you might find you have all you need.

Playing the Perspective Game

There's a fun coaching exercise I sometimes take people through that helps them overcome mental blocks by trying on the perspectives of people they admire. If you're stuck for a solution to a problem, make a list of role models—people who live and work in a way you'd like to. These could be people you know personally or people you've never met. They can be living or dead, historical or religious figures, family members you respect, business leaders, or the top franchisee in your system. Make your list diverse to get as many points of view as possible.

Once you have your list, ask yourself how you think each of these people would respond in your circumstances. It doesn't matter how they would *actually* respond—you're just using your imagination to broaden your perspective and brainstorm options.

For example, let's say a new competitor has opened in your territory and sales have dropped. You're stressed and unsure how you should respond. So ask yourself, what would George Washington do? What would Aretha Franklin do? What would James Bond do?

Yes, James Bond is a fictional character—that doesn't matter. Asking what he would do might still yield some useful answers. If he inspires you, you can still imagine what his answer could be. You might say he'd operate with confidence, keeping a cool head and acting with dignity. He'd consult "Q" to acquire more resources. He certainly wouldn't give up. More than once I've seen people get workable ideas from some pretty outrageous imaginary figures. Have fun with this process—the purpose is to get past whatever's been blocking you and help you think of solutions that you couldn't see before. As long as you have upward targets in your world (or in your franchise), you may as well tap into your admiration of them to expand your thinking.

Choosing the Metrics that Matter

Humans need to feel that they're growing. It's not enough to *be*. You must *do*. And you need ways to measure your progress so that you can know what you're doing is working. When you're not sure how to measure what you're doing, you compare yourself to others, even though the information you get as a result may be misleading. One solution for this is to look at different gauges.

In addition to choosing the right comparison targets, it's also important to choose which key performance indicators (KPIs) to monitor. Some matter more than others. If you don't know the purpose of these metrics and what they actually tell you, it's easy to draw incorrect conclusions and take things too personally. You don't want that. You want objective data that will help you run your business and achieve your goals. Let's look at some of the most important metrics you should consider.

Gross Sales

This is the most basic measurement of a business. It's a good overall number to keep score. Your rankings are probably based on this number, and it matters a great deal to your franchisor, as it's used to calculate their royalty. But how your gross sales compare to other locations is less important than how they compare to your own gross sales from a previous time period. That will tell you the direction your business is headed in, and how quickly.

Rankings

These numbers are only good for two reasons, and there's only one that truly matters. The unimportant one is ego. It feels good to outdo others. Maybe it'll earn you a plaque. But a franchise is not a contest or a way to validate how awesome you are. It's a means to get wealthy (in terms of money, time, and quality of life). The real benefit of rankings is to help you identify what's working, so you can investigate and replicate them.

Profit

This is the truly important number. From a revenue standpoint, it's the metric that should affect all your decisions. It's the true north of your business. If your franchisor could accurately rank locations by this number, the list might look very different from the gross sales ranking. Anyone can lease a high-traffic location or invest a fortune in marketing to drive customers to their business. You can easily spend your way to a top gross sales ranking. But profit? That takes real business acumen. It's the difference between peacocks and owls. As you mingle with your fellow franchisees and talk numbers, try to find out what their profits are, even if it's just as a percentage of gross sales. Then seek to learn from those whose numbers are good.

Growth Rate

This tells you if the business is growing or shrinking, and at what rate. Again, be careful about comparing your number to others. A franchise that goes from $250,000 to $300,000 has grown by $50,000, or 20 percent. A franchise that goes from $1,000,000 to $1,150,000 has grown by 15 percent. As the numbers get bigger, it's harder to grow at the same pace. Twenty percent is more than 15 percent, but $150,000 is more than $50,000. So which is doing better? It's hard to tell unless you can see their expenses and determine what their net profit is.

Customer Satisfaction

I'd put this metric right up there with profit, since customer satisfaction is the number that leads to profit. The happier you make people, the more they buy, the more they talk, and the more you make. This is often measured by looking at a business's Net Promoter Score (NPS), Customer Satisfaction Score (CSAT), or Customer Effort Score (CES). You can also look at star ratings on online review sites. When I ran my franchise, I paid attention to these things. What I cared about most, however, wasn't what customers said on a survey or on a call to their home. I cared about whether they came back or referred a friend to us.

At my stores, we asked every customer how they found out about us and if they'd used us before. Repeat transactions and word-of-mouth are the true measurements of customer satisfaction.

Customer Count

How many people are walking through your doors? Is it the same people or new people? Repeat business speaks to good service, while new business speaks to good marketing, including happy customers doing your marketing for you. To grow, you need to acquire new customers and convert them into regulars. Knowing how often repeat customers come and how much they spend will help you determine their lifetime value. And that number will help you make marketing decisions and calculate your customer acquisition cost.

Ticket Average

This is the amount your customers spend on average per transaction. It tells you how well you're selling. Growth occurs not just by driving more sales but by driving bigger sales. You want to grow both wide and deep. Pay attention to this number and work to boost it. The best way to achieve this is by offering more value. Focus less on upselling and more on up-serving. Strive to make the customer even happier with each transaction.

Employee Satisfaction

You can't make customers happy if you don't make your employees happy. Do you know how your employees really feel? Are they invested and engaged? Are you sure? Measure it. Don't just ask them how they feel—quantify it with numbers, which makes it easier to track over time. This is as important for your star employees as it is for the rest of them. Great team members are professional enough to perform well and seem happy even while they look for another job.

Expenses

We discussed these in Chapter 7. Monitoring expenses is critical for achieving profitability, so wealthy franchisees are always looking for ways to save.

I studied my P&L incessantly, constantly scanning for leaks and opportunities to save money. I looked at which products sold and which ones lagged. There are countless KPIs and reports to help you track performance. Your franchisor has plenty of great, useful data that will help you run your business. Look at your own numbers compared to previous time periods. Comparing yourself to yourself is much more productive than comparing yourself to others. Only look to other franchisees for ways to improve your numbers.

"OK," you may be saying, "but still, am I any good?"

I've already told you: No one cares! Don't worry about being "good." You have nothing to prove to anyone. Just work to be better tomorrow than you are today. Wealthy franchisees aspire to continuously improve, even when they're already at the top of their game. They always want to do better. Strive for personal growth as much as you strive for financial growth. You could try to outperform other franchisees, but you can't control what they're doing. You don't need to win. Just keep learning and building.

If someone else has a better business than you do, there's a reason—and it might be you. Not who you are, but what you're doing, or more likely, how you're thinking. But you can change that. Your way of thinking and your resulting choices are making a difference, one way or another. If you really have been the problem in the past, you don't have to beat yourself up about it. Just focus on changing what you're doing, and how it could impact your business for the better.

If comparison is a source of misery, gratitude is the antidote. Gratitude is about being happy for what you have. The trick is to practice it even when you have less than you want. Appreciate your business and your life, even if others have more. And know that right now someone else is jealous over something wonderful in your life that you take for granted. You are their upward target. Take stock of your good fortune and celebrate it. Be joyful for the wealth you already have, even if other people appear to have more.

PART III

MASTERING THE WEALTHY FRANCHISEE SKILL SET

W ealthy franchisees run excellent operations. They rank high in sales, control costs, and win awards. When they're not on-site, you'll still see engaged employees creating great customer experiences. Wealthy franchisees demonstrate consistent high performance that can be easily observed.

None of this happens by accident. It's the H factor in the formula C + O + H = R (Circumstances + Operations + Humanity = Results). Their mastery of the human elements of their business directly impacts their execution of operations. It's why they're superior.

Figure P–1 on page 160 shows six areas of business operations. Notice the difference in how wealthy franchisees and struggling franchisees approach each one.

Clearly the wealthy franchisee's emotional experience of the business is more pleasant. It's also more lucrative because feelings and attitudes influence our habits, determining not just what we do but also how we do it.

	Wealthy Franchisees	Struggling Franchisees
Sales	Aggressive and active	Passive and inactive
Marketing	Faithful and patient	Cynical and impatient
Managing Employees	Inspiring and engaging	Directive and neglectful
Customer Service	Warm and inviting	Cold and robotic
Partnership w/ Franchisor	Collaborative and trusting	Resistant and suspicious
Expansion	Confident and courageous	Doubtful and fearful

FIGURE P–1. **Wealthy vs. Struggling Franchisees**

Take marketing as an example. It's mysterious and expensive, and its impact may not be felt for a long time. Two franchisees might decide to run identical campaigns for four weeks. At that point, each must decide if they will continue.

One franchisee is patient. They know marketing takes a long time. Many people saw their ad and made a mental note to try the business when they need it. For some, that will be a few months later. Others noticed the ad but won't respond until they've seen it a few more times. Some people will act right away but won't indicate it was the ad that drove them in. This franchisee isn't certain the ad campaign will build their business, but they *are* certain not advertising will allow it to perish. They see other thriving businesses constantly marketing, so logic dictates they should do the same. They have researched the percentage of revenue other successful businesses in their industry spend on marketing and earmarked an equal amount, but they won't be passive about it. They'll track progress and make adjustments. It will take consistency, money, and courage. But like all wealthy franchisees, they're in it for the long haul.

The other franchisee concludes after four weeks that the ad campaign was a failure. They spent more on the ads than they saw in sales. Corporate is only telling them to advertise because it's not their money. They have other bills to pay, including rent, payroll, and plenty of other nonoptional expenses. Why waste money on something that doesn't work?

I tried starting a marketing co-op with all the Edible Arrangements franchisees in Southern California. We held meetings and took votes and brainstormed and debated. All the data suggested it would be more efficient to pool our advertising dollars. But many franchisees resisted. Some were scared to commit to an ongoing financial obligation, while others didn't like giving up control. Still others didn't trust our corporate office and were skeptical of a program they endorsed.

I explained to my colleagues that the marketing co-ops in other regions were doing well and told them we could start off with small weekly contributions. And I offered that if it didn't prove beneficial to everyone, we could tweak the program or just stop.

It was easy to predict who would vote for the co-op and who wouldn't. The franchisees who provided the best customer service, cultivated great teams, and regularly attended the annual franchise convention were enthusiastic. Others were cautious, but ultimately agreeable. Those who were opposed had the biggest problems and the worst online reviews for their businesses. Ultimately, we got the votes, and I was elected to be the co-op president. Unfortunately, I sold my stores a few months later and never had the chance to see it through.

You'll notice there isn't a chapter on marketing in this book. It's not that I don't think it's important. I do—very much so. It's just that marketing doesn't come up much when I ask wealthy franchisees why they're successful. For them, marketing is simply a basic part of running any business. (When we discuss customer service in Chapter 9, I'll explain how marketing can actually sometimes harm your business.)

Wealthy franchisees do talk a lot about their teams, however. That's so important to them that I've devoted two whole chapters to staffing.

In this section, we're going to examine the operational elements that rely on human interaction. How can you delight your customers? How do you build and motivate high-performance teams? How can you best partner with your franchisor and play an essential role in your community? Everyone says they're in the "people business." This section explores what that really means. We'll look at some of the most important operational elements of running a franchise business and how the wealthy franchisee approach will give you an edge. We'll definitely discuss specific tactics. But ultimately, what matters most is the philosophy behind them.

Blow Their Minds, Grow Your Business

"Hello, welcome to Regency Theatres," droned the concessions clerk.

"Welcome to Regency Theatres," echoed her zombie co-workers.

My kids and I had just reached the front of the concessions line and were met with these monotone greetings. A woman in the next line got the same dusty salutation. "Hello. Welcome to Regency Theatres," mumbled her clerk. "Welcome to Regency Theatres," repeated the walking dead chorus.

Management must have recently sent out a memo reminding employees to welcome customers. The clerks were told what to say and they said it. What they didn't do—or even attempt to do—was *connect*.

They said hospitable words, but they didn't convey hospitality. If anything, they conveyed the opposite. Greeting guests was clearly a burden to them. Even my bank's ATM welcomes me with an exclamation point. It was a total downer.

This is what happens when customer service is viewed purely from an operational perspective. As customers, we repeatedly get scripted phrases like, "May I help you?" or "Thank you for shopping at . . ." We're told by a phone recording, "Your call is important to us. Please continue to hold." This stuff is robotic—it's canned retail babble that does nothing to ingratiate you with your customers, especially when said so indifferently. And while speaking in a monotone is bad, overenthusiasm grates on the nerves like a shrieking cat:

"Mr. Greenberg, would you like one key or two? One? PERFECT! If there's anything you need, my name is Brittany. OK? Don't hesitate to call down, OK? Enjoy your stay!!"

Brittany couldn't possibly have been this excited to have me as a hotel guest. She just thought great customer service means being ENTHUSIASTIC. I appreciated the effort, but I saw through it. It's a performance. It's disingenuous.

Your franchisor has probably suggested some best practices for customer service, but none of these practices will be effective unless you and your team have the right mindset. Mindset is to customer service what a melody is to lyrics. The melody dictates how you sing the words in a song and determines the pace and mood of the music. In a business, mindset dictates how you execute your operations and sets the tone for the service you provide. It's the difference between a forgettable transaction and a memorable connection between you and your customer.

The Untapped Opportunity of Customer Service

Customer service is the absolute greatest tool available to you for building your business. More than marketing, more than sales, great customer service is the single most controllable factor impacting your operation.

It should also be the easiest. I can understand someone who doesn't know how to handle marketing. It's complicated and ever-changing, especially in the digital age. Customer service, however, is something we experience as consumers every day. We've all had amazing encounters and terrible ones. We've had word-of-mouth recommendations from friends and read online reviews. We know what we prefer, what we dislike, and what we can expect.

You've probably patronized and abandoned businesses because of how they treated you. You've experienced firsthand how customer service influences your behavior as a consumer, and you know what good customer service looks like.

Why, then, is there so much bad customer service out there? And why do so many franchisees neglect it?

Before opening my first Edible Arrangements, I visited with an owner at his existing location, and we spoke as he assembled fruit arrangements in the kitchen. Ten minutes into our conversation, the front door chimed as someone walked into the store. He blew out a long breath, peeled off his gloves, and marched out to deal with his customer.

Five minutes later, he returned to the kitchen. He made a beeline to a hand sink to wash up and get back to his work. "I hate being interrupted while I'm trying to make arrangements," he complained. "I need to get these done."

This franchisee was spending thousands of dollars on ads to bring in new business. The appropriate response to a new customer should be a fist pump. But he resented his work being interrupted, even by someone who was willing to give him money. He just wanted to make fruit baskets.

Operations have a way of distracting low-performing franchisees from what's most important. They get consumed by everything that needs to get done—often because they're trying to do so much of it themselves. My colleague bragged about how much he was saving on labor by assembling the fruit baskets himself. It didn't occur to him he was losing money by rushing through customer experiences.

He pulled fresh gloves onto his hands and showed me his technique for quickly cutting fruit, but I had stopped listening. Because that was the moment I realized how I would build a competing location that would dominate the Los Angeles market.

Customer Service Is Your Best Form of Marketing

When you advertise, you're hoping to persuade someone to try you out. Most people who see the ad won't respond. The average consumer on the street isn't that valuable.

But someone who's walked through your door? They're worth everything. They're gold. They're the people you've been looking for.

The experience you give customers is the ultimate form of marketing. It will determine how much they spend, whether they'll come back, and what they say to others. When you make a good impression on them, they'll do your marketing for you.

If there's one area of my Edible Arrangements enterprise I'll brag about, it was the experience we gave our customers. From day one, I recognized the importance of treating customers well. I looked at every order as an audition. I had something to prove. I wanted everyone to know that when they walked into our stores, we were going to do more than we promised and give them more than they paid for. I didn't just want customers—I wanted *repeat* customers. I didn't just want them to think good things about us; I wanted them to *say* good things about us. Whether they were sending a basket or receiving one, I wanted to blow their minds.

Most of our competitors weren't thinking this way. My colleague who just wanted to make fruit baskets certainly wasn't thinking this way. I knew how he was treating his customers. I set out to treat them better.

That mindset took us to the top of the rankings and paid my bills. It got us stars and likes and an award. Our ability to make our customers feel great was our best form of marketing.

That mindset also led to superior operations. By having such a clear philosophy—and *mission*—we easily developed practices that improved performance and outdid our competition.

Consider the difference between wanting to make a sale and wanting to earn a repeat customer. If someone is standing in front of you and you want to make a sale, you ask them what they want, give it to them, and take their money. Done. You've made good on your value proposition: They came in to buy the thing they wanted, they leave satisfied, and they go about their day. The average franchisee thinks this is adequate service.

But a wealthy franchisee looks at the person in front of them and sees more than a sale—they see *many* sales. They see a spokesperson who talks to friends and writes online reviews. Mostly, they see someone they can help.

A wealthy franchisee is not predatory. Sure, they want the customer to spend money and come back again. But they know that to win future business, they have to blow the customer's mind today. Give them a reason in *this* transaction to want future ones. Create an experience they'll remember and want to repeat.

So a wealthy franchisee gives their customer a warm welcome, assesses the customer's needs, and looks for ways to exceed them. Some of these ways might cost them a little more; some of them are added value they throw in for free. They may even find a way to save the customer a few bucks. This isn't discounting—it's marketing and making an investment. They've already spent money advertising to strangers who may never come into their store. Doesn't it make sense to spend a little on someone who's already identified themselves as a lead? And how much is it worth if that customer tells others about their business? Their praise in conversation or online will go a lot farther than anything people see or hear in the franchisee's own ads.

But none of this is on the franchisee's mind at the moment. They decided long before this transaction to build their business by making customers happy, so they can leave feeling better than when they came in. That's the franchisee's mission and mindset, and it's the philosophy they instill in their employees. They are not thinking about selling. Rather, they are focusing on how they can make this customer really, *really* happy.

The average franchisee's "satisfied" customer leaves thinking about the next thing they have to do that day. The wealthy franchisee's customer leaves thinking about what a great experience they just had.

That customer goes back to work and tells a few people in the break room, "Have you tried that place on Beverly Boulevard? They're so great!"

How Marketing Can Hurt Your Business

At franchise conventions, there's always a lot of discussion about marketing. Everyone's looking for new ways to drive traffic to their business. But for many businesses, that's not necessarily a good idea.

If you're providing a poor customer experience, marketing can be dangerous because you will be offending that many more people, who all talk and post on social media. And bad reviews spread much faster than good ones. The initial burst in sales won't make up for the bad word-of-mouth.

But even if you're providing inoffensive customer experiences, you're still not maximizing your marketing dollars. People won't complain if you're average, but they'll forget about you. They're less likely to come back, bring friends, or tell others about your business. It's a missed opportunity.

Don't market your business unless you're providing an experience you want everyone to know about. When you do, you may find you don't have to market that much, because your customers will spread the word for you.

Unfortunately, franchisees who market well but serve poorly hurt everyone in the system. They drive business away from the entire company. Disappointed customers don't just abandon one location—often they'll swear off the entire brand. That's one of the drawbacks of franchising. Every time a customer came to my Edible Arrangements after having a bad experience with another location, I cringed. For every customer who decided to take another chance with my store, there were probably many others who gave up on Edible Arrangements altogether. During the last year I owned the business, we received two negative Yelp reviews. Both were because of bad experiences customers had at another location.

But I'm not especially worried about this. I doubt you're giving customers bad experiences—if you were in the bottom 10 percent, you wouldn't be reading this book. My concern is that you're giving your customers typical, forgettable experiences, the kind we're all used to getting. If you are, you're leaving money on the table. You're making smaller sales, getting less repeat business, and missing out on all that free marketing your customers would do if you just adopted the right customer service mindset. And you're leaving your business vulnerable to competition.

Transactions vs. Experiences

In Chapter 3, we discussed how business success rests on a combination of operations and humanity. Nowhere is this truer than in customer service.

Two elements define the customer experience: what the customer gets and how the customer feels. What they get—the transaction—is the operational piece. It's the ice cream cone, the pest control, or the carpet cleaning. How they feel is the human piece. Getting an ice cream cone can be a very different experience, depending on where you buy it. And creating great experiences is the key to building a fan base. Some brands understand this better than others.

Sport Clips Haircuts Founder/Chairman Gordon Logan is a down-to-earth Texan who gets stratospheric results. He attributes much of this to what he calls Sport Clips' "MVP Haircut Experience." I asked him how that differs from a standard haircut.

He said, "Most men can't tell the difference between an average haircut and a great one. But everyone can tell the difference between an average experience and a better one."

He walked me through how Sport Clips creates that experience, going into great detail about the easy mobile app check-in, the sports-themed décor, the consultation, and the cut. Then comes the hot steamed towel, the shampoo massage, and the neck and shoulder treatment. His vivid description made me want to drop my pen and head straight to a Sport Clips. Gordon is very clear that cutting someone's hair isn't enough. "We want people to leave feeling good about themselves," he said.

Getting a haircut is an errand. But having an MVP haircut experience? That's next-level. That's how great salons are built, by improving how people feel rather than just how they look. That feeling is part of the Sport Clips value proposition.

Let's look at another example. There are lots of places selling sandwiches and salads. But at the Mendocino Farms Sandwich Market, their motto is "We sell happy." And they really do. Great food isn't enough. They want everyone who walks through the door to feel good. If they provide an amazing BLT but don't make the guest feel better than when they came in, they consider that a failure. That sandwich comes with a smile, a friendly greeting, and some sort of personal interaction that makes the guest feel welcome. They don't sell lunch. They sell happy. This philosophy is constantly drilled into every team member. I've been to their employee training sessions and have seen how deeply this concept matters to them. It's infused into every part of their operation.

One way they sell happy is through the dining room experience. Part of their mission is to provide a pleasant gathering place. They don't rush to turn tables. They're glad to let you take a meeting or a tutoring session in their dining room, even if you don't order food. If you bring in a drink from another restaurant, they'll refill it for you at no charge. Why? Because they want their restaurant to be a place where people feel comfortable. Looking at the long lines of people who are buying food, I think they've succeeded.

When my son was young, I took him to a pretzel store to help me mystery shop a brand I was about to speak to. The pretzel was great, but the service was just adequate. It was perfectly forgettable. My son told me he loved the pretzel. I asked him if next time we go out for a treat, would he want to get another pretzel or go to our usual frozen yogurt place, Menchie's? He chose Menchie's. When I asked him why, I expected him to say something about the food, but his response surprised me:

"I like Menchie's because when you walk in, they say, 'Hello, welcome to Menchie's!'"

What mattered most to him was the friendliness. Menchie's created a fun, upbeat environment that won the loyalty of an 8-year-old boy. For my son—and for most people—there's more to going out to eat than just the food. The total experience of getting the food is part of the value, and being welcomed is part of that.

For example, while he was president of Moe's Southwest Grill, Paul Damico employed a similar greeting to stand out in the competitive quick service Mexican food market:

"Everybody on staff yelled 'Welcome to Moe's!' whenever anyone entered. That's something that we developed and we owned that nobody could touch," he said.

Wealthy franchisees provide more than products or services and do more than facilitate transactions. Whatever they're selling, they're in the people business. They use their products and services to make people happy. That's why they beat the competition every time.

People are driven more by their feelings than anything else. Logic therefore dictates that the smart move is to enhance your customers' emotional state. Go beyond your operational function and appeal to their humanity. Of course, this can only happen when you're willing to exhibit yours.

Real vs. Robotic

A little while ago, I stopped into a quick-service Japanese food franchise for lunch. I was the only customer in the restaurant, but the cashier still acknowledged me with that familiar phrase, "Next customer in line." Five minutes later she came out from the kitchen with my tray. I was still the only person there when she looked at me and said, "Guest number 36. Your order is ready."

I was literally a number. There was no connection—no humanity. She wasn't rude. I wasn't offended. This wasn't a bad experience. It was an ordinary one, the kind of lifeless encounter we've come to expect. And I'm sure the cashier did what she was trained to do: be quick, efficient, and move things along.

After a recent out-of-town speech, I stopped someplace to grab an order of hot wings. "Have a nice day," mumbled the bored cashier. It was 9:00 P.M.

The next morning, I had breakfast at a well-known diner franchise. After giving me my change, the cashier said, as she was walking away with her back to me, "Thank you. Have a wonderful day. Please come again."

Your job as a franchisee is not to offer someone a wonderful day. It's to provide them with a wonderful moment. But this only happens when you and your employees are present with them.

It's not what you say—it's what you convey that matters. Asking employees to say friendly things is not the same thing as being friendly.

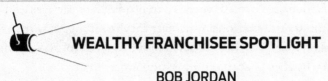

WEALTHY FRANCHISEE SPOTLIGHT

BOB JORDAN

PuroClean

Seattle, Washington

- Opened in 2017; sales doubled from year one to year two
- In year two, performed in the PuroClean highest profit group
- Year three profit was at 22 percent
- Won 2018 PuroClean On the Move Award recognizing business accomplishments within the framework of PuroClean values
- Won 2020 President's Circle Award
- Serves on Brand Ambassador team for potential franchise owners

Bob Jordan is smart. He thinks like an engineer and serves customers like a saint. That combination has made him a quick success in a competitive industry. He wholeheartedly embraces the corporate commitment of "relentless customer service."

"When we pull up, the customer is having a bad day. Our job is to change that and put them at ease," he said.

Bob is a licensed engineer with experience in aerospace, defense, and medical devices. After working for a startup that ran out of money, he found himself unemployed in an industry that didn't seem to be looking to hire a 58-year-old. He was contacted by a franchise coach who found his resume online and introduced him to a number of opportunities. PuroClean, which cleans up properties damaged by water, fire, biohazards, mold, and other major problems, felt like the best fit.

Only a few years later, he's earned a respectful place among a brand of great performers. When I asked PuroClean's president and COO Steve White to recommend an operator to interview, he said they have "an embarrassment of riches when it comes to good franchisees." From those riches, he connected me with Bob.

The feeling is mutual: Bob loves the brand. It's no surprise he was asked to be a brand ambassador to potential franchisees. "I've been in this system for years now and still haven't found the flaw," he said. He listens to his regional directors and never misses a meeting or convention. "They're the experts. I just follow their recommendations. That's enabled me to learn quickly and sidestep a lot of errors," he said.

Bob bought his franchise with a seven-year plan to sell the business (if he wanted to) for $1 million clean. He told me, "To do that, I need a business with low debt, great systems, and 20 percent profit on $3 million of gross sales. We've built this not as a small business but as a corporation."

That's meant no shortcuts, especially with staffing. From the very beginning he took corporate's advice and brought in others to manage sales and marketing (a key strategy that works well in their system). He oversees field operations, culture, and leadership himself. He prefers the people side. Three years in, he's having fun and growing rapidly.

"But you have to be committed. There's going to be high times and low times. You're going to be tired and it won't always go well. You'll be tempted to quit, so you better want to do this."

WEALTHY FRANCHISEE SPOTLIGHT, continued

Bob's Wealthy Franchisee Success Tips

- Don't build a business. Build a corporate empire.
- Make sure you're aligned personally with the work you're doing.
- Make sure you get everything out of your franchisor you can. You're paying a royalty. Take advantage of the expertise you're paying for.
- Work with your franchise neighbors. Be willing to help them and work as a team.
- Be relentless about customer service. Communicate often, explain thoroughly, and take care of them every way you can.

Creating Meaningful Connections

The late German philosopher Martin Buber wrote a famous essay in 1923 titled "Ich und Du," which translates into "I and Thou." In it, Buber discusses two types of relationships: the "I-It" relationship and the "I-Thou" relationship. To keep things simple, I'm going to refer to these going forward as "Me-It" and "Me-You."

In a "Me-It" relationship, we think of another person as an object, or something useful to us. Often the "It" is someone performing a specific function. They might be a cashier, a ticket taker, or a police officer directing traffic. Or maybe you're the cashier, ticket taker, or traffic officer and the "It" is the people you're serving. What characterizes these relationships is that there is little or no human connection, even when there's interaction. There's no meaningful engagement.

A "Me-You" relationship, on the other hand, is all about the connection. These are two people who at some level recognize each other's humanity. The relationship transcends function. It could be a 50-year marriage or a five-second compliment followed by a thank-you. Something about the encounter makes a connection between two people.

Imagine you're having a romantic dinner at a restaurant. You and your partner are looking into each other's eyes, saying sweet things, and sharing a champagne toast. You're totally present with each other. You are connected.

Throughout the meal, a waiter attends to your table. They refill your water, bring you more bread, and scrape crumbs from the tablecloth. At your request, they place your uneaten food in a to-go container. You thank them, and they nod. You go back to your conversation while they go back to the kitchen.

You and your partner are having a Me-You relationship. You and the waiter are having a Me-It relationship. In this situation, both roles are appropriate. If the waiter engaged you in conversation, it would be intrusive.

That's not to say that a connection with wait staff can't take place. The best waiter I ever had was on a cruise ship. We noticed the first night that Marco's name tag indicated he was from Italy. We asked him where in Italy he was from and how he came to work on the ship. He asked where we were from and how we enjoyed the port. Each night we chatted with Marco a little more and looked forward to seeing him at dinner. He perfectly indulged us in conversation while maintaining the formalities of a good server-customer relationship. By the end of the cruise, my wife asked for a picture with him. For a few moments a night over one week, we shared a small but meaningful Me-You relationship with Marco. We left with a good feeling. I'd like to think he left with a good feeling, too. He certainly left with a good tip.

Customer service suffers when franchisees and their employees think of the customer as an "It." That's the result of robotic phrases and impersonal transactions. It's not that every customer engagement should be personal. It just needs to be human.

It also needs to be appropriate. We must maintain the expected social boundaries of our business, which vary from industry to industry.

I sometimes rent cars from a company that used to greet customers with a handshake in an effort to connect, human to human. I applaud the intent, but I question the execution. A handshake implies equality, which isn't always appropriate. If I interact with a lawyer, we'll shake hands. If I interact with a waiter, I don't. It's not that I'm superior to the waiter—in a social environment, we would be completely equal. But in a restaurant setting, the whole idea is to be served. In that context, we're not equal. That's the social contract of the setting.

The opposite is true in a doctor's office. I'm the customer, but I wait for the doctor and almost certainly use their title in our conversation.

It's essential to understand the nuanced social dynamics of your business. What do your customers expect? How do your customers want to feel? What kind of interaction will make them feel that way? Determining these things is critical to creating meaningful, memorable experiences. It's how you make customers feel welcomed and comfortable.

Why Connections Matter

Earlier we discussed the importance of making customers happy. Research on human happiness clearly concludes that nothing makes people happier than feeling connected to others. One of the most famous studies is the Harvard Study of Adult Development. For more than eight decades, researchers have tracked hundreds of men from both Harvard and some of Boston's poorest communities. They also began to look at their spouses. Researchers have monitored their subjects' careers, finances, marriages, health, and other major aspects of life. The study has shown that, more than high income or low cholesterol, close relationships are the best predictors of happiness and longevity.

Our desire to relate to other people is rooted deep in our being. We need to bond with others in our species. Even relationships that are limited to occasional social media exchanges allow us to feel a sense of connection with others.

Some of our human connections are long-term and familial, while others are brief. Recently, I was having breakfast at an IHOP with my son and the song "Call Me" by Blondie came on. Across the room, I noticed a mom around my age bobbing her head and singing, just as I was. We made eye contact and smiled at each other as we continued to sing. We never spoke. We didn't have to. For just three seconds, as our kids looked at us with embarrassment, we shared a moment we couldn't share with our kids. It wasn't an intimate encounter, but it was nice. It felt good, like we were part of the same club.

When customers come to us for products or services, they're still people. Finding a way to connect with them, appropriately and professionally, will make them feel good. Those feelings build trust and loyalty. You don't want them to see you as a proprietor. You want them to see you as person. That promotes connection, and making connections builds wealth. But customers can't see you as a person if you act like a robot.

Connecting with customers doesn't mean you have to become friends with them. It just means relating to them, human to human. We like doing business with people we trust and like. But most of the time we don't even notice the people we do business with because we don't even relate to them as people. We hold something back. That undermines our professional relationships.

I go to the gym each day at 7:00 A.M., and I always see the same guy at the front desk. At that hour, he's tasked to make collection calls to members on the East Coast with expired credit cards. Though we see each other every morning, he doesn't usually say hello, since he's on the phone. He rarely even makes eye contact. Our interaction is limited to him scanning my membership card.

Here he is, the human face of the brand, and instead of a friendly greeting, I get to hear him make not-so-friendly requests for payments from other members. Every morning, I'm reminded of how the company sees its customers.

It doesn't offend me. It's just a lost opportunity for the gym. He could be welcoming us by name. He could make us feel like members of a *community*. Instead, we're just walking bar codes.

I come to the gym to exercise, not to socialize. I don't need to have a conversation with the guy. But it would feel good to hear "Good morning, Mr. Greenberg" or "Hi Scott, this is your cardio day, right?" All it would take is three seconds to make me feel acknowledged and valued as a customer. It's not time-consuming or expensive. It's easy to make people feel good. I go to this gym because it's three blocks from my house, but I'd abandon it in a second if another gym opened nearby.

Business is about relationships. That's not a novel idea, but too many of us ignore it. Whether you're selling fruit baskets, gym memberships, or any other widget, never forget you're really in the people business. Top franchisees build wealth by first building a community.

Clarify What Business You're *Really* In

Most franchisees don't understand what business they're really in. They think they're selling cheeseburgers, lawn services, or plumbing. These are the products and services they offer. But in every case, there's something more beneath the surface—something that affects customers at a deeper, emotional level. Understanding what that thing is will directly impact your bottom line.

I call this the "Above/Below Effect." The "Above" is the transaction. It's the tangible product or service customers pay for. The "Below" is what customers feel as they get it. It's their emotional experience of interacting with your business. When you can laser in on what customers need emotionally from the transaction, it's easier to say and do the things that matter most to them. Remember, consumer behavior is driven much more by emotion (pathos) than logic (logos). If you want loyalty, repeat business, and bigger tickets, you need to be conscientious about how you and your employees make customers feel.

At Edible Arrangements, I initially thought I was in the fruit basket business. We posted menus by our telephones with our selections and serving sizes. When someone called to place an order, the first question we asked was how many people they wanted to feed.

But as I got to know my customers better, I realized they weren't calling us because they were hungry. They were ordering fruit arrangements because someone they loved was having a birthday or an anniversary. They were calling to thank a colleague or congratulate a friend. They were sending a basket to a new mom or sending gifts for Valentine's and Mother's Day. Finally, it hit me. I wasn't in the fruit basket business. I was in the *celebration* business. We existed to help people celebrate the special moments of their lives.

That realization transformed our operation. It changed the questions we asked and led to different conversations. Instead of asking how many people they wanted to feed, we asked what occasion they were celebrating. Then, rather than launching into the sale, we'd celebrate with them. "That's great news!" "How wonderful!" "She's a lucky lady—you're going to make her so happy!" We trained our employees to engage customers in the occasion and then do everything to help them celebrate it. They'd suggest arrangements and upgrades that best fit the occasion.

We steered away from questions like "What's your budget?" or "How much do you want to spend?" Instead we'd ask, "How important is this occasion?" "How big an impression do you want to make?" or "Do you think she'd like her strawberries dipped in chocolate?"

Clearly we were upselling, but we trained our team not to operate from a place of greed. Instead, they were to give customers options to enhance their order. Our job was to help customers create the most wonderful arrangement possible. I wanted to make sure that everyone who saw one of our baskets was blown away. We were in the celebration business. We were selling joy and happiness.

We were also in the peace-of-mind business. Customers placing orders were often concerned about whether we'd get the order right and deliver it on time, so in addition to celebrating with them, we needed to offer reassurance. After they ordered, they needed to put the phone down *knowing* they no longer had to worry about sending a gift. If my employees didn't offer customers this certainty, we were shortchanging them.

I enjoy helping my franchise clients clarify what business they're in. When I worked with Tommy's Express Car Wash, their franchisees realized they weren't in the car-washing business but the "new-car feeling" business. They were there to help customers regain that pride of owning a new car.

Bruster's Real Ice Cream franchisees determined they were actually in the social gathering business. They existed to provide people with an activity that bonds family and friends closer together. Tim Davis told me that The UPS Store isn't just in the shipping, packing, or printing business. "We're in the business of making complicated things easier for people," he said. And Miracle-Ear senior vice president Vera Peterson told me with a proud smile that they don't just sell hearing aids—they "help people rediscover all the emotions of sound."

These distinctions are important. They affect your messaging (your marketing) and the experience you provide. Ice cream vendors just hand over the product, but Bruster's creates a whole atmosphere that's fun, friendly, and conducive to people hanging out together. A great ice cream cone is just one part of their multifaceted value proposition. That's why they can command more money per transaction. It's also why people will pay a premium for a cup of coffee at top coffeehouses: They're gathering places that allow their customers to feel comfortable, sophisticated, and connected. Getting coffee at a convenience store is not the same experience.

The franchise locations that get the most business are the ones that go beyond their products and services and instead offer people an experience that appeals to both the head and heart. They facilitate encounters customers want to tell others about. They think beyond the widgets they sell.

Ask yourself what emotional or psychological needs your products meet. What is the feeling your customers are chasing? The business that best elicits that feeling is the one that wins.

By this point, let's assume I've persuaded you to commit to serving your customers well. You understand that the best customer service practices won't work unless they're driven by the right mindset, philosophy, and culture of making people happy, and now you know what that looks like. But even the best customer service mindset won't work unless it's properly instilled into the minds of the people who really matter—your employees. We'll look at how to do that in the next chapter.

CHAPTER 10

Assembling Your High-Performance Team

Chapter Features

- Team building vs. team cohesion
- Defining your ideal business culture
- What to look for when hiring employees
- The most common biases that impact recruiting
- Using a hiring matrix to evaluate candidates

M y employees exploded with cheers when they learned our location had won the "Best Customer Service" award out of more than 1,000 Edible Arrangements locations worldwide. The recognition validated something I already knew about them: They were rock stars. They'd been blowing our customers' minds for a while. It showed in our glowing online reviews and our growing base of repeat guests. It was only a matter of time before our corporate office honored them. I was soon asked to speak at our annual franchise convention about how to build a great team. The invitation amused me, because if you'd asked me about my employees just a few years earlier, I'd have told you they were my biggest headache.

The Challenge of Having Employees

"Scott, can I talk to you?" my manager asked one day.

That never heralded anything good. I invited Jessica into the office.

"I don't want to be a snitch, but I thought you should know. Sarah is stealing from you," she said.

"Really? *Stealing?*" I said. "Sarah? What's she stealing?"

"Time."

Jessica explained how over the past few weeks, Sarah had been calling the store when she was running late to ask the other employees to punch her in. Sometimes she'd be on the clock for 45 minutes before she actually showed up. She'd asked Jessica to do this a few times, and it was making her uncomfortable. When I checked our security camera footage, it verified the discrepancy between the time clock and Sarah's actual arrival times. I was so disappointed. I liked Sarah. But she had crossed a line from which she couldn't return.

It wasn't the first time this had happened, and it wouldn't be the last. It was one of countless issues I had with employees those first few years in business. Stealing, tardiness, complacency, conflict, flakiness—all despite my best efforts to be a cool boss. I thought my motivational speaker sensibility would immunize me from having problems with employees. It didn't. My employees drove me crazy. At the time, I thought they were the worst part of running my franchise.

I was a bit naive about managing employees when I came into the business, assuming the concepts I'd recited so glibly onstage would translate to my own operation. Some did, but many did not. This wasn't a classroom—it was the real world. Employees didn't respond the way leadership gurus said they would. They couldn't be classified by personality profiles. It didn't matter that there was no "I" in team. They didn't care what I knew, once they knew I cared. These were complex people with unique backgrounds, driven by different motives. Academic Jedi mind tricks were totally ineffective on them.

I called my first manager's references when I was preparing to hire her, flew her to Connecticut for training, and offered her good compensation and lots of perks. She still quit three months into the job. I warmly communicated my open-door policy and my support of a respectful work environment. There was still infighting among my workers. I emphasized "integrity" as a major company value. But some employees still covertly ate chocolate-covered strawberries from the walk-in cooler. I used "When you X, I feel Y" statements. Their eyes glazed over. I did everything by the book, but apparently, my employees never read it.

Sometimes the issue wasn't managing employees but finding them. We'd hang a help wanted sign out front, ask team members to reach out to their friends, post ads on the hottest recruiting website, and increase the starting salary. Half the people who responded never even showed up for the interview, and most of those who did show didn't impress us. Some lacked communication skills. Many were obvious job hoppers. Some seemed good but had too many time conflicts.

One of the hardest jobs to fill was our delivery driver. This job attracted people who wanted to work by themselves, but they would be the face of our business. We needed someone friendly and poised, and they had to be willing to accept less pay than they'd get working for a big shipping company or driving for a rideshare. It was a tall order.

One of the first people to apply was a charming gentleman from Australia. He had delivery experience back in Melbourne and was full of enthusiasm. He seemed perfect until he requested his checks be made out to his cousin. I stopped the interview right there.

I often felt tempted to lower my hiring standards, and sometimes I did, so I could check "fill the position" off my to-do list. Invariably, these hires added new problems to my list.

I just wanted to run a fun, profitable fruit basket business. I was willing to give people jobs, pay them fairly, and treat them well. Why were they making this so hard? Was I doing something wrong? Were American workers really this bad? Most of my fellow franchisees thought so:

"Young people are so entitled."

"No one wants to work."

"They have no loyalty."

"Screens have ruined this generation."

It took a few years of trial and error. I went through a lot of employees, tried many management techniques, and took a lot of Advil, but eventually I turned a corner. I got better at hiring, learned how to motivate employees and engage them in the business, and got them working as a team. Morale increased, along with retention. I used to complain about my employees, but now I was giving thanks for them. They would win awards, earn stellar online reviews, look out for the business, solve problems, and have each other's backs. They'd enable me to stay home or travel to a speech. They'd save me time, reduce my stress, and make me money. By the time I sold the business, most of my team had been with me for years. I'm still in touch with most of them.

I've come to believe that never before has the work force offered such a great pool of candidates. In the right environment, today's young people will work hard and produce, remain loyal, collaborate, and innovate. All this while still checking their cell phones.

Team Building vs. Team Cohesion

Anybody can assemble a group of talented people and call them a team. But that's like buying flour, sugar, and butter and calling them a cake. It's not enough to have the right ingredients. What matters is how they combine.

Wealthy franchisees don't just fill positions. One person at a time, they carefully construct a supergroup of employees who excel individually and work together to support one another. They cultivate *cohesive teams*. Cohesive teams do more than fulfill their responsibilities—they work to become a stronger, tighter, and better working unit. They're in it as much for each other as for themselves. Their shared purpose is at the center of their bond. Think of a great sports team growing closer over their mutual desire to be champions, or an aspiring rock band connecting over a shared dream of hitting it big. They're emotionally invested in their work, not just out of personal interest, but because that's how they experience their connection to each other. As we discussed in Chapter 9, nothing makes people happier than making meaningful connections to others. If you can give your employees a feeling of belonging, they'll care a lot more about their work. That's good for them and good for business.

Team cohesion among hourly workers isn't some idealistic fantasy. It happens all the time. You can facilitate those bonds among your own team, but only if you hire the right people and are deliberate about building your company culture.

Defining Your Culture

Every business has a culture—some by design, most by default. Within every group, there is a shared set of beliefs—sometimes unspoken—and a set of behaviors that determine how things are done and how it feels to do them.

Wealthy franchisees have a deliberate focus on the culture of their business. They use that word a lot, too:

"We spend a lot of time working on our culture."

"They need to share the same values as our culture."

"I only hire people who fit with our culture."

I hear comments like these constantly from wealthy franchisees. They understand that how employees feel working together directly impacts the quality of the work they do together. The relationships within a business are as vital as the systems in that business.

In Chapter 3, we discussed the franchise success formula: Circumstances + Operations + Humanity = Results. Your employees' work reflects the operational elements, while their social dynamics reflect the human elements. Like all human factors in business, their relationships hugely affect their operational performance.

One summer in college, I was one of the original bellmen at a new luxury hotel. There was no formal leader among us and no team building of any kind. We were simply told what our duties were and given our schedules, so we developed ways of doing things on our own, some of which didn't breed goodwill among employees.

Because of my class schedule, I started my first shift a week after the hotel opened, and I was trained by one of the more "experienced" bellmen. He explained that during training, the new person carries all the luggage and the trainer keeps all the tips. This wasn't official hotel policy. It was simply a ritual that had developed, most likely created by an employee with a more dominant personality. I resented it, but it was "how things were done."

Much of what's "done" isn't about work, but about social interaction. How do people greet and support each other? Are they competitive or are they collaborative? Do they work as a team or do they break into cliques? Do they speak lovingly or critically about customers? The answers to these questions will remain in your business longer than the employees who created them. Team members come and go, but culture remains. If you don't purposely establish the behavioral norms of your business, they evolve on their own.

Aptitude and Attitude

As we discussed above, our franchise success formula, Circumstances + Operations + Humanity = Results, also applies to employees. These are the things we look at when evaluating them.

Employee circumstances are obvious things like age, availability, or physical ability (if the job requires it). There's not much gray area when it comes to their circumstances. We should be able to check for these (legally and appropriately) before the interview.

The in-person meeting is about operations and humanity. The operational piece is their aptitude: Do they have the abilities and skills they need to learn and perform the required work?

The humanity piece is their attitude. Do they have the right willingness and energy level? Do they have sufficient social competence? Can they work with a team, or, if the job requires it, can they excel on their own?

Some franchises require applicants to come in with certified aptitude. Massage and beauty concepts generally require licenses. Urgent care franchises need doctors and nurses on their teams. No matter how good an applicant's attitude is, if they lack official certification, they're a nonstarter in these situations.

Fortunately, most jobs in the franchise world don't have these requirements. The systems and processes created by your franchisor can easily be passed on. With the right training, aptitude can be acquired.

Attitude, however—the human factor—should be great from the start. That doesn't necessarily mean they must be outgoing and energetic. It just means they should demonstrate the soft skills needed to thrive in your culture. Most workplace problems are rooted in attitude, so keep that in mind when staffing. Wealthy franchisees hire for attitude and train for aptitude.

Learning from Franchisors

Given how important staffing is, it would seem reasonable to expect your franchisor to help. Unfortunately, the legal climate here in the U.S. has made many franchisors reluctant to advise in this area. Concerns over joint employer status have limited how involved they can be, and they need to maintain some distance. These are your employees, not theirs. You're on your own.

Having said that, franchisors are building their own cultures, too. Every franchisee they recruit impacts the human elements of their system, one way or another. Smart franchisors are very discerning about who they bring into their business community, and we can learn from their methods.

While he was CEO of Naf Naf Grill, Paul Damico personally had dinner with every franchisee prospect to determine if they were a good cultural fit for the company. Having spent years as president of both Focus Brands (Carvel, Auntie Anne's, Schlotzsky's, Cinnabon, McAlister's Deli) and Moe's Southwest Grill (at which he famously appeared on *Undercover Boss*), he understood the mindset needed to run a restaurant. He knew what to look for and what to avoid. He admits he was resistant to selling franchises to practicing doctors and lawyers.

"They could invest, but I wouldn't let them anywhere near the operation," he said.

With total respect for those professions, he wanted the restaurants run by committed operators who loved food and would embrace the system. His franchisees needed a very different skill set that could only come from an all-in commitment to the business.

Since my first conversation with Paul, he's become the CEO of the much larger Global Franchise Group. While he can't personally meet with every interested prospect, he still maintains high standards, instructing his team to vet every potential franchisee for a good cultural fit.

I'm not saying you should take every job applicant out to dinner. But you do want to find some way to ensure they're a good fit for your team. What are the characteristics a prospective employee needs to ensure they'll enhance your work environment? What are the characteristics that might harm it?

Jersey Mike's Peter Cancro also spends time with every franchise candidate at Discovery Day. By the time prospective franchisees meet him, they've already been financially vetted. At this point, it's all about culture. Why do they want to invest in a Jersey Mike's? Do they share the same values? Do they want to make a difference or just make money?

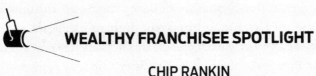

WEALTHY FRANCHISEE SPOTLIGHT

CHIP RANKIN

MilliCare

Wilmington, Delaware

- Four units in mid-Atlantic U.S.
- One location ranked number one in system
- Combined units make him the largest franchisee in the system
- 97 percent customer retention rate
- Two-time winner of MilliCare President's Award as well as awards for revenue and growth
- Three-time winner of the Delaware Quality Award
- Won Delaware state chamber of commerce Superstars in Business award

I catch Chip Rankin at his vacation home in Celebration, Florida, where he plans to retire one day. Chip's been working in the flooring business since he was

---

WEALTHY FRANCHISEE SPOTLIGHT, continued

a college student. If you've ever walked the clean carpets of Baltimore/ Washington International Thurgood Marshall Airport (BWI), you've seen his work.

Chip never set out to spend his life caring for floors. But as a finance student, he saw an opportunity to do something hugely profitable, as well as something meaningful. It's easy to hear his enthusiasm as he describes it:

"I like the sustainability story of our product," he said. "We're keeping carpet out of a landfill. It's the best product to use inside of a building for indoor air quality, so it helps people work better. Everything is at a higher level."

"Higher level" is a great way to describe Chip. He certainly has the numbers. He attributes his success to the team he's built. From the beginning, he wanted to set up systems within his business that would allow him to scale and expand it. That meant building the best team he could. Early in the business he even hired a "teamwork coach" who administered a personality profile to help assess his values and better identify employees who were a good match for his temperament. That proved invaluable. Of the 22 people on his leadership team, 15 have been with him for more than 20 years. Chip rewards this group with a "teamwork" bonus, splitting 7 percent of revenue (after hitting breakeven) among them.

Chip's Wealthy Franchisee Success Tips

- Focus on your team. Find people who share your values.
- Create replicable systems that don't require your direct involvement.
- Plan for success. Create systems that will accommodate the size of the business you want to have, not the one you currently have.
- Have someone do a personality test on you to better understand the kinds of people with whom you can build trust and collaborate.

WEALTHY FRANCHISEE SPOTLIGHT, continued

◆ Build up enough money to ensure you can make the right decisions and hire the right people when you need them. That's the only way to create the capacity to grow.

◆ You don't have to love the business, but you do have to love its model for success.

Sport Clips Haircuts uses a third-party assessment tool for their vetting process, which scores applicants for their levels of "drive," "independence," "sociability," and other characteristics needed to run a salon. All that happens before being invited to Discovery Day. Only 5 percent of prospects are extended an offer.

What if you were that selective about who you brought into your business? It would be inconvenient and take longer to staff up. It would also align you with some of the most successful franchise brands in the world. You can do at a small scale what they do at a large scale and get similarly great results.

Hiring Bias

As with other areas of running your franchise, hiring requires a great deal of self-discipline. Emotions can cloud your judgment, causing you to overlook good people and hire the wrong people. For effective hiring, you need objectivity and clarity of mind. That can't happen until you look inward and recognize your biases.

Labor laws protect workers from mistreatment and help level the playing field by prohibiting bias based on what a person "is." That's good for employers as well. It forces them to look beyond stereotypes and consider quality candidates their prejudices might have ruled out. The world is better with less prejudice. It's morally wrong and bad for business.

But everyone brings their unconscious preferences into hiring, even with the best intentions. It's easy to take mental shortcuts that lead to inaccurate conclusions.

Psychologists have identified many biases that cause people to rush to judgment. For example, there's the *halo effect*, where a person clings to one quality they like in someone and disregards everything else. The opposite would be the *horn effect*, being unable to let go of that one thing you don't like. Focusing too much on the things you have in common with someone is an example of *affinity bias*. *Confirmation bias* causes us to seek out others who share the same perspectives. *Beauty bias* speaks for itself.

I used to remind my manager Jennifer to keep an open mind for the entire interview. That meant being open to *not* liking a candidate until the end of the interview. Important information that needs to be considered may not come up until late in the conversation. Often a candidate makes a good first impression, so we start asking questions that confirm what we want to be true about them. It's hard to hold off judgment, especially when you're eager to hire someone and get a task off your plate.

Here's an example. Mother's Day was approaching and we were short-staffed. I needed to get someone hired and trained. The first few people I met didn't impress me, so I greeted Nina with a great deal of hope.

Nina had spent more than a year working for a competitor, so she already knew how to make fruit arrangements. She could put on an apron and go right to work. With the holiday approaching, we could really use her skills. I was excited. (Activate the halo effect.) I'd noticed that she was a bit cold and not too friendly during the interview, but I disregarded that. We just never got applicants who were already trained to make fruit arrangements, so I said, "Welcome aboard!"

Her skills were great, no doubt about it, but culturally, she was absolutely a bad hire. She made no attempt to connect with our other team members. She'd punch out after a shift and leave without saying goodbye to anyone, scowled when co-workers joked around, and refused to participate in employee potlucks. Her attitude bummed people out. When Nina was on shift, morale and productivity both dropped. Was she being paid to socialize? Of course not. But we did expect her to contribute to a positive team environment. We were in the celebration business, so we needed a friendly, upbeat workplace. That was our culture. Her standoffish nature was obvious during the interview, but I was blinded by her bright, skill-based halo into deciding I liked her way too quickly. It was a relief when she finally quit.

One of my first hires was a founding member of a well-known rock band I liked in high school. I was surprised he was applying for an hourly job at Edible Arrangements, but I was still excited to meet him. We had a great conversation and really connected over music (affinity bias). A more objective employer would have spotted the red flags (arriving late, unstable work history), but I thought it'd be cool to have this guy on staff. It wasn't. He came to work late. Sometimes he'd forget to come in at all. He didn't last long.

I made a lot of mistakes those first few years, but I also got lucky and acquired some winners. Reflecting on these hires over time, both good and bad, helped me refine our hiring practices. By knowing what to look for and exercising more self-control, it became easier to identify the right people and weed out the wrong people.

Likable Candidates vs. Qualified Candidates

There are four possible outcomes from employee recruiting:

1. You hire the right person.
2. You don't hire the right person.
3. You hire the wrong person.
4. You don't hire the wrong person.

Your goal is to hire the right people and not hire the wrong people. But most employers don't have a good process for this. They just meet applicants and hire the ones who feel right. "I go with my gut," they often say.

If your gut consistently identifies the right people, then keep going—you're doing better than the rest of us. Most people's guts are unreliable. They hire people they like, but they don't always work out. And even if you have good instincts, it's hard to pass them on to your managers.

Likability is what we look for socially. For a job applicant, we need the most qualified candidate and the best cultural fit. That could include someone who's likable, but that's not enough to go on.

Unchecked, our emotions and subjectivity can lead to bad hiring decisions. To minimize this risk, we need to create objective, replicable hiring systems. I recommend using what's called a *hiring matrix*.

Using a Hiring Matrix

A hiring matrix will allow you to numerically score a candidate against a list of traits you believe are most important for the job you're trying to fill. The candidate with the highest cumulative score is the one most qualified for the job.

The first step is to identify the essential characteristics for each position. I like to look at my best current and past employees and list the traits they share. Different jobs will require different characteristics. Employees who interact with customers need different qualities than ones who work in the back, for example. For each position you have to fill, what are the most important qualities you need in a person doing that work?

Once you have your list, decide if any of these qualities are considerably more important than the others. For example, maybe you've noticed your best salespeople are extremely driven. For you, "drive" may be twice as important as other traits, such as "experience."

This list of traits is the criteria by which you or your managers will evaluate job candidates. For each trait, you'll assign candidates a score. A simple one to five scoring system works for me, but you may want to go to ten. For any traits you've decided are the most important, double the score. After the interviews, you can add up the scores and see who has the highest number.

Clearly there's still plenty of subjectivity in the process. But at least now you and your managers are focusing on specific traits rather than just deciding if you like the person. If multiple people are evaluating the candidates, you can combine all your scores and use that total to decide whom to hire.

Let's look at an example of how this might work. Say you own a senior in-home care franchise and need to hire another caregiver. You've worked with many people over the years and have determined that the following are the five most important qualities shared by the best caregivers:

1. Responsibility
2. Availability
3. Empathy
4. Compassion
5. Experience

Empathy is by far the most important, so you'll double the score for that one. Your hiring matrix will look like the example in Figure 10-1, below.

After advertising for the position and looking at resumes, you decide to bring in two people for interviews, Caroline and Cathy.

Caroline arrives on time for her interview at 9:00 A.M. She's dressed professionally in a navy pantsuit and gives you a warm smile and a

	Candidate	Candidate
Responsibility		
Availability		
Empathy (x 2)		
Compassion		
Experience		
Total:		

FIGURE 10-1. **Blank Hiring Matrix**

confident handshake. You invite her to sit down, and she immediately points out your Duke University mug, saying that she, too, loves college basketball. She shares a funny story of losing her basketball tournament pool to a friend who just flipped a coin to make his picks. It doesn't surprise you to learn that she was a cheerleader in high school. She's very energetic, friendly, and a good conversationalist. She's also been in the caregiving industry for four years, having previously worked for some of your competitors. She's heard good things about your company and would love to join. You've scoured through a lot of unimpressive resumes by this point, and you're finally feeling hopeful.

Cathy is scheduled to come in at 11:00 A.M. A half-hour before that, she calls and tells you there's been an accident on the interstate. Her GPS says she'll arrive at 11:20. She apologizes profusely and asks if 11:20 will still be OK or if you'd like to reschedule. She also offers to start on time over the phone if that would be more convenient. You're annoyed, but you have the time; 11:20 A.M. will be fine.

Cathy arrives at 11:15 A.M., dressed in a simple black skirt and white blouse. She wears no makeup and has her hair pulled back in a ponytail. She shakes your hand and apologizes again. No worries, you lie, and invite her to sit. She places her hands uncomfortably on her lap and waits for your first question.

Cathy is thoughtful, perhaps a little nervous. She pauses to consider her words before answering, and her responses are intelligent and complete. You describe some of your clients. She nods her head as you talk about their unique needs. "Sounds like you have a lot on your plate," she observes. She asks a few more questions about the clients and the services you provide. Her resume shows that she's worked at the same preschool for three years. "It's been a great experience and I really love the kids. I'd just like to learn something new," she says. She shares that her own father has dementia. She's appreciated his caregivers, and that inspired her to apply. She and her siblings can't afford full-time care for him, so she looks after him on Tuesday and Thursday evenings. She assures you that's her only conflict.

"Anything else you'd like to share?" you offer. She thinks and reveals a nervous smile. "No, I think that's it."

You stand up and shake her hand. "Thanks for coming in."

"Thank you for your time," she responds. "And again, I know how busy you are, so I'm sorry for holding you up."

You sit back in your chair and think about the two interviews. Caroline makes a really good first impression. She's outgoing, personable, and fun. She's a lively person with infectious energy and great stories. She reminds you of your favorite cousin. Plus, she's experienced and completely available. You like Caroline a lot.

Then there's Cathy. You didn't appreciate that she came late, but she did call. She's only had the one job, and it's working with kids. Then there's the availability issue. Most of your clients need daytime care, but when evening care is requested, the Tuesday/Thursday conflict isn't ideal. Cathy was also kind of quiet. She answered all your questions and even asked you a few, but you did most of the talking. Overall, she was professional and polite, but you didn't feel the same connection you had with Caroline.

Your gut tells you to hire Caroline.

But this whole exercise is about going beyond your gut. The goal isn't to choose the candidate you like. You want the one that fits.

Caroline was fun, outgoing, and likable, which are all good things, but they're not on your list of traits. You take a deep breath and try to look beyond your first impression. It's time to use the matrix.

You do a side-by-side comparison of Caroline and Cathy, assigning each one a numeric score from 1 to 5 against the five criteria you established before interviewing. Your scores are admittedly still subjective, but the added structure forces you to think more deeply about the two candidates.

First there's responsibility. Caroline arrived on time. That's rule number one. But her resume shows she's had four jobs in three years. She had explanations for this, but it's still a question mark. Will she last with you? You're not sure. You give her a 3.

Cathy came late. Not good. When caregivers don't arrive on time, your clients get nervous. But she did call a half-hour in advance, apologized, and offered to accommodate your schedule. If she's ever running late for a client, you're confident she'll give them a heads-up.

She's also held the same job for three years, which says something about her reliability. You give her a 3 also.

Next is availability. Caroline is always available and can start right away. That's an easy 5. Cathy is unavailable two nights a week. She also said she'd need to give her current employer three weeks' notice. That's not ideal, but you respect it, and you like the idea that she'd extend you the same courtesy. It won't improve her availability score, but you decide to boost her responsibility score to a 4. For availability, she gets a 3.

Now we score empathy. This is the most important trait, so all scores are doubled. Caroline didn't make much of an impression here, and her answers to your questions, though totally fine, didn't provide much insight. You play it safe and give her a 3, which is doubled to 6.

Cathy, while on the quiet side, was definitely listening to what you had to say. Your clients like to tell their own stories and appreciate being heard. In her apology for being late, she acknowledged that you had a busy schedule. Having a parent with dementia should also help her understand what your families are going through. Cathy definitely has a strong sense of empathy. You give her a 5, doubled to 10.

You give both candidates 5s for compassion.

When it comes to experience, Caroline has more than Cathy, but not for long stretches, since she's worked so many different places. Cathy hasn't worked with the elderly, but caring for kids requires many of the same skills. Plus, her time spent caring for her dad is meaningful experience. Both women get a 4.

Your hiring matrix now looks like Figure 10–2 on page 198.

Cathy has the higher score. Does this automatically mean she gets the job? Of course not. But the exercise does move the process forward. First, it should make you take a closer look at Cathy. She may not be someone you want to hang out with after work, but she might excel at this position.

It also highlights where you need more information from Caroline. Perhaps you could contact her previous employers to learn more about why she didn't last. You may also want to call her and ask a few more questions to better gauge her level of empathy. The additional information could change her scores.

	Caroline	Cathy
Responsibility	3	4
Availability	5	3
Empathy (x 2)	6	10
Compassion	5	5
Experience	4	4
Total:	23	26

FIGURE 10–2. **Complete Hiring Matrix**

Another step you could take is to create a standard list of questions that shed light on each of these traits. For example, to check for compassion, you might ask, "How can you tell when someone needs help?" or, "Tell me the steps you go through to provide comfort." For responsibility, you might ask, "Under what circumstances have people depended on you?" You can research the web for other questions associated with just about any trait you can think of. Experiment and see what works best. The farther you can get away from, "Tell me a little bit about yourself," the greater the chance you'll get the information you need.

Change the process however you like, but keep it simple. The overall goal is to move away from likability and broad subjective impressions and focus on what really matters.

Spend time on your staffing. Hire slowly and carefully. Your employees are the stewards and ambassadors of your business. You're putting your wealth in their hands, so hold out until you can find truly great people.

Then prepare for the most important work you'll do in business—*keeping* them great.

Managing Your High-Performance Team

Debra operates a midsize flower nursery in upstate New York. She approached me after my presentation at a large horticulture conference, wanting advice on how to motivate her workers.

"I don't understand. I treat them so well. I buy them lunch, I throw them parties, I give them little gifts. But they just don't seem to want to work," she said.

I hear this a lot. Well-intentioned employers breaking their backs to show respect, express gratitude, and make work fun—only to find little or no boost in employee performance.

Debra, like many others, mistakenly believes good management means being nice. Treat your employees the way you want to be treated. Show them you care about them as people. Kill 'em with kindness.

Being nice is, well, nice. It feels good. People appreciate it. But it's not enough. Kindness makes people like you, but it doesn't make their work better.

This is also true for tough management. Scaring employees is equally ineffective at sustaining high performance—especially when you're not there to crack the whip. Your goal is to get employees to do great work even when you're not there. You can't promote independent excellence when you rely solely on either carrots or sticks. You need to expand your managerial repertoire, and that starts with expanding your thinking.

Managerial Mindset

As with everything else in this book, your mindset about leadership will determine what kind of team you have. Your beliefs about employees and your approach to leading them directly inform their performance.

Wealthy franchisees see their employees as the lifeblood of their operation. They know they can't grow their business unless they grow their team. Developing employees isn't a burden—it's the most important work they do. They don't believe in the adage "Hire good people and stay out of their way." Instead of "lighting a fire under them," they light a fire *within* them. Then they work constantly to keep the fire lit.

Employees today love their cell phones, but wealthy franchisees don't judge them—they ask questions to understand them and learn how to motivate them. They realized long ago that compensation isn't motivation. How people are treated matters much more. Wealthy franchisees take care of their people, and in return, their people take care of the business.

Wealthy franchisees are friendly with their employees, but they're not their friend—that just doesn't work. They have clear boundaries. Employees like their wealthy franchisee bosses, but they also respect them and understand what's expected of them. If objectives aren't met, there's going to be a conversation. If rules are broken, the conversation won't last long. Wealthy franchisees also insist on healthy collaboration.

They defend the company culture and have no tolerance for anyone who threatens it.

Wealthy franchisees understand that they're in the people business, and their employees are the most important people. They're more important than the customers (they're certainly harder to replace). They value their team, coach them with love and respect, and appreciate what they have to offer.

I'm not saying wealthy franchisees don't have employee issues. The highest-level employers still wrestle with personnel problems. It's stressful. But with the right strategies in place, you'll have more influence and fewer problems.

Your Role as an Employer

Your perspective on this may make the difference between having a dream team and a nightmare. Struggling franchisees look at their team as hourly workers who exist to perform tasks. All training and feedback focus on completing those tasks. Everything is about the work.

Wealthy franchisees see their team as growing people who exist to become leaders. All training and feedback center on their development. Everything is about their growth.

The difference between getting work done and nurturing people is crucial. By cultivating leadership instead of directing work, wealthy franchisees enjoy higher productivity and fewer headaches.

My grandfather never fully appreciated this. "Pop" ran one of my father's restaurants. He was two generations older than most of his employees, an army veteran and an old-school manager. He had a very simple approach to leadership: "I tell you what to do and you do it. That's what I'm paying for. That's the deal." Oddly, my grandfather was actually a very sweet, loving person when he wasn't running the business. He was constantly joking and making friends. The way he ran things at the restaurant wasn't a true reflection of who he was as a person—it was just the only management style he knew. The fact that it didn't work very well caused him a lot of frustration.

"I just don't understand," Pop used to complain. "I'm paying all their salary. Why aren't they giving me all their effort?"

This seems like a logical question. On the surface, the relationship between employer and employee is transactional: One person pays for the work and the other does the work.

The problem with this logical question is that there's an emotional answer. These were human beings he was managing, and like all people, they were driven by a lot more than a financial agreement. There was fear, insecurity, boredom, resentment, and a whole other spectrum of emotions directly impacting their job performance. You may be fully funding my paycheck, but speak to me disrespectfully, and you're not going to get my best effort. Even if you're good to me, I still may not meet your expectations if a co-worker is slacking off, if a customer is rude to me, or if I'm having problems at home.

That's why trained employees still need managers. They need ongoing guidance, assistance, and support to keep them at the level you want. Actively helping them do their job shouldn't be seen as a burden. It's the *manager's* job.

As a franchisee, you're the head of a family. Nurture it. Be present and attentive. Don't expect automatic excellence. Foster it. Make the job less about the work and more about the people. The result will be better work.

Coaching Employees for Higher Performance

The role of a coach is to give team members the knowledge, skill, and motivation they need to succeed. They train their people to fulfill their roles, provide ongoing feedback to foster constant improvement, and inspire their teams to maintain their confidence, enthusiasm, and drive. If they do this well, the team will excel.

Most franchisees and managers claim they're too busy to coach. Running a business is a lot of work—there's accounting, ordering supplies, scheduling, paying bills, marketing, and often helping customers on the floor. Doing much of the work yourself is a great way to keep labor costs down.

But busyness is the enemy of leadership. If you're actively part of the system, it's harder to lead the system (or grow it). It's tough to play and coach simultaneously. Every minute you spend working is time away from coaching. Sure, stuff has to get done. But nothing is more important than developing your team.

I made this point during a franchise keynote speech, and a guy came up afterward saying he has way too many employees to provide them with adequate coaching. That's like saying you have way too many kids to feed them all. Employees need their minds fed. If your team is too large for you to coach, bring on more managers. Don't complain about poor performance if you're not willing to provide leadership. Management is not an expense—it's an investment.

If you coach your employees well, it'll actually save you time. You might even find yourself standing around, watching them thrive and wondering what you should be doing. That's when you can focus less on running the business and more on growing it.

I've spent a great deal of time studying coaching methodology with my business partner, Mario Del Pero. Mario has worked in the restaurant space his whole life and is best-known for cofounding the Mendocino Farms Sandwich Market restaurants with his wife, Ellen Chen (which you read about in Chapter 9). Both of us have managed a lot of employees, trained a lot of managers, and seen what works and what doesn't. We've also experienced some horrible and wonderful bosses ourselves.

Our discussions helped us create a new employee management program we teach called 30-Second Leadership. In the program, we use the metaphor of a doctor who doesn't take time to diagnose his patients. He just prescribes the same treatment to everyone and sends them home. Such a physician would be guilty of malpractice.

Most franchisees are guilty of managerial malpractice. They're too busy to diagnose what their employees need, so they prescribe the same management style to everyone. Then they complain about poor performance. With management like that, it's not the employees who need curing—it's the coach.

What follows are some of the main ideas from 30-Second Leadership that will dramatically boost *your* performance as a coach. Using this process will engage your employees, save you time, and grow your business.

Determining What Employees Need

In the last chapter, we discussed the two operational and human qualities to look for in job candidates: aptitude and attitude. Once these candidates join our team, these traits evolve into *skill set* and *mindset*. Aptitude measures a person's ability to learn a new task, while their skill set is the mastery of that task. We measure their skill set by asking two questions. First, can this person state the necessary steps to complete the task? Second, can they consistently demonstrate these steps? If the answer is yes to both questions, their skill set is high. If it's no to either question, their skill set is low.

Attitude is their willingness to complete a task, and mindset is a combination of the emotion, psychology, and humanity they bring to that task. You measure it by looking at their confidence and enthusiasm. It's subjective, but do your best to determine if their overall mindset is high or low.

Their skill set is what they know, and their mindset is how they feel. Both are equally important for high performance. These are the two factors you should look at to diagnose what an employee needs from you.

But before we start, I have to address one essential component to this coaching process: *The diagnosis must be specific to one job function.* Your first inclination may be to evaluate an employee's overall performance. That's useful for determining if a team member has earned a change in job status, but for coaching, it's unhelpful. When you see a good doctor, they don't generally diagnose you as "healthy" or "unhealthy." They look at your heart, lungs, eyes, ears, and so on and evaluate each bodily system independently to see which ones are OK and which ones may need treatment. You can look at a student's grade point average for an overall picture of their performance. But if you want to help the student improve, you need to look at their performance in each individual class. For some subjects, they might need a tutor. For others, they can *be* a tutor.

Your employees perform numerous functions at work. By evaluating their skill set and mindset separately for each one, you can customize your coaching to their unique needs.

Making Your Diagnosis and Choosing the Best Coaching

Measuring skill set and mindset as either high or low leaves you with four possible combinations for a given function:

Low Skill Set	Low Skill Set	High Skill Set	High Skill Set
High Mindset	Low Mindset	High Mindset	Low Mindset

Each diagnosis requires a specific coaching method. Let's look at each one.

Low Skill Set, High Mindset

This employee is probably grateful for the opportunity and excited to learn the task. Their mindset is in good shape. Your job is to boost their skill set before they get discouraged and lose their mindset. This person needs *training*.

Most job training is inadequate. The struggling franchisee quickly goes over how to do something, looks at the employee, and asks, "Got it?" Most likely the employee nods. They don't want to look stupid or incompetent. Of course, at this task, they *are* incompetent, but it's not their fault. *No, I don't get it,* they think. *I'll figure it out later.* But since they were poorly trained, they never excel.

Wealthy franchisees want their employees to be great. They spend as much time as necessary on training and don't let the employee perform a duty unsupervised until they can state the necessary steps and consistently demonstrate them.

As a wealthy franchisee, your approach to training comes in four steps: tell, show, watch, and review. Explain to the employee all the steps needed to do something well. Then demonstrate it a few times. Watch them do it. Then provide feedback. Repeat this process until their skill set is high.

You or your manager don't have to do all the training. Any employee who has a good skill set can handle it. In fact, giving a skilled employee a chance to train someone will be great for *their* mindset. It keeps them challenged and prevents boredom. Culturally, staff training staff promotes camaraderie.

Don't rely on encouragement for these employees—their mindset is already high. Pushing a nonswimmer off a boat and saying, "Don't give up! I believe in you!" is a great way to kill their mindset (and them). New swimmers need instruction to survive.

Also, if an employee has a high skill set for one task, that doesn't necessarily mean they'll have a high skill set for all tasks. If they're doing something new—especially if they've recently been promoted to a leadership position—they need training for the new task.

Low Skill Set, Low Mindset

Employees reach this point when they're not well-trained. That's our fault as franchisees because we have not given them the knowledge they need, and now they're discouraged. This person needs *training and encouragement*. This includes all the above steps for training, combined with emotional support. This is urgent. It's in this phase that many people decide their job isn't right for them. Your instincts when you hired them were probably correct. You can still salvage your new hire by providing the information and inspiration they need to improve.

Keep supervising, set them up with easy wins, and notice when they do something right. Share stories of other people who struggled with this task to normalize their feelings. Recognize that they're down on themselves, which makes it harder to learn.

Sometimes an experienced employee who is underperforming is actually in this state. Management may misdiagnose them as having an attitude (or mindset) problem when in fact they got by without ever really mastering a skill. Unless you know with certainty that this person has a high skill set for the task (i.e., they can state all steps and demonstrate them), don't assume the problem is mindset. Always confirm their skill set and provide training—with encouragement—when necessary.

High Skill Set, High Mindset

This is where you want your employees to be. Your role now is to keep them there. You shouldn't micromanage them, but you do want to actively support their ongoing success by preventing them from feeling bored, complacent, or unappreciated. This person needs *reinforcement*.

Give this superstar (for this job function) lots of praise, publicly and privately. Don't assume they know how much you value them. They need reminding. Challenge them to get even better, ask them what would make the task more interesting, and solicit suggestions for improving things. The question will show how much you respect them—and they'll probably have some good ideas, too.

An employee with a high skill set and high mindset can be very helpful for boosting others' performance. They usually appreciate the opportunity—it keeps them engaged. But be careful not to dump too much work on this person. That happens a lot. And remember, if you promote them or assign them a new task to help keep them challenged, they need training on it, just like any other employee.

High Skill Set, Low Mindset

This is where most personnel issues arise. When you focus more on operations and less on the human elements, it's easy for someone who's mastered a skill to see their mindset fall. When this person's performance goes down, additional training will worsen their mindset. They already have the skill. Retraining will anger them. This person needs *reengagement*.

To reengage someone with skill mastery, you need to ask questions to determine why their mindset has dropped. Begin the conversation carefully so they don't get defensive.

Start by acknowledging their skill set and then express concern over the lowered performance. You might say something like, "Normally you're so great at this. Everything OK?", or "Hey, what's wrong? I've seen you do this so well before." Approach it from a place of concern, not accusation.

Then listen. Their reasons might be job-related, or they could be personal. It might have nothing to do with you, or it might be because of how you've spoken to them in the past. Often they've just lost interest or gotten too comfortable in the job. Try to figure out the underlying cause and respond accordingly. They might need some encouragement, or they might need some tough love. Or maybe they just need a day off to deal with whatever's going on at home. Don't offer this as punishment, but do explain that in order to work their shift, they need to muster the attitude their teammates and your customers expect. As Mario says, "Hang your bummer at the door." Franchisee Burke Jones from The UPS Store actually has a taped line on the floor separating the "backstage" and the "stage." When employees step onto the stage in view of customers, they had better bring the happy.

30-Second Leadership won't always direct you to the precise solution for personnel issues, but it's a pretty good compass. Let's look at an example and see how it might help.

Imagine you own a coffee franchise. Mary has been one of your top employees for two years. She excels at every function and is always upbeat and energetic—a total superstar. She's thrilled to be promoted to assistant manager.

A month later she comes to you expressing frustration. She's struggling with two team members, Natalie and Alex. Neither's been doing a good job cleaning the espresso machine, despite her repeated requests. This morning the coffee bean hopper got clogged, preventing shots from pulling correctly, and customers started complaining about the long wait for drinks. That's not acceptable, so you agree to help her figure out what's going on.

First, you approach Natalie. She's been working for you almost as long as Mary has. She's cleaned the espresso machine hundreds of times, so you know she has the skill. But she does seem to be lacking energy today.

"Natalie, word is Captain Joe isn't getting cleaned during your shift," you say. "Everything OK? Usually you make this thing sparkle."

It takes a little back and forth, but eventually you uncover the truth: She's angry. She wanted the assistant manager job, and she doesn't understand why Mary got it instead. Her mindset is low because she's feeling underappreciated. She needs reengagement.

You explain your decision while also expressing how much you value and believe in her. You assure her there'll be a leadership role for her too at some point. You'll help her get there. Right now, though, she needs to step up and support Mary. She agrees and apologizes. You thank her for her honesty and receptiveness.

Then you speak with Alex. He's been working for you for a few months, but now that you think about it, you realize you've never actually seen him clean the espresso machine.

"Hey Alex, quick quiz," you say. "What are the six steps for cleaning Captain Joe?"

He smiles, embarrassed. "Uh . . ."

That's all you need to hear. "Sounds like you're not sure?"

"Well, I've been cleaning it, but it makes me nervous," he admits. "I'm afraid I might break something. I'd much rather make drinks than clean the machine."

Alex has both a low skill set and a low mindset for cleaning the machine. You've seen him work the counter, and customers love him. He has a high ticket average. As far as customer service goes, he's a rock star. That's helped him skate by on cleaning the espresso machine. For that, he needs training and encouragement. You have an idea.

"Hey, Natalie, got a second?" She walks over. "Alex needs some help learning how to properly give Captain Joe a bath. Can you tell him the six steps?" Natalie rattles off all six, and you give her a high-five. "That's how it's done. Can you spend some time with Alex and get him up to speed?"

"Sure. Alex, watch the master at work." Both laugh.

"Don't be too impressed, Alex," you say. "It took her six months to get it right."

"Hey!" she replies, feigning offense.

The two conversations took only a few minutes. While both employees had underperformed for the same task, your assessment of each person's skill set and mindset led you to different coaching approaches. You also further reengaged Natalie by having her train Alex as a sign of respect. Then you made a little joke at the end about how long it took her to learn the task, making Alex feel a little better about his own struggles cleaning the machine.

But you're not quite done. One more person needs to be coached—Mary. As assistant manager, she should have been able to handle this situation. It's not her fault, though—it's yours. When you promoted her, you didn't train her adequately on management. She can make drinks, serve customers, and clean Captain Joe, but leading employees? That's new to her. She didn't have the skill set. By throwing her into the deep end too early, you allowed her mindset to drop.

You fill her in on what happened and apologize for failing to prepare her. You promise to provide more guidance (teach her 30-Second Leadership!) and assure her you know you made the right decision promoting her.

Consider how all that might have gone without a coaching structure. What would most managers do? What would they say? "C'mon, you guys, you need to do a better job cleaning the machine!" Good luck with that.

It's easy in a fictional situation to get employees to respond to coaching. I'm well aware how tough it can be in the real world. But as long as you distinguish between skill set and mindset and adapt your management style accordingly, you'll improve your odds of helping your employees. Of course, that's only if you make the time to do it.

After presenting 30-Second Leadership at a franchise conference, I had a woman approach me saying she just realized her development person, a guy she hired to bring in more business, had a low skill set and high mindset for his job. (She failed to limit her diagnosis to a specific job function, but let's ignore that.) He was enthusiastic, but just didn't know how to sell.

"So do you think I should get him some training?" she asked me.

Would it be wise for her to provide training to the person she's relying on to bring in new business? Should she help him acquire the skills he needs to do his job?

Yeah, maybe get him some training.

"The thing is, I'm just too busy running around to train him myself," she complained. "I'm not sure what to do."

There it is: the busyness problem. What other part of her business is more important than empowering her only salesperson?

WEALTHY FRANCHISEE SPOTLIGHT

AMY LINN

PrideStaff

Dallas, Texas

- Ranked number one in sales in system
- Operates at 29 percent profitability
- Multiple-time winner of Office of the Year
- Winner of PrideStaff Mile-High Award for operational excellence
- Winner of ClearlyRated Staffing Industry Diamond Award
- Listed on *Dallas Business Journal*'s "Best Places to Work"

Amy Linn is a problem solver. Her focus isn't on filling positions or building sales. She's all about developing long-term relationships and meeting the needs of everyone her business touches. She often looks to the PrideStaff mission statement for operational guidance on how to best accomplish this.

"If we have a question in mind as to which way to go in decision making, we literally refer to the mission statement," she said. "What does it mean 'to consistently provide client experiences focused on what they value most'?"

Her "clients" include the companies that pay for staffing, the field associates she places, and her own in-house team. To her, the last group is the most precious.

"The average in-house staffing employee lasts nine months," she said. "We set out to build a culture with much better retention. Our average tenure is 7.5 years. Because we're not constantly recruiting and retraining for ourselves, we can focus on serving others. That's the number-one thing we've done to hit our profitability goals." Her partner, Julie Vicic, actually started with her as a college intern before working her way up in the business.

WEALTHY FRANCHISEE SPOTLIGHT, continued

I asked Amy how she's created this culture. "Leading from a place of transparency and trust," she said. "And we have fun! That keeps people engaged."

She also engages them by reinforcing their sense of purpose. She kicks off each morning's staff meeting with the same question: "Who has a mission story to share?"

Amy is passionate about serving companies and understanding the human elements that matter to them.

"It's about emotional currency," she said. "Our client is looking to us for so much more than filling in for a receptionist."

With so much focus on others, Amy has to be deliberate about taking care of herself. She's operated her business through three economic downturns, and it hasn't always been easy. "You need to focus on what you can control," she said. One way she maintains a clear head is her morning walk with her husband.

"We talk about everything we have rather than on everything we might lose. This daily ritual keeps me grateful and calm."

Amy's Wealthy Franchisee Success Tips

- You bought a franchise for a reason. Follow the model.
- Clarify your mission and stick to it.
- Hire, train, and retain people who align with your mission.
- Your most important client is your team member. Take care of your team.
- Make yourself indispensable as a problem solver, and you'll build an incredible network of promoters.
- Your business can always prosper. You just have to find the opportunity. Continuously reflect, reframe, and find new ways to meet new needs.

Be more than a boss. Be a coach. Assume your employees want to succeed and have the potential to do so. They just need your involvement to make it happen.

Motivating Employees

"OK, guys, who'd like to make some more money?" My team whooped with excitement. We were having an after-hours company meeting, and I was introducing a new contest to boost our ticket average. I devised a two-week bonus program based on sales. The more they sold, the higher the prize. I also offered financial incentives for selling our new $500 fruit arrangement.

The plan worked—for a while. Team members ran to answer phones, engaged customers, and suggested upgrades to their orders. Sales increased, and many employees earned bonuses, so I decided to extend the program.

After a while, their enthusiasm petered out. Employees talked less about their sales, and the ticket average went back to normal, even with the same bonuses still available.

My thinking was flawed in two ways. First, by incentivizing my team to boost the ticket average, it made them predatory. Their focus was on selling rather than serving. That's shortsighted. Our customers are our family, not our prey. I wanted long-term relationships with them, and that would only happen if we provided the best possible experience. Eventually I realized that, and we discovered that we enjoyed serving more than selling. It became our way of doing things, and it lasted. Interestingly, that's when we built the highest sales. Employees also seemed more grateful receiving $10 Starbucks gift cards for good online reviews than $50 cash bonuses for high sales.

The second mistake was my belief that more money meant more motivation. It didn't, not after the initial burst of activity. The continued opportunity to earn bonuses had no lasting effect. On other occasions I tried reengaging complacent team members by giving them raises. They were appreciative of the extra money, but their performance didn't improve.

Giving employees more money doesn't necessarily motivate them the way you think it would. Human motivation is complicated. There's more to it than rewards and consequences.

Extrinsic vs. Intrinsic Motivation

Our behavior is driven by two types of motivation. *Extrinsic motivation* describes the use of external incentives to drive performance: compensation, prizes, rewards, or promotion. Generally, it's provided by an authority figure such as a boss, parent, teacher, etc. It's all the rewards we're offered to behave a certain way. This form of motivation works to stimulate short-term bursts of activity: "If you eat your vegetables, you can have some ice cream." External motivators require someone else's input.

Intrinsic motivation comes from within. It's an internal, emotionally satisfying payoff. It's when we do something just because it feels rewarding. Think of all the things you do just because they're fun or fulfilling, such as hobbies. You don't need outside stimulation. You do them all on your own, because you want to.

People who thrive most in pay-for-performance jobs such as commissioned sales or driving rideshare derive more from their work than financial gain. For them, the money is also a satisfying measurement of progress, a way of keeping score. Yes, that Uber driver wants the extra $150 for completing a certain number of rides. But there's also an internal payoff in the sense of fulfillment that comes from achieving a goal. The reward is as emotionally satisfying as it is financially beneficial. That pushes people to work harder.

After big holidays, many Edible Arrangements franchisees would take pride not just in their sales, but also in how many orders they filled or in how they ranked. Those numbers have nothing to do with profit. Still, they were meaningful statistics to many people. They liked the achievement itself. That was also true for my employees—they always asked how many fruit baskets they had produced and how we did compared to other locations. The answers had no effect on their paychecks, but it really mattered to them. It motivated them to give holidays everything they had.

That's intrinsic motivation, and that's what you want. You promote it by creating an environment that taps into what your *employees* want.

Promoting Intrinsic Motivation

Intrinsic motivation for your employees is like great service for your customers. It's about creating an experience that appeals to the things they care about most. Remember, we humans are driven most by pathos, or emotion. Anything that makes us feel good is intrinsically attractive. The key, then, is to create a work environment that aligns with what your team cares about most. Employees show up for the financial payoff, but they *step* up for the emotional payoff.

The problem is that many franchisees make assumptions about what drives their employees, and often they think it's just money. I once surveyed the employees of a restaurant group that was underperforming. The general manager complained to me that he wasn't allotted enough funds to pay them well. I asked the employees in a survey to rank what they wanted most from their job. Out of 12 items, salary came in at number four. What they wanted most (statistically by far) was to feel appreciated for their effort. Many told me in interviews that management provided little positive reinforcement. I told the GM that instead of throwing money at them, he needed to pat them on the back. Don't just pay them; *praise* them. It's what they really want. And it's cheaper.

I've done these surveys many times and gotten similar results. I even did it with my own employees. I figured that if I could identify what mattered most to them and appeal to those values, it'd be easier to motivate them. Take a look at how ten of them answered the question in Figure 11–1, on page 216.

Of the seven options, only three were chosen: pleasant work environment, growth within the company, and for one team member, personal growth and learning. (A tenth person responded in the comments, echoing similar feelings as the others.) That led to more conversations about what these things meant to them. What did they like about our work environment, and what would make it even better?

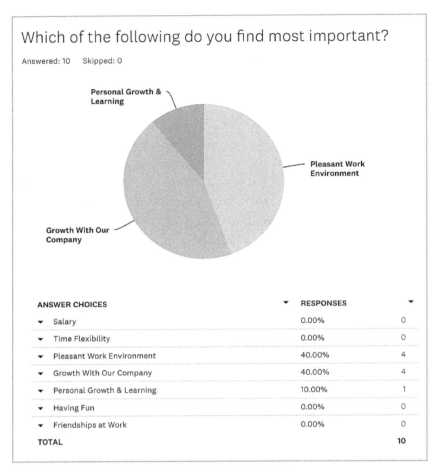

Which of the following do you find most important?

Answered: 10   Skipped: 0

ANSWER CHOICES	RESPONSES	
▾ Salary	0.00%	0
▾ Time Flexibility	0.00%	0
▾ Pleasant Work Environment	40.00%	4
▾ Growth With Our Company	40.00%	4
▾ Personal Growth & Learning	10.00%	1
▾ Having Fun	0.00%	0
▾ Friendships at Work	0.00%	0
TOTAL		**10**

FIGURE 11–1. **What My Employees Valued**

What new positions, job titles, and opportunities could we create so team members felt like they were progressing? What things beyond their operational responsibilities would they like to learn about? It didn't take long to identify what they wanted, and it didn't cost much to provide it.

We did for our team what we did for customers—identified what was most important to them and did our best to provide it. Our employees loved that we made the effort. Honestly, they loved that we even asked them in the first place. It created an "Me-You" relationship that made all the difference. Their performance was fine before. Now it got even better, without us having to constantly be on them.

Mr. Rooter Plumbing's top franchisee, Vinnie Sposari, is also big on creating an intrinsically satisfying environment. He's got a team of 65 people, many out in the field, and he needs them to operate independently.

"I don't micromanage. I give them ownership in the work they do. They appreciate that, and they take their work personally. They feel a great sense of pride in being number one in sales," he said.

So how do you promote that sense of "ownership"?

"Find the right people who are energized by the work you're doing," he said. "Then you have to be there for them. Make them feel cared about. Help them grow. That connects them to the company culture and makes them feel proud of their contributions."

Promoting his team's independence has done more than build the top sales in his franchise system. It also saves him time and enhances his quality of life. While his franchise continues to run, he's now able to leave the state with his wife to spend winters in Palm Springs.

There are reasons to pay people well. Higher salaries attract more applicants, increasing the pool from which you get to choose. Higher salaries, when combined with a good work environment, also encourage people to stick around when they have other options. Good compensation attracts and keeps great people, although it doesn't *create* great people. But trying to motivate a mediocre employee to do better by paying them more simply doesn't work. Sustained great performance only comes when employees are intrinsically motivated.

I devoted two chapters to creating and managing high-performance teams because it's simply that important. Make this a top priority. As an employer, think of yourself as a farmer. It's not enough to acquire good seeds. You need to plant and cultivate them. If you tend to your crop, you're likely to harvest more wealth.

Of course, there's another relationship that also needs tending . . .

Improving the Score with Your Franchisor

"Sent under protest!"

This was the message PIP Printing franchisee Justin Tracy used to write on the monthly royalty checks he mailed to corporate. Justin was angry. He and his family had been with PIP from the very beginning. Things had gone well for a long time. But after multiple changes in corporate leadership, buyouts, and a major reduction in the number of locations, he had lost faith in the home office. Sometimes he'd withhold the royalty check just to see how long it would take them to notice.

"I didn't see any value for my royalty," he told me. "They weren't helping me at all. I felt like they should come out and thank me for the money I was basically giving them every month."

I've heard these feelings many times over the years from franchisees. I try not to take sides. I'm interested in the relationship between franchisee and franchisor and how disagreements are managed.

Justin wrote a bitter letter to PIP's new president, Catherine Monson, expressing his outrage. She was a big believer in engaging directly with franchisees, so she called Justin and said, "Let's get a date on the calendar. I'm coming over."

Catherine traveled to Justin's location and spent three hours listening to his concerns. She promised action where appropriate and offered to connect him with other franchisees who might be of help in finding solutions. She worked her magic—what Justin referred to as "her Catherine personality"—to defuse his anger and shift the conversation from what had happened in the past to what could be done for the future. That redirection helped reengage Justin and made the conversation constructive.

Justin did the right thing by communicating his concerns to the franchisor. Letting bad feelings fester helps no one. He told me, "You have to attempt to have good communication. If you don't be the squeaky wheel, you're not going to get any grease."

Many of the franchisors I've interviewed used the "squeaky wheel" analogy, encouraging their franchisees to make their concerns known rather than remaining quietly dissatisfied. But Justin's "squeak" was pretty aggressive. Catherine described it as outright negative. He told me that was necessary in order to get corporate's attention. I asked Catherine if this was true.

"No," she replied. "Justin could have gotten better service and support from PIP Printing years earlier if he wasn't being so negative. There were a lot of management mistakes that were being made and some real reasons for his anger. But if he'd had been more constructive rather than negative, he would have gotten more."

But instead of debating this issue, both Justin and Catherine chose to move on, positively and productively. It helped that Justin was open-minded and willing to collaborate once he felt he'd been heard. Equally important were Catherine's thick skin, passion for franchisee success, and willingness to run toward the anger.

Justin and Catherine forged a strong, mutually respectful relationship that exists to this day. (Both gave me permission to share this story.) Justin once told Catherine he would remain unhappy until pigs could fly, so she made it her mission to change that. When he finally admitted she had succeeded, she sent him a flying pig toy to commemorate the occasion.

This story has a happy ending. The franchisor and franchisee were able to work through their differences and get back to building wealth together. It took patience, good communication, and a willingness to work on the relationship, not just the business.

But far too often, that doesn't happen. Tension between franchisor and franchisee impairs collaboration, preventing great people with a sound concept from earning all the money they could be making. Their circumstances are fine and their operations are solid. But that human factor? That's what they need to work on.

Computers in a network don't second-guess the information that comes from other terminals, hold back critical information, or share it with some computers on the network and not others. They don't say one thing and mean something else or attach too much meaning to what's said.

Humans do. We're burdened with psychology and emotion and pathos that sometimes make coexistence challenging. Human interaction is impacted by our humanity, for better and for worse. There's generosity and greed, honesty and deceit, ambition and complacency, what's said and what's heard.

Wealthy franchisees build strong working relationships with their corporate office. They engage at a higher level than most franchisees by participating in councils and committees. They read corporate communications and watch their videos. They follow the system while suggesting ways to improve it. They don't just look to their franchisor for help running their businesses—they partner with their franchisor to help build the brand.

Wealthy franchisees sometimes disagree with their franchisor, but they handle those disagreements constructively. They communicate well, appreciate their role in the relationship, and understand the importance of trust.

Franchising isn't immune to bad leadership or unethical behavior. If you sometimes question your franchisor's actions, it's possible your concerns have merit. Franchises, like any other business, are institutions run by humans. Not all of them are good partners. I've absolutely encountered some that don't operate in their franchisees' best interest, and most unhappy franchisees are convinced that's who they're in business with.

But those franchisors are the exception. The overwhelming majority of franchisors are smart, ethical people who want to make money by building a strong franchise system. They genuinely want their franchisees to thrive and work tirelessly to support their local partners while trying to manage their own corporate enterprise. And they have a tough job. If you've run a business, you know how hard it can be to manage employees. Now imagine having to wrangle hundreds or thousands of independent, strong-minded personalities spread out over millions of square miles. We franchisees can be a real motley crew!

Franchisors and franchisees are equally responsible for building trust. But franchisors are people, just as we are. They feel joy, frustration, excitement, and fear. They get upset when they're yelled at. Sometimes they lose their temper and do the yelling. Ideally, they'll behave professionally—and so will we—but everyone makes mistakes. We're all out there living our lives and doing our best.

While I acknowledge it takes two to tango, this book is for franchisees, so we're going to focus on *your* role in the relationship. It's the only part you can control, so make sure you're operating in the most constructive manner possible. Do that, and you'll have a more positive influence on your corporate partners—and hopefully enjoy a much more productive relationship.

The Importance of Trust

Trust is the foundation of any relationship. The essence of partnership is a belief that someone else has your back, and a willingness to put yourself in their hands. It's the single most important element of franchising.

Some franchise systems understand this better than others. They're transparent and communicative, act with integrity, and pursue trust as aggressively as they pursue profit.

I discussed this issue at length with Tropical Smoothie Cafe CEO Charles Watson. His company believes so deeply in the importance of building trust that they even use the word as an acronym to encourage the following qualities in their franchisees:

- **T**ransparent: "Be honest about what's going on."
- **R**esponsible: "We've got our responsibilities, and you've got yours. We have to build the bicycle, but you have to ride it."
- **U**nique: "There's value in you being your unique self." Charles called this "bringing your whole self to work"—celebrating your true self.
- **S**ervice-oriented: "We need to drive a servant leadership mentality all the way through the organization."
- **T**enacious: "A great franchisee in a poor system can still be successful because they're really going to get after it."

After she left PIP in 2008, Catherine Monson went on to become CEO and president of Fastsigns and chair the International Franchise Association (IFA). She defines the three criteria of franchisor excellence as the following:

1. Franchisee profitability/economic viability
2. Franchisor has high moral character and focuses on franchisee success
3. Positive franchisee-franchisor relationships

How awesome would it be to have a franchisor who focuses on these three elements? Many franchisees actually do—they just don't realize it. Our trust level isn't just based on someone else's behavior; it's also based on our perceptions. A person can be completely well-intentioned, but if you doubt them, your level of trust decreases. That doubt could be the result of something they said, did, or didn't do. It could also be because of a rumor or an incorrect assumption on your part. It doesn't take much to cloud our perspective.

That said, I've definitely encountered brands that don't meet Catherine's criteria. I don't know your circumstances, so I won't defend your franchisor. But what I see most often are franchisees with great franchisors who suffer needlessly because they don't have all the facts. They don't know their corporate team, the work that team is doing, and the reasons behind that work. That breakdown in communication weakens the system. Honest franchise professionals with a great concept can't get wealthy in a poor relationship.

In the 2017 *Harvard Business Review* article "The Neuroscience of Trust," neuro-economist Paul J. Zak shared some fascinating data he and his team collected about trust in the workplace. They found that, compared with people at low-trust companies, people in high-trust companies experienced lower levels of stress and burnout (and fewer sick days), as well as higher levels of energy, productivity, and engagement. Their research also correlated trust with an increase in production of a brain chemical called *oxytocin*. Often referred to as the "love hormone," oxytocin is associated with empathy, social bonding, and maternal care. The greater the production of oxytocin, the stronger our relationships and the better our work performance. I'd love to see a franchise whose mission statement reads: "To increase the oxytocin levels in our franchisees, employees, and customers."

While I don't know who you're in business with, I do know there's a reason you chose them. Hopefully you believed in them as much as you believe in what they sell. If you did your homework, your instincts were probably right. It's in your best interest to build and maintain a strong bond with them. That might mean letting go of the unsubstantiated beliefs that make trust difficult.

Tug of War with Your Franchisor

I spend a lot of time getting to know my franchise clients. Sometimes I'm researching multiple brands at the same time, interviewing both franchisees and their corporate offices. They're usually pretty open about their feelings. I hear great things and occasionally some not-so-great things, often from franchisees within the same company. If I don't have my notes in front of me, it's easy to forget which franchise I'm dealing with, since the complaints all sound so similar:

"They don't care about helping franchisees. They just want to add more dots on their map."

"We offer them so many tools to run their business, but instead of using them, they complain we're not doing enough."

"They'll sell anyone a franchise at any location, in any geographic area, even if there is not a chance in hell of the franchisee being successful."

"Every time we offer a new idea we get pushback. We've done the research. Why don't they trust us?"

"They're completely out of touch with what's happening at the store level."

"We really do want to hear from franchisees. How can we help if they complain to each other but don't communicate with us?"

"The incompetent leadership and dictatorial attitude of corporate personnel is sucking the life out of the organization."

Franchisors struggle with franchisees they believe are noncompliant, resistant to change, or unwilling to invest what it takes. Franchisees feel their corporate office doesn't care, doesn't understand *their* market, or doesn't know what they're doing. They think the franchisor's only priority is selling more franchises.

These perceptions say less about either side than they do about the delicate connection between them. Relationships of any kind are volatile. A franchise is a powder keg. It's a long-distance relationship with financial ties. The model is loaded with tensions, areas where franchisees and franchisors can easily be at odds. Consider the issues listed in Figure 12-1 on page 226 and the different perspectives each side might have.

All these land mines are there, waiting to be tripped. When you throw in personality clashes, it's a miracle any franchise functions.

But many do. There are countless franchise families where all parties enjoy profitable, flourishing relationships. They work through

Issue	Franchisee Perspective	Franchisor Perspective
Freedom	Wants independence to do things based on own experience	Wants franchisee to adhere to the system and to do things based on brand standards
Focus	Wants to grow own business in local market	Wants to grow brand nationally/globally
Income	Personal income from net profit	Corporate income from gross sales
Franchise Agreement	Individual franchisee is vetted and personally committed for the duration of agreement	Company is vetted, but leaders and team members may change at any time
Products/Suppliers	Wants to control costs	May be the supplier or receive rebates from suppliers
Marketing	Wants franchisor to do more	Wants franchisee to do more
Problem Solving	Wants franchisor to do more	Wants franchisee to do more
Franchisee Innovation	Willing to do it. It works for them.	Willing to test it. Will it work for everyone?
Franchisor Innovation	Sees risk and costs of making changes.	Sees risk and costs of not evolving.

FIGURE 12–1. **Franchise Tensions**

their differences on all the above issues to find common ground and ensure everyone's needs are met. Sales are made, bills are paid, royalties are taken, and supplies are purchased. Both franchisee and franchisor grow their companies, and at least once a year they have a pleasant drink together at the annual convention.

WEALTHY FRANCHISEE SPOTLIGHT

NICK CROUCH
Tropical Smoothie Cafe

St. Augustine, Florida

- Co-CEO of Dyne Hospitality Group
- Operates more than 62 locations in six states with development agreements to reach more than 100 cafes in the next few years
- 2016 Franchisee of the Year
- 2018 IFA Franchisee of the Year
- Member of multiple committees and councils within TSC system

As a young, aspiring entrepreneur and franchisee, Nick Crouch studied *Multi-Unit Franchisee Magazine*'s top operators around the world, showcased in each issue. His vision was never to own a restaurant, but to build a restaurant company with many locations and grow a "best in class" company culture. He obsessed over learning operations and growth strategies from people who were already doing it. Today, people are learning from him. Take a look at the Q4 2019 edition of *Multi-Unit Franchisee Magazine,* and you'll find Nick and his partner, Glen Johnson, on the cover.

Nick formed the company with fellow franchisee Glen in 2017, making them the largest Tropical Smoothie Cafe operator in the system. It's a far cry from his first cafe. He personally worked in the business just about every day during his first year and even slept there several times to ensure the place looked and ran just the way he wanted it.

Like many wealthy franchisees, Nick and Glen are highly active in the Tropical Smoothie Cafe system, participating in every committee they can. They especially love testing new ideas before they get rolled out.

"We want to get it, work through it, give input, and get ahead of it," he said. "We want to be the first to try new systems and procedures. We want to be at the forefront of changes."

His thoughts on success are the same as many other high performers: "We're in the people business. We just happen to sell smoothies, wraps, sandwiches, quesadillas, salads, etc."

The "people" Nick talked about most were his team. If he had a secret sauce, it'd be "building culture and developing the best talent in the industry." He's all about creating a strong team community that elevates everyone, both personally and professionally. All prospective employees watch their culture video on the homepage of the Dyne Hospitality Group website, in which Nick and Glen talk about the work environment, passion, and company culture they're committed to maintaining. No one joins their team unless they can get onboard with the values they discuss. Nick makes it hard to resist. "We all have to work," he said. "I say, let's have fun doing it."

Nick also explained that to keep great people, you need to provide opportunities for career growth. "One of our primary reasons for constant expansion is to ensure there will always be high places and opportunities for our team members to advance. We want them to grow with us."

Nick's Wealthy Franchisee Success Tips

- Live, breathe, and understand the brand.
- For long-term success, you have to be passionate about the work.
- Take a risk—go for it!
- Make sure you're ready financially.

> **WEALTHY FRANCHISEE SPOTLIGHT,** continued
>
> ◆ Be prepared to be challenged. It's not going to be easy. Work hard. Have fun!
>
> ◆ Find great people, establish a great workplace culture, and work toward the common goal together.

But this doesn't happen by accident. As with any relationship, franchises must be deliberate about building their culture and attentive to the human factors that influence social interaction.

Anticipating Conflict

Experienced parents warned Rachel and me about adolescence. They told us our sweet, young children would become moody teenagers. They'd talk back, push boundaries, and want to spend less time with us and more time with friends.

They were right. Our kids have changed exactly as predicted. They're rolling their eyes, closing their doors, and leaving the dinner table as soon as we allow them. We don't always enjoy it, but knowing what to expect has prevented us from being too concerned. Their behavior is normal.

Similarly, tension between franchisees and franchisors is normal, and predictable. It's more of a reflection of human psychology than a statement about the qualifications and morality of the players involved. When you know this going in, you'll be less alarmed when it happens.

Social scientists know that people go through normal phases of development. So do groups. We can look at the maturity level of a franchise system and pretty accurately anticipate the social dynamics that will occur. Understanding these dynamics will help you navigate through them more peacefully.

One of the most famous models of group development was created by psychologist Bruce Tuckman in 1965. Tuckman defined four stages

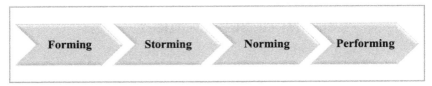

FIGURE 12–2. **Tuckman's Stages of Group Development**

(which he eventually expanded to five) that normal, healthy groups go through as they come together and collaborate. The four stages are most often represented sequentially, as displayed above in Figure 12-2.

Here's what happens at each stage:

Forming

This is the creation of the group. In the beginning, people figure out what their combined purpose is, what the rules are, and what everyone has to do. For a franchise, this includes Discovery Day, signing the franchise agreement, and setting up shop. At this stage, everything is new, and people tend to be on their best behavior. Often this is called the "honeymoon period." Either there hasn't been enough time for disagreement, or people aren't yet comfortable expressing it.

Storming

After some collaboration, there tend to be growing pains. The reality of life together is beginning to set in and emotions start coming to the surface. Idealism has worn off, questions arise, and personalities clash. Group members begin to test boundaries. Most of the tension is around personality styles and approaches to work.

Everyone is excited when they buy their franchise and open. They trusted the franchisor enough in the beginning to make the investment. But once they get going, franchisees start to perceive the difference between their expectations and the reality of running a business. It's common to experience dissatisfaction, and that causes friction.

This phase is scary to people who aren't secure in their group. They see tension as a failure in the relationship, when really it's just a deeper level of engagement. It's the next step forward in the process.

Norming

With communication, patience, and perseverance, groups can resolve their differences. Roles are clarified, culture and group norms are defined, and trust is rebuilt. This is the stage where everyone clears up misperceptions and figures out how to work together. One of the advantages of attending your brand's convention and regional meetings is to be able to speak with your franchisor face-to-face to address any issues in the most direct and productive setting possible. Well-run franchise advisory councils (FACs) and associations can also promote better relations. Sometimes all it takes is one good phone call between an owner and the corporate office to get to this stage. Norming requires both franchisor and franchisee to be honest, polite, and committed to collaboration.

Performing

Here the group experiences flow. Everyone knows their role, what to expect from each other, and how to accommodate different personalities. This is where they become most productive. Franchises in this stage are characterized by harmony, productivity, and hopefully, profitability.

Adjourning or Mourning

Tuckman added this fifth stage to his model years later. Some groups have a stopping point, such as a team that reaches the end of a season or a committee working on a finite project. It would also include a franchisee who departs the system upon selling the business or when the franchise agreement expires. This can be an emotional phase. Saying goodbye to franchise partners, colleagues, and employees can be difficult. There's a need for acknowledgement and closure. Many people in this stage are in transition and feel uncertainty, especially when there's a change in ownership. They must now enter a new "forming" stage and repeat the process, probably with new people.

There's a lot more information out there about group dynamics you can explore. The important thing to know now is that experiencing some dissatisfaction, mistrust, and tension in your system doesn't necessarily mean the relationship is broken or that you've partnered with the wrong people. It means you've partnered with *people*. Cooperation is tough—throw money in the mix and it's *really* tough. Don't let this scare you. Stay constructively engaged in the relationship, and you're more likely to break through to a prosperous partnership.

Franchise Triggers

Tuckman's group development model tells us to expect conflict in the "Storming" stage, a little while after a new group comes together. But in franchise systems, storming doesn't just follow the formation of the partnership. It also occurs when, after a comfortable period in the "Performing" stage, something changes. New systems, new policies, or new leaders throw people off and trigger tension. This dynamic is described in another rendering of Tuckman's model in Figure 12–3, below.

Change is uncomfortable and threatening. It could also cost a lot of money without an adequate ROI. At the same time, we're paying our franchisor to innovate and keep us successful in an evolving, competitive marketplace. Putting aside for the moment the question of

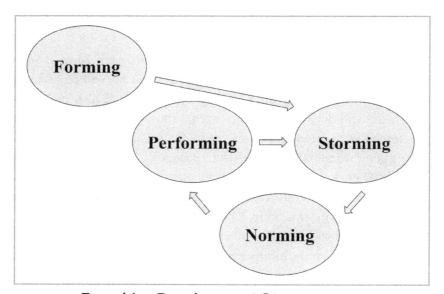

FIGURE 12–3 . **Franchise Development Stages**

whether a specific change is good or bad, it's important to understand that the change itself may cause us to storm.

I've observed a lot of changes in franchises and the conflicts they create. Understanding that these are normal sources of tension may help keep things in perspective. Here are the most common:

New Policies

As franchises grow their network and acquire more exposure, they become more bureaucratic. Ad hoc policies will no longer cut it—they need more structure to support the larger system. That's hard to adjust to if you're used to looser practices. A good franchise will also continually change the way it does things to improve, stay relevant, and respond to market conditions.

It's easier to embrace new policies when we know the reasons behind them, but some franchisors do a better job explaining them than others. I discussed this with Tropical Smoothie Cafe CEO Charles Watson.

"There are some franchisors who don't express the 'why.' Franchisees want to know the reason behind a decision. Franchisees should be pushing for the why. It all gets back to communication, but real communication . . . you've got to work through the situation together," he said.

Just because the policy doesn't make sense to *you* doesn't mean it doesn't make sense. Ask questions with an open mind and remember that your franchisor is looking out for the entire system. Withhold judgment until you have all the facts.

New Ad Fund Contributions

If you haven't previously had to make them, or if they've been kept lower than the requirements in your franchise agreement, being forced to fork over another point or two doesn't feel good. It's worse if you don't know or don't agree with how the money is being used.

At first, many new franchisors don't ask franchisees to contribute to an ad fund, even when their franchise agreement allows for it. That's because they want to make it as easy as possible for franchisees to come aboard. There may also not be enough contributors in a new system to accumulate a meaningful sum.

If it's in your agreement, expect to start contributing at some point. But the ad fund is actually one of the benefits of franchising. Pooling your marketing dollars can help pay for ad campaigns you probably couldn't afford on your own.

Remodeling

Many franchisees don't put money aside for capital improvements. While the concept of freshening up your retail business makes theoretical sense, who wants to pay for it? But as we discussed in Chapter 7, there's evidence to suggest that remodeling correlates with an increase in sales, even if that possibility is rarely comforting for the franchisees who are forced to fund it. Many go into remodeling kicking and screaming.

Chances are your agreement requires periodic upgrades and makeovers. Expect it to happen, and expect to dislike it. Still, it's necessary, it's standard, and it's most likely best for the business.

New Products and Services

Do they make sense? Will people buy them? Everyone has an opinion.

It was always controversial at Edible Arrangements when our franchisor introduced a new fruit. We had to learn how to source it, store it, clean it, and prepare it for arrangements. Then we had to sell it. None of us really knew how the new fruit would sell, but we all had feelings about it.

Every business needs to innovate to keep customers interested, and that means creating new offerings. Hopefully your franchisor has a good process for testing them.

Some of our new fruits sold better than others. Some were surprising successes and others were disappointing duds. All of them got people talking. Your brand's innovations may or may not generate profits, but they'll definitely generate emotions.

New POS/Computer Platforms

I hear about this one a lot, and I experienced it at Edible Arrangements. We get attached to our software environment, so learning a new system is hard. The switchover can be really stressful. Expect to feel this and don't judge the system until you've learned it.

New Leadership

In some cases, franchisees are extremely grateful for a new CEO, CMO, or field rep. Other times they mourn the loss of a trusted partner. And if a private equity group comes in, that brings a whole other layer of mystery that leaves folks uneasy. You can't control who comes and goes at your corporate office. But you can actively work to build a productive relationship with them. Expect there to be changes and always be ready to form new partnerships.

Drops in Sales

It's tempting to blame the franchisor. "They're not innovating enough." "They're not marketing enough." Maybe that's true, maybe it isn't. Whatever the real reason for the falling sales numbers, they put franchisees on edge. There's going to be tension. Keep the lines of communication open. Keep your *mind* open. And always find constructive ways to address the problem.

Changing Suppliers

If you like what you're getting and who you get it from, being told to get it elsewhere doesn't feel good.

These dynamics are common points of contention in the franchise world, so you can see the importance of good communication from franchisors. If they consult the franchise advisory council, keep franchisees informed, and be clear about why they're changing suppliers, they can do a lot to minimize pushback.

In reality, their strategy may be sounder than their messaging. Many well-intentioned franchisors get this wrong all the time. Help them out by not rushing to judgment. Your business is their business. It's all they do. They're working with a lot of data, so ask questions, try to understand their reasons, and be open to their ideas. Contribute to the conversation, but don't feed into the drama.

Engaging with Your Franchisor

One common trait I've noticed among wealthy franchisees is a high level of engagement in the brand. These people get involved. They communicate, participate, volunteer, and assist fellow franchisees. That helps them cultivate stronger relationships with their franchisors and gives them a say in what goes on. Most of the franchisees profiled in this book are active within their franchise systems beyond running their own operations.

Charles Watson told me that most of Tropical Smoothie Cafe's best franchisees are heavily involved in the system. They're active on various volunteer councils and committees and fly to the corporate office at their own expense for meetings. Back at their business, they maintain strong ties to the home office and proudly represent the brand.

"It's all about engagement," Charles said. "Our best franchisees don't miss webinars. They follow the system. They block and tackle very well. They fully understand that they bought into a system. They understand that to be the most successful, they need to be the best executors."

Miracle-Ear senior vice president Vera Peterson had similar thoughts about how franchisees should stay connected to the network.

"Communicate," she said. "Take advantage of everything we give to you. Be open with field support. Attend our meetings and conferences. If you're angry about something, don't boycott the convention. Show up and protest! It's like an election. You can't complain if you don't vote. Hold your peers accountable if they're damaging the brand. At the same time, collaborate with your peers as much as possible. They're going through the same thing as you."

Vera told me that all her top franchisees are as active with the brand as they are with their own territory. They mentor other franchisees, both to help their fellow operators and to help the brand. They understand they're not working in a vacuum. The better all franchisees do, the stronger the company. And the stronger the company, the more prosperous each location is. She also pointed out that struggling franchisees tend to be more receptive to wealthy franchisees' advice than the franchisor's. Sometimes it's easier to learn from a peer.

Active engagement correlates with individual franchise success. It's part of the wealthy franchisee way. Catherine Monson shares in her Fastsigns Foundations Training that franchisees who actively engage in their system are 3.8 times more likely to report strong profits than those who don't. That's significant—who wouldn't want to almost quadruple their chances of building strong profits?

Even if you don't formally join a committee, it's important to be part of the conversation. "It's incumbent upon the franchisee to raise their hand," Charles Watson told me. "You've got to communicate to your franchisor the issues that you're having. The onus is on the franchisee to kick up the information about what's not working."

But what about those struggling franchisees who say their corporate office doesn't listen to them? Many franchisees complain about this. I posed this question to Charles.

He said, "My usual response to that is 'Have you sat down and had a conversation or have you sent a snippy email or left a jerky voicemail message?' I've had plenty of hard conversations with franchisees in my career. I have yet to have a conversation where I didn't get off the phone seeing closer to eye to eye."

Of course, you've got to speak up constructively. He continued:

"We're all human beings, whether you're a franchisor or a franchisee. It's still Charles and Sally. When Sally calls screaming at me, I, Charles, the human being, am a little taken aback. You get more flies with honey than vinegar. You need to have a businesslike attitude going into it and try to solve the problem vs. yelling and screaming and it's all someone else's fault."

But at least in this example Sally is communicating directly with Charles. What I often see are franchisees communicating only with each other, indulging in what I call . . .

The Franchisee Venting Loop

"Hi, Barb. It's Diane over at the Rancho Park store. How are you?"

"Oh, hi, Diane. Hanging in. Did you see that email today from corporate? Here we go again."

"I know. Can you believe it? It never ends with these people!"

If I didn't know these were two franchisees, I'd think they were high school kids. Conversations like this are taking place today between business owners in almost every franchise system in the world, who habitually call each other to vent. Each conversation reinforces their negative feelings.

I'm all for franchisees supporting each other. It's important to connect with people fighting in the same trenches. Having colleagues is one of the great advantages of owning a franchise. But there's a difference between supporting each other and riling each other up.

Few things influence us more than the peer groups we choose to join. I pay attention to who my kids hang out with. Their friends will either lift them up or hold them down. Fortunately, my kids have found friends who are ambitious, kind, and positive. They mutually reinforce each other's values.

Franchisees also join peer groups with like-minded colleagues. It's human nature, but it's not always good business, because your peers may be reinforcing counterproductive perspectives.

This is an example of confirmation bias. It's no different from seeking out radio or cable news shows that support the beliefs you already have. Looking for agreement and looking for the truth are not the same thing.

My father and I used to talk all the time about our Edible Arrangements stores, and we often gave in to the temptation to blame our corporate office for any troubles we were having. When one of us would hear something, we'd call the other to reinforce our beliefs. We really worked each other up sometimes.

Then we'd travel to the annual convention, meet our franchisors face-to-face, and get their perspective. We shared our concerns, got their responses, and interacted with the flesh-and-blood people running the company. Somehow they didn't seem quite as sinister in person. We didn't always agree with them, but we always left calmer. On the trip home, we'd brainstorm all the things we could start doing to improve our businesses.

One of the challenges of the franchise model is geography. Even with visits from corporate field representatives, the home office feels far away. It's easier to depersonalize people we don't see, and we can easily start to build up an image of them that may be inaccurate.

I was once copied on a mass email started by a disgruntled franchisee from another brand who wanted to share a complaint about his franchisor. That first message set off an avalanche of negative "reply alls" in which everyone unloaded their frustrations. Sometimes the complaints would change, but the general message was the same—corporate was the enemy.

What could have been a productive exchange of solutions turned into a bitch thread, with each email driving the wedge deeper between franchisees and corporate. It's not that there wasn't some truth to the concerns—it just wasn't a useful conversation. The web has a way of intensifying feelings. It's easy to lash out with your keyboard.

Wealthy franchisees associate with other wealthy franchisees, not just because they want more wealth, but also because they're attracted to people with a similar sensibility. They gain nothing by talking to complainers. Rather, they seek out solution-oriented colleagues who help them maintain their enthusiasm. Because they're calm, respectful, and directly involved with the franchisor, they're better able to tackle tough issues and get results.

Don't get sucked into the venting loop or let others intensify your anger. It won't help. Instead, keep a clear head, check your facts, and communicate directly with those who are in a position to take action.

This chapter may have given you the impression that I'm on the franchisor's side. Most of what I've shared are ideas for playing your role in the franchise relationship, which may have left you feeling defensive.

I promise, if I took sides, I'd be on yours. I'm still a franchisee at heart. I want you to succeed and get wealthy. But to be helpful, I need to give you something to do.

Once, a brand's franchisee association hired me to speak to their members, and I asked the association officers to share the challenges their franchisees face. Everything they said was a complaint about the franchisor. They couldn't come up with a positive message for franchisees. Did they want me to spend an hour criticizing their franchisor? I didn't doubt their perspective, but for me to be helpful, I needed to give franchisees some action to take. I had to come up with a message about something that was under their control.

That's my intention here—not to put all the responsibility on you, but to empower you where I can. Put me in a room in front of a bunch of franchisors and I'll have plenty to say to them as well.

But let's get to the question that's likely been on your mind this entire chapter:

What If My Franchisor Really Is That Bad?

Get out. Sell. Cut your losses. If you really have the wealthy franchisee mindset, if you're really keeping a clear head, inspiring your employees, wowing your customers, and doing all you can to partner well with your franchisor and are certain, absolutely *certain* that the problem is them, then it's time to leave. I would say that about any detrimental circumstance you can't control.

It's hard to take a loss. But if you're willing to apply the concepts in this book, the sooner you get into better circumstances, the sooner you can start building wealth.

Ideally, you can sell. If not, maybe you can last until your franchise agreement runs out. Or maybe you can negotiate your way out of the agreement. Resist the urge to cut and run. That's not the wealthy franchisee way. Seek out counsel on how to exit properly.

When I started this book, I imagined I'd be done at this point. But after meeting so many great wealthy franchisees, I noticed one more thing they all have in common . . .

Bigger Picture, Bigger Payoff

I did a poor job painting my daughter's room. She was away at a weekend camp, and I wanted to surprise her with the new color. I had two days to transform her room into the lavender princess quarters she'd always wanted. Eager to get started, I moved the furniture and began slathering pinkish purple all over her walls, rushing through the most important part of any paint job, the preparation.

Before applying color, you're supposed to fill any holes and repair the drywall. You need to remove faceplates from outlets and light switches, tape off any vulnerable spots, and carefully lay out your drop cloths. Then you apply primer and allow it to dry. It's a long, arduous process that doesn't feel productive. Do it right, however, and the paint goes on quickly and the room looks great.

My daughter's doesn't. A close look reveals uneven lines between the white ceiling and colored walls. Dried drops of lavender freckle the white baseboards. The walls are bumpy in places where I didn't adequately sand down my patches. My daughter was happy when she saw the new color, but each imperfection bothers me to this day. She deserves better. I wish I'd done it right.

Many franchisees similarly rush through their prep work or skip it altogether, eager to open and start selling things. They get busy running their business without developing the formal operating philosophy they need to run it well. That limits their performance.

I've observed a lot about top franchisees over the years, but what really jumped out as I researched this book was this one, final common behavior among them. Wealthy franchisees spend time upfront envisioning the larger context of their enterprise. They ask big questions and consider what they want their business to achieve besides profitability. Instead of thinking only about what they want to get, they also think about what they want to give and who they want to be. That context, that larger perspective, remains on their minds at all times. They excel at all the little things because they never lose sight of the big things.

Wealth is built not by chasing it but by attracting it. The more value you put out there, the more money tends to flow in your direction. Franchisees who focus on something bigger than their own interests make more impact, boosting quality of life for themselves and everyone their business touches. Their wider perspective helps them make smarter business decisions—and, consequently, more money.

Running a franchise enables you to do some pretty cool things. Important things. That may be the key to building wealth. It's certainly one of the habits of wealthy franchisees.

What, How, and Why?

There are three important questions worthy of deep consideration. Your answers will yield practical benefits and help you make decisions. On the surface, they seem merely philosophical, and if you don't make use of the answers, they will be of no benefit. But if you incorporate them into your daily activities, they'll become valuable tools that will take your operation to the next level. The questions are:

1. What do you do?
2. How are you doing it?
3. Why are you doing it?

Let's walk through each one. Check out Figure 13-1 below to see how they line up with your mission, values, and purpose.

What Do You Do?

What's your business's daily assignment? What's its specific, important contribution? What's its role in the big picture? Think beyond personal gain or what it's meant to do for you. What's your business putting out into the world? Your answer will define your *mission*.

How Are You Doing It?

Not tactically, but morally. How do you want to be as you do this work? What principles will you stand for as you fulfill your mission? What

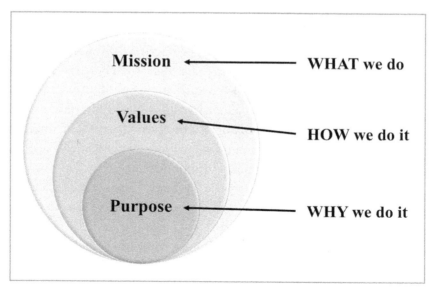

FIGURE 13–1. **What, How, and Why**

guidelines will determine how you operate? These answers are your *values*.

Why Are You Doing It?

What's your reason for doing all this? Why does your business exist? How does it improve the world or enhance life? Your answers to these questions make up your *purpose*.

Your mission, values, and purpose combine to determine how your business will run—if you use them. Plenty of companies write mission or value statements and immediately ignore them, posting these grandiose proclamations on their websites for the world to see and never looking at them again. It's pretty rare to find someone who can recite their company's official working philosophy.

Whether or not you realize it, *something* is influencing your decisions. It could be your passion or your fear. You might be chasing success or running from failure. You might do what's best for customers or what's best for your ego. Clarifying your philosophy will ensure that you work, live, and operate deliberately, according to predetermined standards.

Thinking Big Beyond Your Business

If your motive is just to make money, you'll probably make less of it, and it won't be worth it—it's too darn hard. Building a business requires a Herculean level of effort. Not one wealthy franchisee has ever told me success just happened for them. They've all invested long hours and endured a lot of headaches. Many of them shared stories of wanting to quit. It's so much harder than having a job. Resilience isn't just an advantage for a franchisee—it's a basic requirement.

Having a strong sense of purpose is a powerful source of resilience. As Friedrich Nietzsche once said, "He who has a *why* to live, can bear with almost any *how*." When you have a strong reason to fight for something, you can fight harder and longer. I've learned that as a parent. I'll let myself go hungry, but I won't let my kids. For them, I'll work a lot harder to put food on the table.

But most people want to take care of their families, so that isn't enough to elevate your thinking to the place where magic happens. You need to see your business as a vital part of a larger family.

That's a perspective I consistently see among the great people of the franchise world. Their ambition exceeds their business, which is just one part of many aspirations. They play on a much larger field, and that broader perspective helps them run a better business.

A great example of this is Fastsigns' Catherine Monson, whom you read about earlier. You'd think being CEO and president of an international sign franchise would place enormous demands on her time. But ambitious people always seem to make more time for the things that matter. Catherine's also found a way to chair the IFA, participate in a number of franchise committees, serve on the board of multiple franchises and a print industry association, and maintain an active speaking schedule. I asked her why, with so much already on her plate, she takes it on herself to advocate for the entire franchise industry rather than just focusing on Fastsigns.

"If the franchise business model is harmed, this great thing I get to do goes away. I'm a big believer in personal responsibility. I think that's key in everything in life. So I better be in Washington, DC," she said.

Doing all this work outside the franchise exposes her to more ideas, relationships, and resources for the franchise. She can represent her company's interests and have more influence on the conversations and policies that directly impact it. She looks out for her home by looking out for her entire neighborhood. Being more than a CEO has made her a better CEO. Just ask her franchisees— they're thriving.

Catherine gave me a tour of the Fastsigns world headquarters in Carrollton, Texas. The building is a single-story labyrinth decorated with beautiful images throughout. (They're in the sign business, after all.) She was eager to take me on a stroll down "Inspiration Hall," a long corridor with its walls covered in motivational quotes. It's a powerful experience to move through a space adorned with nothing but wise, inspiring messages. (I aspire to say something profound enough to be immortalized there one day.)

A visitor could walk through these offices and not even know what business the company was in. It was so much bigger than signs. Just as that thought occurred to me, I noticed the company motto on the wall: "More than fast. More than signs."

More than a CEO, more than an association chair, more than a board member, Catherine demonstrates what's possible when your purpose is bigger than your business.

So does Taco John's franchisee Tamra Kennedy. I met Tam at the FaegreBD Franchise Summit, where she appeared on a panel discussing brand devotion and customer experience. As the only franchisee on the panel (and one of few to attend the conference), she brought a unique and important perspective to the conversation.

Tam is a franchise crusader. In addition to operating nine Taco John's franchises in two states, she's an active member of the board of directors for IFA and chairs the IFA Franchisee Forum. She's been awarded the IFA Franchise Action Network Member of the Year. Tam lobbies Capitol Hill, has testified before Congress, and has written op-eds in *The Wall Street Journal* defending the franchise model and advocating for its protection. She's also a partner in a consulting group that advises franchisees and participates in a variety of franchise events around the United States. And she's a grandmother. All this while running a multimillion-dollar restaurant business.

What allows Tam to do so much so well is the way she thinks. She sees her business as a piece of something much bigger. She doesn't just want to make money—she wants to make an impact. Her broader perspective allows her to do both remarkably well.

Thinking Big *Within* Your Business

The wealthy franchisee mindset isn't just about working in a bigger world. It's also about doing bigger, more meaningful work within your business. That larger meaning is communicated in your mission, values, and purpose. You may think these things aren't important, but the data increasingly shows that they mean a lot to your customers.

According to the 2018 Cone/Porter Novelli Purpose Study "How to Build Deeper Bonds, Amplify Your Message and Expand the Consumer Base":

- 78 percent of Americans believe companies should impact society as well as make money.
- 77 percent feel a stronger emotional connection to companies that exhibit a social purpose.
- 66 percent would switch from a product they regularly buy to one from a purpose-driven brand.
- 68 percent are more willing to share content from a purpose-driven brand on social media than content from a traditional company.

These things mean a lot to the people you're trying to hire as well. According to the PwC 2016 report "Putting Purpose to Work: A Study of Purpose in the Workplace," Millennials are more than five times more likely to stay in a job when they have a strong connection to their employer's purpose. Non-Millennials are more than twice as likely to do so. Employers acknowledge this data but have been slow to take it seriously. While 79 percent of business leaders agree on the importance of purpose for their success and longevity, only a third of them agree that it's used for leadership decision making.

Using it for your decision making will make a difference. It does for wealthy franchisees. All the great ones I meet are deeply concerned about the philosophical infrastructure of their business. They take the time to carefully articulate their goals and principles and infuse them into every aspect of their business—and that gets them results.

The UPS Store superstar franchisee Burke Jones (profiled in Chapter 5) has his mission statement posted on the walls, in the back, on his business card, and even in his bathroom:

"We deliver a five-star experience to our customers, co-workers, vendors, and community by merging world-class customer service with world-class business solutions, delivered with a world-class positive attitude."

You can't go anywhere near his business without seeing his operating philosophy. His mission statement isn't artwork or a slogan. It's a working set of guidelines that drives every element of his business.

Tropical Smoothie Cafe's largest franchise operators Nick Crouch (profiled in Chapter 12) and his partner Glen Johnson are also experts in defining and communicating their philosophy. Their website says:

"Our Culture is much more than a page on a website or an inspirational poster on a wall. To us, our culture is who we truly are and what we love to do. We use it to make every decision in our company. We encourage our team to live by it and hold each other accountable to it. We base hiring, promotions, team member reviews, performance and communication off of it."

The page then describes the "four pillars" that outline their operational philosophy. You won't find a word about food or smoothies—it's all about culture and human behavior. They could easily start a business in another industry and use the same language.

Tam Kennedy trains her morning shift at Taco John's not just to serve breakfast but to fulfill their mission. "People are tired, running late, and not ready for the day," she said. "We need to be the sunshine inside that they may not be feeling outside." Her competitors are just selling breakfast burritos.

Tam's mission extends to her team members. Just as Jersey Mike's Peter Cancro started as a 14-year-old working at a sub shop, Tam started as a server at Pizza Hut making $2.30 an hour. Some people see fast-food work as a dead-end job, but she saw it as a launching pad. She still does. She's passionate about giving her employees a good start in life. When I asked her what her reason (or purpose) was for running her restaurants, she told me:

"I want to give a home to those people who are looking for a place to learn, a job they can be proud of, and lessons they can use to make better choices when they leave. I want to help young people not drop out of their lives. Then I want them to come back and say this was the best job they ever had."

This mission doesn't conflict with generating revenue. If anything, it helps her generate more. Her business is solid and her team is stable.

WEALTHY FRANCHISEE SPOTLIGHT

DOC COHEN

Great American Cookies

TCBY

Coffee Beanery

Pretzelmaker

Houston, Texas

- Second franchisee to be chair of the International Franchise Association (2006–2007)
- First franchisee inducted into IFA Hall of Fame
- First franchisee to earn the IFA Certified Franchise Executive (CFE) designation
- First franchisee inducted into the Great American Cookie "Cookie Hall of Fame"
- Three-time Great American Cookie/IFA Franchisee of the Year
- Two-time Franchisee of the Decade
- Chaired IFA Foundation for two years

Doc Cohen is a legend in the franchise industry. For more than 40 years he's enjoyed enormous success running as many as 31 franchise businesses from four brands in seven states. He's made money, won awards, and possibly baked more cookies than anyone else on earth. To Doc, the most horrifying image is an empty cookie tray, unless there's a new tray coming out of the oven to replace it.

Doc's accomplishments as a franchisee are rivaled only by what he's done for the franchise industry as a whole. In addition to chairing the International Franchise Association, he spent two years chairing the IFA Foundation. He continues to be involved in the IFA today, working to strengthen the industry. He

---

WEALTHY FRANCHISEE SPOTLIGHT, continued

also devotes a lot of time to mentoring business leaders and other franchisees. "I just feel the need to give back to what made me successful, which has been franchising," he said.

And while he's big on sticking to the system, he's rarely scared off by others telling him what's not possible. He shared a story of having to staff his business with high school students. Everyone else older had taken jobs on the high-paying offshore oil rigs in the area and it seemed like teens were all that was left. Colleagues warned not to hire a 19-year-old to manage his business. That 19-year-old helped him build the first $1 million cookie store in the system. Today he's the president of Doc's company.

Doc likes hiring someone who's never had a job before. "I like growing young people as leaders and teaching them about responsibility and integrity," he said. "If you can earn their trust, you can help them in a positive way. You can mold them into a higher-level employee."

Doc has worked hard; in the early years he personally ran his operation from open until close. It wasn't easy. "Mindset is critical," he told me. "You have to believe you can do it. You can't let anyone tell you that you can't."

Doc's Wealthy Franchisee Success Tips

- Pick a franchise you like.
- Do your homework. You've got to research the franchise you intend to buy. Call as many franchisees as possible before buying into the system.
- You're a steward of the brand, so always try to do the right thing.
- Protect the brand by sticking to the system.
- Invest in people, even when money is tight. That's when it's most important.
- Commit to success—refuse to fail. Do whatever it takes.

Formalizing Your Philosophy

Purpose, mission, and value statements shouldn't be written to impress your customers. They're meant more for internal use. They define the company for your team members.

The way your philosophy sounds is less important than the action it inspires. *That's* what impresses your customers. Having said that, carefully expressing your philosophy in written words will make it easier to communicate it to your team.

Companies use the phrases "mission statement," "purpose statement," and "value statement" interchangeably. There's no right or wrong name for it. Nor is there one correct format. Don't get too hung up on what you call it or how you present it. What's most important is that it codifies your overall philosophy in a way that's useful.

It's likely your franchisor already has a formal mission statement for your brand. If that works for you, embrace it. If not, create your own. Just make sure your philosophy aligns with theirs.

Write your philosophy statement with as few people as possible. Some organizations try to get buy-in by making the process very inclusive. This rarely works, because groups can't write. I've taken some through the process, and it's really hard. It's much easier to have one or two leaders draft something and then solicit feedback.

Or don't ask for feedback. This is your business, and you've paid for the privilege of defining your own culture. You can decide what you want to achieve and who you want to be and then build the business around your preference.

I'll admit I didn't do this when I owned my Edible Arrangements stores. I absolutely had a philosophy, but I didn't take the time to write it out. I wish I had—it would have helped me make decisions. It also would have been very useful for recruiting, training, and motivating my team. If I could go back, here's what I would've written:

At Edible Arrangements, we create delicious, attractive fruit arrangements (our mission) that help people celebrate the important occasions in their lives (our purpose). Every move we make is guided by the following principles (our values):

- *Teamwork.* We accomplish more when we work together.
- *Family.* Whether it's the family we're from or the family we create, everything we do will strengthen our relationships.
- *Personal Growth.* All of us should develop, learn, and grow from doing this work.
- *Courage.* We will acknowledge our feelings but always do the work necessary to accomplish our goals.
- *Continuous Improvement.* We will constantly learn and evolve in order to remain the best at what we do.
- *Profitability.* We will bring in more money than we spend in order to sustain the business and continue accomplishing our goals.
- *Enhancing Life.* Our business should improve the lives of everyone it touches.

This philosophy may or may not resonate with you, but that doesn't matter. It's mine. It's the way I want to run *my* operation. Anyone who wants to work with me will need to get onboard with it. If they don't, they're a bad fit. Clarifying your philosophy will help you recognize the practices and the people who are a good fit for you.

Architects don't just envision a building. They draw blueprints. That enables others to take the architect's ideas and make them real. Writing your philosophy statement will make it less philosophical and more practical. And it will mean you can share it with everyone you want it to influence.

Operationalizing Your Philosophy

A mission statement is like any other tool: It only works if you use it. Great businesses make their statement a regular part of their operation.

The Ritz-Carlton is well-known for their daily shift lineup meetings. Each day, every employee in the company worldwide is pulled from their work for 10 minutes to discuss daily operations and some element of Ritz-Carlton's philosophy. They review their service principles and their purpose as outlined on their "credo card." This card is a required element of their uniform that must be on their person at all times. I visited the Ritz in New Orleans, and every employee I met proudly flashed their card when I inquired if they had it. Their executive chef allowed me to watch the lineup he led with his kitchen staff, and I asked one of the cooks if this daily conversation really makes a difference. "Some days we feel it more than others, but we never forget why we're here and what's expected," he said. This is why Ritz's guests can expect so much.

Staffing franchise PrideStaff encourages their franchisees to review and discuss their mission to "consistently provide client experiences focused on what they value most" each day with their teams and talk about what that means. I interviewed a number of franchisees, and all the top franchisees I spoke with do—every day.

In fact, most of the franchisees profiled in this book have formal rituals and processes that consistently promote their philosophy to their team. Whether it's part of their employee onboarding and training, their performance reviews, or in conversations about how to address issues that arise, it's always there.

Don't let your philosophy blend into the background. It must be continuously broadcast. Your team needs regular reminders of the big what, why, and how of their work, or they'll just be busy. Don't forget—busyness is the enemy of leadership. It poses as productivity. You don't want your team spending their shift dully pushing through tasks. You want them out there swinging a sword and fighting for your business.

Being a Community Hero

"We love you, Edible Arrangements!" screamed the walkers.

"We love you, too!" replied my team. "Whooo!"

Never had I seen my employees in such good spirits. We celebrated birthdays, held potlucks, and threw holiday parties. All were fun, but none brought out the same energy in them as AIDS Walk Los Angeles.

One Sunday a year, thousands of people marched by our store to raise money and awareness for the AIDS epidemic, and we made it our mission to support them. We set up in front of our store cheering the walkers and passing out free fruit. One year it was strawberries. Another year it was pineapple. They'd cram in around our tables to enjoy whatever juicy treats we had to energize their trek around the city. Kids would want selfies with whichever one of us was wearing the strawberry costume.

The first year, I figured the walkers would appreciate it, but what surprised me was how my employees responded. They loved it! It was more than just a break from business as usual—they really enjoyed helping out and supporting a great cause. They laughed, high-fived the walkers, and told me I didn't need to pay them for their time. Donating it for charity was more meaningful. (I paid them anyway. I don't mess with labor law.)

My employees made more than minimum wage, but not much more. Our business model didn't allow it. Many of them were single parents who could use some help themselves. But when they were given a chance to do something charitable, something inside them came alive. That internal payoff brought the team together and deepened their connection to our work.

Many franchisees don't appreciate the potential social impact of their business, seeing it only as a means to make money. It can do that, but it can do so much more. In fact, doing more may actually make a lot more money. It's certainly part of the wealthy franchisee playbook.

Wealthy franchisees, by definition, do well financially. It sounds counterintuitive, but they accomplish this by not obsessing over profit. They focus on bigger things. Their goals are loftier and their vision is wider. They're on a mission to make an impact, and it turns out that making an impact makes more money.

The best franchise brands have major community-service programs. Few do it better than Jersey Mike's. During the month of March, the restaurant chain invites guests to come into their locations to donate to local charity partners. The campaign culminates with their annual "Mike's Day of Giving" on the last Wednesday of March. One hundred percent of the day's sales systemwide are donated to the local partner charity. To date, they've raised tens of millions of dollars for various causes. But they don't stop there.

CEO Peter Cancro proudly told me about Jersey Mike's "Coach Rod Smith Ownership Program." The program is named after the football coach who gave Peter the financing to buy his first sub shop when he was 17 years old. In the same spirit, Jersey Mike's now identifies the most deserving managers in the system and sets them up with their own shop. He said, "We're signing the lease and putting up all the money." The owners who lose their manager in the process will be given a small percentage of the proceeds for three years. Everyone wins.

Peter actually got a bit choked up as he told me about the program. As well as he's done for himself selling sandwiches, replicating the opportunity that was given to him seems to be the mission closest to his heart.

Sport Clips Haircuts is another brand that constantly works to serve the community. Through their "Haircuts with Heart" program, they actively seek to make a difference for veterans, families, and children. They have national partnerships with Veterans of Foreign Wars, the St. Baldrick's Foundation, and the American Red Cross. They also have a relief fund set up for franchisees and team members should anyone ever find themselves in need. Founder/Chairman Gordon Logan takes this work very seriously.

"I know this is supposed to be good for marketing," he said, "but we do it just because it's the right thing to do."

Gordon went on to quote Zig Ziglar, saying, "You can have everything in life you want if you will just help enough other people get what they want." Interestingly, Burke Jones of The UPS Store referenced the same quote in my interview with him. Wealthy minds think alike.

During my visit with Gordon, he invited me to sit in on their national franchise advisory council meeting and speak with franchisee Liz Crawford. Liz runs a solid operation in Tallahassee, Florida, and credits much of her success to their community service.

She told me, "I see Sport Clips doing so much at the national level. I wanted to create that same culture of service among my own stylists. We all want to give back to the community. The customers feel that, and it really makes a difference."

Charles Watson from Tropical Smoothie Cafe told me, "Most of our franchisees really want to serve the communities where they operate. They want to have a positive impact. They believe in the higher calling." Many struggling franchisees have a hard time wrapping their brains around the concept of a "higher calling." They're just trying to make money.

Miracle-Ear franchisees support and raise money for the Miracle-Ear Relief Fund, which supplies hearing products for needy Americans. Their top franchisee organizes an entire golf tournament to raise money for the fund.

All these examples are from companies and people who do really well for themselves. Wealthy franchisees are givers, not takers. If you want to have what they have, you must do as they do. Charity is part of their formula for success.

Cause Marketing

Cause marketing is a company's promotion of their social work. The messaging focuses on the brand's charity work rather than on its offerings. The goal is to make a positive impression on consumers while making a meaningful impact on a cause. It works, and people like it. Many folks who took free strawberries from us during the AIDS walk returned at a later date to buy some.

Some people see cause marketing as duplicitous and question the company's motives: "These people don't really care about the community. They're just looking for another way to advertise."

But the beneficiaries won't care. If they get the help they need, they're happy for you to get some recognition. And keep in mind, people often start working in community service for one reason and then continue for others. Many people wouldn't think to do it if there wasn't a tangible benefit in it for them. But once they've personally felt the joy of giving, they're inclined to continue, even without getting something in return.

If you're going to market your business, you may as well help others in the process.

Giving vs. Giving Back

You need to shift your thinking away from the concept of "giving back." Giving back implies you received something in the first place, but community service shouldn't be a quid pro quo. It shouldn't be about returning a favor or paying a debt. Too many people wait until late in their lives to volunteer, be of service, or donate.

Give first. Donate first. Serve first. Even if you're young, new, or sales are down, start serving your community now. Do it without thinking of it as a tactic to grow your business or expecting anything in return. If you do, you'll receive payoffs that far exceed (though totally include) money. Life will give back to you.

I hope this chapter has somehow widened your mind and opened your heart. But if all you really care about is maximizing revenue, the action you have to take is the same. Think big, and think *give*.

CHAPTER 14

Final Thoughts

I wrote this book to help the millions of people who work in the franchise industry to do better, live better, and serve better. I want franchisees and their team members to grow personally as well as professionally. I want them to use their products and services to improve the lives of the millions of people who visit their businesses every day. While I stand behind the ideas in this book as a strategy to make more money, my hope—my *purpose*—has been to make the world a little better, one franchise at a time.

There are so many intelligent, hardworking, deserving people out there ready to run a successful business of their own. They just need a concept and a little guidance. The right franchise can be their opportunity to thrive.

If I had only 30 words in which to share my message instead of 80,000, it would be this:

*If you want to run a successful franchise business, keep a clear head,
stick to the proven system, and use your business to improve the lives of
everyone it touches.*

That's really it. Everything else is just the details. Do these few
things consistently, and you'll be leaps and bounds ahead of most other
people.

I'd love to be an ongoing resource for you and your franchise system.
I present keynotes, workshops, and trainings, both live and virtually. I
provide one-on-one coaching for franchisees, write blogs and articles
and record video messages, and stay active on social media. If you'd be
interested in attending a Wealthy Franchisee Bootcamp to collaborate
with other franchisees and apply these concepts to grow your business,
please let me know. My website is https://www.scottgreenberg.com/.
Reach out any time with questions. I'd be delighted to hear from you.

Doc Cohen often cites a poem called "The Bridge Builder" by
Will Allen Dromgoole that was included in his University of Georgia
fraternity handbook. It inspired his approach to life and offers a simple
but powerful message for the rest of us:

> An old man going a lone highway,
> Came, at the evening cold and gray,
> To a chasm vast and deep and wide.
> Through which was flowing a sullen tide
> The old man crossed in the twilight dim,
> The sullen stream had no fear for him;
> But he turned when safe on the other side
> And built a bridge to span the tide.
>
> "Old man," said a fellow pilgrim near,
> "You are wasting your strength with building here;
> Your journey will end with the ending day,
> You never again will pass this way;
> You've crossed the chasm, deep and wide,
> Why build this bridge at evening tide?"
>
> The builder lifted his old gray head;
> "Good friend, in the path I have come," he said,

"There followed after me to-day,
A youth whose feet must pass this way.
This chasm that has been as naught to me
To that fair-haired youth may a pitfall be;
He, too, must cross in the twilight dim;
Good friend, I am building this bridge for him!"

What we build for ourselves matters less than what we build for others. In the end, we can't take anything with us. All that will matter then is what we've left behind. Wealthy franchisees make plenty of money for themselves, but more important, they leave a legacy for the rest of us. Work in a way that contributes to your legacy. Maybe that's what being wealthy really means.

Acknowledgments

Let me first apologize to those I'm going to fail to mention. Writing a book is like running a franchise: It's highly collaborative. I've accomplished little in my life without a lot of outside help. I fear I may overlook a few folks who've enabled me to write this. That says more about my scattered brain than it does about anyone's contribution. Sorry about that.

Those I'm fortunate to remember and appreciate:

First, to my editor Jennifer Dorsey and the gang from Entrepreneur Press: You saw what this could be before it was anything. Thanks for getting in the weeds with me and doing the hard work. I'm proud to be associated with the Entrepreneur brand.

To my agent, Wendy Keller: Every writer should have a guardian angel like you. Thanks for taking this on and pushing it through. Your boldness and perseverance are rivaled only by your kindness and compassion. You'd make an amazing franchisee.

To my manager Sheldon Senek and the team at Eagles Talent Speakers Bureau: So great to work with you. What wonderful hours we've wasted together joking around on Slack.

To Katrina Mitchell from the Speak! Franchise Speakers Bureau: I'm so grateful for the doors you've opened. You definitely know the franchise world—it's all you do.

To my other speakers bureau partners around the world—thanks for keeping me busy!

I'm so grateful for the time and wisdom of my clients and franchise colleagues who sat for interviews, answered questions, and provided input, including Rhoda Olsen, Paul Damico, Chuck and Becky Bongiovanni, Catherine Monson, Peter Cancro, Gordon Logan, Chuck Runyon (awesome Foreword, Chuck!), Erin Walter, Vera Peterson, Charles Watson, Heidi Morrissey, Tim Davis, and Tamra Kennedy.

To the wealthy franchisees profiled in this book: Thanks for your time, your insight, and your role modeling. You're proof of what's possible in franchising.

To the many other franchisees (some wealthy, some typical, and some struggling) who've given me their time and shared their perspectives over the years: You're my brethren.

To my former employees at Edible Arrangements: Thanks for showing me how great people can be and what excellent, cohesive teamwork looks like. Yes, you *can* find good help these days.

To my former Edible Arrangements general manager, Jennifer Satzman: Thanks for taking the journey with me. They say you're not supposed to be friends with the people you hire, but I'm so glad I broke that rule with you. May our adventures together continue.

To Steve Callaghan, Rodel Delfin, Evan Katz, Erin Fischer, Cleve Tzung, Ross Kramer, Shelley Fine, Lee Broekman, and Scott Winter: Here's proof your encouragement works.

To my business partner Mario Del Pero: You've championed this project from the beginning. I'm so excited for what we're creating together. Look out, world.

To my dear friend and fellow Script Jerk Adam Nathan: You've been supportive of this project and every other endeavor since we met in film school. I'll never forget that—unless this book takes off, in which case it's likely I'll forget all about you. You CBS.

To Ron and Diane: I couldn't ask for better in-laws. I won't even try. Thank you.

To my brother Brent: You nagged me to do this for years and cheered me on once I started. You were the first reader of the first draft, and you probably saved me from a lot of embarrassment. Thanks, bro.

To my sister Kelli: You had virtually nothing to do with this book, but I still love and appreciate you.

To Mom and Dad: You've supported everything I've ever done. I won't trust your review of this book, since you'll love it no matter what. I love you no matter what.

To my kids, Bailey and Peyton: I hope that for even a moment this book makes you as proud of me as I always am of you. Please thank my readers for helping us pay for college.

And finally, to my wife, Rachel: You're always my girl. If you're reading this, it means I finished the book. You're probably more relieved than I am. I hope you never write a book. I wouldn't want to go through what I put you through. Thanks for continuously supporting my success but never needing it in order to love me. I can write a book about franchising, but to convey how I feel about you, I just don't have the words. ATTO.

About
the Author

Scott Greenberg is an internationally recognized speaker, author, and coach who helps leaders grow their businesses, build high-performing teams, and create unforgettable customer experiences. He's given presentations in all 50 U.S. states and throughout the world with franchise clients that include McDonald's, Great Clips, GNC, RE/MAX, Smoothie King, Global Franchise Group, and countless others. For ten years, Scott was a multi-unit franchise owner with Edible Arrangements. His operation won Best Customer Service and Manager of the Year awards out of more than 1,000 locations worldwide. He lives in Los Angeles with his wife and two kids. For more information, visit https://www.scottgreenberg.com/.

Index

CPSIA information can be obtained
at www.ICGtesting.com
Printed in the USA
JSHW032011160821
17857JS00002BA/2